D1606332

Disciplines in Art Education: Contexts of Understanding
General Series Editor, Ralph A. Smith

Books in the Series

Art Education: A Critical Necessity
Albert William Levi and Ralph A. Smith

Art History and Education
Stephen Addiss and Mary Erickson

Aesthetics and Education
Michael J. Parsons and H. Gene Blocker

Art Making and Education
Maurice Brown and Diana Korzenik

Art Making and Education

ART MAKING
AND
EDUCATION

Maurice Brown and
Diana Korzenik

UNIVERSITY OF ILLINOIS PRESS
Urbana and Chicago

This book is printed on acid-free paper.

This volume and the others in the series Disciplines in Art Education:
Contexts of Understanding are made possible by a grant from the Getty
Center for Education in the Arts. The J. Paul Getty Trust retains all
publishing rights to the individual essays in the series. The views expressed
in the volumes are those of the authors and not necessarily those of the
J. Paul Getty Trust.

Library of Congress Cataloging-in-Publication Data

Brown, Maurice, 1932–
    Art making and education / Maurice Brown and Diana Korzenik.
        p.   cm. — (Disciplines in art education)
    Includes index.
    ISBN 0-252-02007-3 (cl). — ISBN 0-252-06312-0 (pb)
    1. Painting—Study and teaching (Higher)—United States.
    2. Painting—Technique. 3. Creation (Literary, artistic, etc.)
    I. Korzenik, Diana, 1941–. II. Title. III. Series.
    N105.B76   1993
    751.4—dc20   92-35667
                                                           CIP

Contents

General Series Preface   ix

General Editor's Introduction   xi

Acknowledgments   xix

Part 1. Beyond the Crossroads: Reflections on Painting

Prologue   3

1. The Grandchildren of God   7

2. The Medium   18

3. Some Other Factors: Style, Impulse,
   Eclecticism, Color   38

4. The Studio   50

5. Creativity   72

6. The Classroom   91

*Part 2. Education's Four Competing Traditions
   of Art Making*

7. Bringing Art Making into the School   107

8. Looking at Our Personal Histories
   and Educational Legacies   115

9. Transition to the Traditions: Art Making
   as Study Skills   128

10. Art Making for Jobs   140

11. Art Making for the Spirit   160

12. Art Making for Understanding Ourselves
    and Others   173

13. Conclusion: Who Chooses?   193

Index   203

General Series Preface

Since the early 1980s, the Getty Center for Education in the Arts, an operating entity of the J. Paul Getty Trust, has been committed to improving the quality of aesthetic learning in our nation's schools and museums. According to the organizing idea of the center's educational policy, teaching about the visual arts can be rendered more effective through the incorporation of concepts and activities from a number of interrelated disciplines, namely, artistic creation, art history, art criticism, and aesthetics.

The resultant discipline-based approach to art education does not, however, mandate that these four disciplines be taught separately; rather, the disciplines are to provide justifications, subject matter, and methods as well as exemplify attitudes that are relevant to the cultivation of percipience in matters of art. They offer different analytical contexts to aid our understanding and aesthetic enjoyment, contexts such as the making of unique objects of visual interest (artistic creation), the apprehension of art under the aspects of time, tradition, and style (art history), the reasoned judgment of artistic merit (art criticism), and the critical analysis of basic aesthetic concepts and puzzling issues (aesthetics). Discipline-based art education thus assumes that our ability to engage works of art intelligently requires not only our having attempted to produce artworks and gained some awareness of the mysteries and difficulties of artistic creation in the process, but also our having acquired familiarity with art's history, its principles of judgment, and its conundrums. All are prerequisite to building a sense of art in the young, which is the overarching objective of aesthetic learning.

Although no consensus exists on precisely how the various components of aesthetic learning should be orchestrated in order to accomplish the goals of discipline-based art education, progress toward these objectives will require that those charged with designing art education programs bring an adequate understanding of the four disciplines to bear on their work. It is toward generating such needed understanding that a five-volume series was conceived as part of the Getty Center's publication program. To narrow the distance separating the disciplines from classroom teaching, each book following the introductory volume is coauthored by a scholar or practitioner in one of the disciplines (an artist, an art historian, an art critic, and a philosopher of art) and an educational specialist with an interest or competence in a given art discipline. The introductory volume provides a philosophical rationale for the idea of discipline-based art education. It is hoped that the series, which is intended primarily for art teachers in elementary and secondary education, for those who prepare these teachers, and for museum educators, will make a significant contribution to the literature of art education.

Ralph A. Smith
General Series Editor

General Editor's Introduction

In this volume, two art teachers in higher education, one with a special interest in painting, and the other a painter with a special interest in teaching art to the young in the schools, provide insightful perspectives on artistic creating and making.

Maurice Brown, the author of the first set of chapters, was raised in the South and attended the University of Tennessee, where he majored in painting, and Ohio State University, where he completed his doctorate in painting and philosophy. He has taught at Bradley University, the University of Wisconsin, and, since 1963, at the State University of New York at New Paltz. He has received a number of awards and fellowships and his paintings are represented in major collections throughout the country. Brown's achievements as a painter and his teaching experience constitute a background that makes him unusually qualified for setting down for an educational audience his reflections on the nature of artistic creation.

In his reflections on painting, Brown emphasizes the importance of respecting and exploiting the potentialities of the medium, especially the pliability of oil paint and the sensuous and expressive uses of color. He distinguishes between making a start on a painting and its inception, which comes only after the artist has worked the medium for some time. Brown fixes the real beginning of a painting at a crossroads, that is, at the point when significant artistic decision making sets in. "Art" lies beyond this crossroads, its task having become that of carrying a painting to completion. During the accomplishment of this task, certain possibilities and options are cast aside in favor of the path chosen. Work now continues within the restraints and limitations of the sensed artistic resolution. Such, at least, is the way Brown views his own way of working.

How, then, does one arrive at the crossroads of a painting and move beyond it, and what are the necessary equipment, background, and attitudes that allow one to do so? About such matters Brown has much to say that is interesting, instructive, and, I think, particularly relevant at this moment in culture. Through an approach that is aphoristic, metaphoric, dualistic, and, in essence, dialectical, he invites his readers to share his distinctive understanding and appreciation of artistic creating.

Keeping this characterization of Brown's writing in mind, we are better able to savor his fascination with oil paint and its special properties; grasp the reason for his frequent references to the object as a dialectical, interactive partner in artistic creation; and understand his musings on the function of the studio as a source of ideas and feelings that at times makes this environment seem to be part of the work itself. Central to Brown's discussion is his description of how images come together and how ideas emerge while he composes within the medium. "One does not, at first, really have ideas," he writes, "they are fully gotten only through the work, and not unless the work toward them is allowed to have its say can one have them." It is important to note, however, that for Brown artistic ideas are images, connections, and feelings. They arise from a not always conscious preoccupation with several themes — for example, the golden section of antiquity, the cruciform shape of Christianity, the human face, landscape, certain figure groups, and so forth — that appeal to him for both their formal and their humanistic interest. It is with an insistent mindfulness of such themes and the continual interaction among the images, feelings, shapes, and forms associated with them that Brown's artistic interest is most closely identified, although he does not deny that contemporary social issues leave their traces on his work. Indeed, metaphoric vision, the propensity to see one thing in another and the capacity to join together disparate phenomena, lies at the heart of Brown's creativeness. Hence the quotation from Herman Melville that serves as the epigraph to his first chapter.

But if a personal, dialectical encounter with paintings and their themes and objects is characteristic of Brown's efforts in the studio, his dualistic as well as synthetic frame of mind is just as evident in his written reflections about creating. Brown emphasizes the movement toward and beyond a crossroads in painting, with the most important work being done neither at the start nor at the end. His thinking is likewise done in the middle, in that he characteristically rejects extreme attitudes and prefers to find something sensible or useful in opposing views. He chooses his ideas as eclectically as he does the sources for his painting. Thus while he realizes that words cannot go very far in describing works of art, he nonetheless understands the need for discourse and appreciates the knowledge and wisdom of others who have addressed his concerns. Obviously, Brown's own considerable cultural literacy — amply attested to by his references to history, literature, philosophy, and criticism — confirms the value he places on the written word. Like Joshua Reynolds, the English painter to whom he refers, Brown has laid up much in his cognitive and allusionary base that serves him well. What is more, he believes that reason and its tools are not necessarily opposed to impulse and sensation. Indeed, the scholar's interest in truth and the preservation of memory strike a responsive chord in him. If Brown found it congenial to write within the framework of a discipline-based approach to aesthetic learning, it is because of his easy conversance with the disciplines involved.

Brown's preference for the middle, or perhaps better, for the insights gleaned from contrasting viewpoints and positions, is evident throughout his discussion of various topics. He speaks, for example, of both the piety and playfulness of artistic creating and believes that drawing and color do not constitute opposites. He pays due respect to both the transient and the timeless, to tradition and the contemporary, to the tale (the work) as well as the teller (the artist); and he acknowledges both the modesty and nobility of artistic creating. He is not unduly impressed with originality even though he strives for a modicum of it. He understands that the wellspring of motivation for painting lies in the work of others as much as it does in some supposedly autonomous self. In his dealing with numerous other polarities, opposites, and dichotomies, Brown is similarly prudent, self-effacing, modest, and often wise.

Brown affectionately remembers his parents and the teachers who had such an important part in his development and encouraged his love of painting — a love that perhaps stands out more than anything else in his reflections. He could never, for example, regard painting as a mournful act. His outlook and his view of history, it is worth noting, are psychological and personal. It is a living past that informs his work and personality, a sense of the passage of time that locates people, objects, and events not in some long-gone era but through a measure of life-spans of eighty years each. In a striking image Brown places us within approximately six life-spans from the summit of the High Renaissance. His vision, in short, is humanistic, and it is central to what he calls the existential factor of creating, the E Factor. Finally, however, Brown's proven facility with words and the very considerable store of knowledge he draws on do not make him a highly cerebral artist; he has too much respect for mystery, the unforeseen, the enigmatic, and the accidental to be so regarded.

The principal responsibility of the discipline specialist (art historian, philosopher of art, art critic, and artist) in the series of which this volume is a part is to describe the discipline in question, while the coauthor, an educational specialist with an interest in the same discipline, is responsible for the issues of teaching and curriculum design. Thus it was not Brown's task to present a list of teaching suggestions or methods; but he has nonetheless provided some. Just a few of the educationally relevant points that come to mind concern the inculcation of a reasonable respect for technique, knowledge, and tradition; a sensible attitude toward preparation for artistic creating, not to be overdone but not to be slighted either; a suspicion of strongly previsioned ends so as to permit inspiration and discovery to have their way; an appreciation of limitations as well as possibilities; the maintenance of a balance between impulse and judgment; an openness to life's difficulties and multiplicity; and so forth. At a time when nothing seems to be done in moderation and extremisms of many kinds hold sway, Brown, the teacher, provides the student and novice with sound advice.

Diana Korzenik was raised in Brooklyn, New York, and attended Vassar College, Oberlin College, and Columbia University, where she studied art history. At Yale University and the New York Studio School of Painting she continued study in painting, drawing, and sculpture, and her doctorate, received from the Harvard Graduate School of Education, reflects her work in cognitive studies and art education. Most of her career has been spent at the Massachusetts College of Art, where she was chair of the Art Education Department from 1973 to 1988.

A writer about art and a historian as well as an artist, Korzenik has made notable contributions to the history of art education. Among her publications are chapters in *The Arts and Cognition, The Educational Legacy of Romanticism,* and *Pilgrims and Pioneers: New England Women and the Arts.* Her *Drawn to Art: A Nineteenth-Century American Dream* received a number of awards. In past years she has devoted considerable efforts to the teaching of art making to young children. Korzenik's background as an artist, an art teacher in the public schools, and an academician and theoretician in the field of art education thus lends a multifaceted perspective to her reflections on the creative artist as a source for ideas for teaching art. What virtually ensures the usefulness of her remarks for today's art teachers is her consistent, unblinking respect for the educationally feasible — as opposed to the desirable or ideal — in the world of schooling. She repeatedly cautions us that we have to keep reality in mind.

Some of these realities are seemingly immutable, while others may be capable of melioration and should therefore be addressed. Among the latter she includes the gulf that so often separates theory from practice. "While the philosophers sort out their treatises, the lawmakers are in committees recommending legislation, and the professors are at their conferences, the children are with their teachers in classrooms." The books and articles of art-educational theorists, she cautions, must not be be mistaken for the experience of the classroom art teacher.

Korzenik's intention, then, is not to add to that body of professional literature that is only tenuously related to what actually goes on in schools. Instead, she writes with the classroom clearly in mind, for it is here that we encounter one of the educational realities so important to her: the autonomous teacher. Teachers, rather than policymakers and philosophers, decide not only what activities will be engaged in in the art classroom but also why these activities are considered important. Korzenik thus pays teachers the professional compliment of casting them as potential theoreticians as well as practitioners. Teachers of this stripe would not be well served by more directives from on high; hence Korzenik assures her readers that she has not tried "to select any best way." Still, even autonomous teachers can use some assistance in becoming conscious choosers of their own direction; they need to be made aware of what they are choosing from.

But since the aim is to teach art making, teachers have to bring their work into some kind of relationship to the paradigmatic art maker, the creative artist. Here again a strong sense of realism asserts itself in Korzenik's observations. The work habits of the studio artist, she says, are diametrically opposed to the manner in which schools have to operate, and therefore such habits "cannot be lifted, whole-cloth, unchanged, and placed in the school." Only those artists can make an educational contribution who are willing to submit to the school's institutional arrangements and the agendas pursued on behalf of children.

Korzenik thus recognizes that while the studio artist's universe of adult concerns provides a wealth of suggestions for art teaching, it also creates dilemmas. For this reason she turns her attention to the other half of the artist/art teacher tandem, that is, those art practices that educators have actually admitted into the curriculum and that have managed to thrive in the school environment. She discovered that these practices — and more especially the justifications provided for them — can be separated into four paths or traditions. She sees these four traditions as the efforts of artists to excerpt from their studio something that can accommodate the constraints of schools. Such practices contain strong elements of the studio artist's thoughts that can mesh with children's needs and the schools' obligations.

The description of the four traditions — their origins, evolution, and contemporary manifestations — occupies the core of Korzenik's chapters. The first tradition, art making as a tool for the improved teaching of other school studies, suggested itself when adults observed children's earnest absorption in their artlike activities and realized that art's potential for concentrating the attention of students could be harnessed for more general learning purposes. In the second tradition, art making for jobs, the justification for art in the schools assumed interesting variants. Drawing, for instance, was first touted as a preparation for specific well-paying jobs. Later art instruction was supposed to foster such general traits as manual dexterity, powers of observation, and a sense for design, which were thought to make young people more employable. But as industrial processes became increasingly fragmented and alienating to workers, the teaching of art in the schools took on a therapeutic function. With the artist held up as a model, students were encouraged to seize opportunities often lacking outside the school: to see the making of an object through from plan to finished product. Perhaps this concern for restoring a sense of wholeness to young people anticipates the next path, art making for the spirit.

This third approach, which justifies the inclusion of art in the curriculum on the basis of the personal benefits students are supposed to derive from it, has been widely embraced as the authentic mission of art education. In its early phase, when "being good for the spirit" was equated with the promotion of aesthetic as well as moral refinement through beauty, the ambivalence of Americans toward cultural matters prevented this path from being argued for convincingly. But once goodness was understood in psychological terms, that is, as mental health and the furtherance of proper child development through creative self-expression, this tradition established itself as a powerful force in art education.

One could say that the fourth path, art making for understanding oneself and others, takes children one step further, from having expressed themselves in art to becoming reflective about what they and others around them have externalized. Korzenik believes that the accepting, democratic atmosphere of the art classroom provides an ideal context for teaching children not only to learn more about themselves but also to appreciate cultural differences as they present themselves in the art products of students from various ethnic origins. This fourth path, which can serve as a conduit for the current interest in multicultural education, is younger than the other approaches. Still, it is not as novel and unprecedented as its proponents often believe. Korzenik points out such antecedents as the nineteenth-century enthusiasm for collecting art from all over the world; the "homeland exhibitions" that celebrated immigrant traditions and were very popular earlier in this century; and the vision of cultural pluralism embodied in

Chicago's Hull-House. Always ready to present a balanced account, Korzenik also cautions that multiculturalism can imprison as well as liberate since its effort to preserve traditions may inhibit individual growth: "The romanticizing of ethnicities has its own inertia. Students feel pressured to conform to the available group prototypes."

One reason that art educators should be grateful for Korzenik's account of paths taken by art making in the schools is that combined these four narratives amount to an excellent historical overview of art education. To be sure, the important names, ideas, and developments make their expected appearances. But readers should be careful to receive them in the spirit in which Korzenik wants them to be understood. She does not simply compile the usual list of the "movers and shakers" of the field. "Never in any era," says Korzenik, "was teaching the sole invention of a single expert, no matter how influential a certain leader may have been." What allowed certain persons to become influential was not their ability to think of things others could not, but their ability to articulate notions toward which others were already groping, for which a need already existed. Furthermore, "to a much greater extent than we might imagine, whether the ideas were ever acted upon depended on the actions of a multitude of individual teachers."

Persons who have been regarded as leaders and innovators in art education are thus less giants to be looked up to than participants, along with today's art teachers, in a centuries-old conversation that, Korzenik urges, must be carried on into the future. In an age that glorifies originality — often achieved through willful ignorance of the history of a profession — it is refreshing to encounter a writer who acknowledges the contributions of the past (most of our ideas are hand-me-downs, she says) and invites her contemporaries to find their place in the tradition.

The chapters by Brown and Korzenik share something important. Like Brown, Korzenik is no enemy of the word and is sensitive to the role of tradition in making and teaching. One need only consider her discussion of the four traditions of making and her belief that most contemporary ideas have historical antecedents. In other words, Korzenik not only respects the contributions of others but, like Brown, values the narratives, stories, and influence of parents, teachers, and friends. Her outlook, too, is personal and humanistic. The two sets of chapters thus reveal kinship and connecting threads that help to make this volume a text that readers should find rewarding.

Ralph A. Smith

Acknowledgments

Both before and after this book was contemplated, my thoughts on its subjects were affected by far too many of my friends, colleagues, and students to mention; however, I wish in particular to acknowledge the patience of Dr. William Klenk, Alexander Martin, Dr. Henry Raleigh, and Benjamin Wigfall in considering my various expressions of them.

I am grateful for permission to reproduce the following illustrations in part 1 of this book:

Mill by the Water. Piet Mondrian. Ca. 1905. Canvas mounted on cardboard. 11⅞×15 in. Museum of Modern Art, New York.

Women of Algiers. Eugene Delacroix. 1836. Canvas. 71×90 in. Louvre, Paris. Giraudon/Art Resource, New York.

Maids of Honor. Pablo Picasso. 1857. Canvas. 76⅜×102⅜ in. Picasso Museum, Barcelona. Copyright 1991 ARS N.Y./SPADEM.

The Wife of Tobias with the Goat. Rembrandt. 1645. Oil on wood. 7⅞× 10⅝ in. Staatliche, Berlin. Marburg/ARS, N.Y.

Alba Madonna. Raphael. Ca. 1510. Oil on wood transferred to canvas. 37¼ in. diameter. National Gallery of Art, Washington, D.C. Andrew W. Mellon Collection.

The Hunt of the Unicorn. Detail from no. 4, *The Unicorn Defends Himself.* Late fifteenth-century French or Flemish. Silk, wool, with metal threads. 12 ft. 1 in.×13 ft. 2 in. From the Chateau of Verteuil. Metropolitan Museum of Art, New York. Cloisters Collection. Gift of John D. Rockefeller, Jr., 1937. (37.80.4).

Untitled (figure 8). Maurice Brown. Ca. 1981. Ink on paper. 12×14 in. Artist's collection.

Travels. Maurice Brown. 1988. Mixed media. 37×31 in. Private collection.

Green Truck. Maurice Brown. 1962. Canvas. 30×55 in. Rose Art Museum, Brandeis University, Waltham, Mass. Gift of the Ford Foundation.

Untitled (figure 11). Maurice Brown. 1984. Canvas. 12×31 in. Artist's collection.

The Knight, Death and the Devil. Albrech Dürer. 1513. Engraving. 9⅝×7⅜ in. Metropolitan Museum of Art. Harris Brisbane Dick Fund, 1943. (43.106.2).

—M.B.

Thanks to the many graduate students with whom I have discussed these ideas over two decades. Each research project they undertook tested and enriched the framework I present here. Thanks too to the state of Massachusetts for providing them with a public independent art college, Massachusetts College of Art, where students who otherwise might never afford to attend an art school pursue the work described herein. Special thanks also to Andrew Dibner and Sue Quinn, who from perspectives outside the art education field offered their early and valuable criticism of this manuscript. Thanks also to Bernice Buresh, Evelyn Davis, and Kathryn Kirshner, who encourged me in this work.

The following have kindly provided permission to reproduce the photographs used in part 2 of this book:

Geology Lesson. Drawn by Harold Korzenik. Photographed by Larry Scheinfeld.

Baby at Play. Thomas Eakins. National Gallery of Art, Washington, D.C. John Hay Whitney Collection.

All other photographs are by Mark Wise, Department of Education, Museum of Fine Arts, Boston. © Museum of Fine Arts, Boston. All rights reserved.

—D.K.

PART 1

Beyond the Crossroads: Reflections
on Painting

Prologue

Artists intent on discussing their own procedures are caught in a bind that is familiar to those who have analyzed such accounts, but particularly to other artists. As a developing painting can "uncover its own direction," so extensive statements of this kind have a way of steadily drifting, as with an internal logic, toward the autobiographical and personal. To resist that drift too greatly is, in a sense, to misrepresent what artists are most qualified to offer, particularly those who are convinced that creation is based in, or at least includes, individual character. However, to surrender wholly to it is to run the risk of blunting the explanatory purpose with yet another, perhaps interesting, but undisclosing statement.

Therefore, the most effective such statements are continual adjustments of both interests, as if one could not adequately describe, reveal, or discuss creation without allowing a prominent role to personal experience and opinion. Clearly, an honest attempt to explain one's creation requires the same nicety as the creation. Neither scientism nor egoism employ this nicety or provide us with the revelations we find in reading van Gogh, Max Ernst, Fernand Léger, Audrey Flack, or Robert Irwin on how and why their works were made. Most of Picasso's singular disclosures, for example, strike me as purely personal and at the same time observations of obvious but generally unrecognized fact. These kinds of statements admit a definitely common ground, but their peculiarities ask more than usual of the reader if both the ordinary *and* the peculiar, the plain *and* the complex are actually to serve up insights into something as intricate as creation.

In my view, there are inevitable consequences of such a blend, and a few of them may turn up in my example of it as well. One is an arbitrary pattern of concentration similar to the capriciousness exercised in making images. Both the work and the thoughts on its origins are circumstantial. (Nothing, whether the subject, the history of its treatment, or anything else, seems to require that the figure holding up Christ's legs in Titian's *Entombment* have a bald pate. Similarly, I would not defend the brief consideration of impulse in chapter 3 against every other possible subject.) Another consequence is sudden swings between detail and generality, between easygoing simplicity and dense compression.

A single sentence may be contorted with the mood-swings of creation. Yet another, one particularly demanding of the reader, deserves a brief examination.

Even without considering the most illustrious creators, I would say of those devotedly or more than usually involved in creating that they tend not to ask or expect of life easily digested explanations or a detailed set of directions, maps, and scorecards. A fundamental quality of "the creative," teachers and others, is their relative ease in arriving at the many personal and productive meanings of phenomena — a quality that of course presupposes their paying attention. Amid the arguments about whether this is good or bad or even true, they become inured to finding and evaluating their own way. (And they do so amid the confusions of simultaneously heeding — or at least maintaining an awareness of — the pathways already paved.) I believe artists' elliptical prose and the leaping connectives of their narratives, descriptions, and explanations reflect this personal, daily attitude. That is, just as they themselves process raw existence, the eternal chaos as well as the deep order, the gloomy and the bright, gearing their responses to it and caging it in their works, they assume that others will meet anything more than halfway and *make* something of the often raw material of their own observations, even if these too are incomplete and dappled with confusion, method, the grave, and the ridiculous.

As far as I know, the first obvious reflection of this attitude is in Montaigne's essay "On Vanity" (the famous discrepancy between many of his essays and their titles is itself a perfect case in point). Because it is how makers seem to find all matters, his authorial pronouncement in that piece also characterizes the maker's communication: "I want the matter to make its own divisions. It shows well enough where it changes, where it concludes, where it begins, where it resumes." He disdains "interlacing" his essays with guides for the careless and, as if that were not guide enough, quotes Seneca: "Nothing is so useful that it can be of value when taken on the run."

Without this disdain, I have tried to organize my discussion and guide the reader through a many-faceted subject. However, in keeping with what may be my version of Montaigne's approach, I may have made some more than usual interpretive demands on the reader. They may stem from the fact that I occupy the confusing ground *between* some points of view now taken to be exclusive, forever defined, and all too clear. More important, however, they stem from the *personal* nature of art making and any individual's consequent, honest attempt to cover it within usually strict limitations. Another way of putting it may be to say that there are basically three approaches to the topic:

(1) a more or less objective, scholarly overview or compendium of views; (2) a purposely selective view that wishes to confirm a predecided position; (3) the one taken here, an art maker's recollections and observations. Obviously, like an individual's art, the third will in any case omit a great deal and can never satisfy every interest.

Consequently, I have no doubt strained some implemental expectations where I felt compelled by other priorities. In leaving specific applications largely to the reader, I have trusted his or her ability, and especially the teacher's, to conceive particular connections from a broad and sometimes general examination. Such trust is usually more agreeable when the commentator enjoys great notoriety — if we could read it, Mary Cassat's mere opinion of bridges would perhaps sprout a flock of applicable meanings. Nonetheless, I feel that those who must "read" students and speculate on the best paths of action will find relevance here. Like artists, teachers are fed by the whole world and all of their lives, not just the sanctioned and "professional" parts. They honor the feeling and thought that rise from their own direct experiences. Ideas and inspiration — connections — may come from a store window, an argument among zoologists, a movie, a meal, or an essay. And it need not have been pre-stamped "Art" or "Education" (a point I take up in discussing eclecticism in chapter 3).

I have trusted, too, my own experience as a teacher: invariably, the most operationally detailed book is the least useful — at least until my conditions match those of the author. Once convinced of significance or persuaded to view it anew, I can usually figure out how it might be demonstrated or identified in my own circumstances. Therefore, I have devoted more effort to staking out a fuller range of the subject than to the classroom presentation of smaller pieces of it.

Though of course interrelated and arranged in a designed sequence, the chapters are also freestanding. A deep involvement with language is said to heighten one's sense of its delicate, problematic nature. Curiously, something of the same may also result from the image maker's relative estrangement from language. If so, the problems will loom no greater than when the image maker turns to a candid, extensive commentary on his or her art. Appropriately, then, the first chapter begins my commentary with an old and reconsidered relation between image makers and language. Creation may be considered from the standpoint of personality, the created product, or the society in which it takes place, but the second chapter emphasizes the response to its medium — paint, in this case — as a key to understanding it. From the long list of qualities and practices that might be said to stand out in the painter's process, I have selected four (style, impulse, eclecticism, and color) as subjects for brief emphasis in the third chapter. The fourth chapter consists of further probes into the grounds of picture making and some personal experiences and ruminations of the kind that usually condition those grounds. After a short appraisal of the contemporary atmosphere in which differing concepts of creativity contend, the fifth chapter argues the continuing educational significance of creation. In the sixth chapter I relate some of my own relevant experiences as a student and conclude with some recommendations for teachers of art making.

What follows, then, is not only a testament, in the sense that it reports on or bears witness to much that is involved in the making of my own work and some of what seems to me to pertain to art as a whole, but also, I hope, an essay of direct use for those who see art and the studies connected to it as educational necessities.

1

The Grandchildren of God

In placid hours well-pleased we dream
Of many a brave, unbodied scheme.
But form to lend, pulsed life create,
What unlike things must meet and mate:
A flame to melt — a wind to freeze;
Sad patience — joyous energies;
Humility — yet pride and scorn;
Instinct and study; love and hate;
Audacity — reverence. These must mate,
And fuse with Jacob's mystic heart,
To wrestle with the angel — Art.
— Herman Melville

In a sense, artists of all kinds can be said to dare their audience to regard art without the aid of explanations. If artists seem to ask for such regard, it is not only because they may wish to encourage the imagination and independence of each member of their audience. It is also because they have faith in the independence of their art. Though easy to forget if one does not ordinarily produce them, a symphony or a painting are as distinct from words as from one another. The clown feels it is a poor performance that needs the introduction "This is funny" and afterwards a verbal summary. Likewise, artists take for granted the completeness of their forms.

Because I sympathize with it as a part of my own, and because I am a painter who with this essay departs from it, that outlook and its significance is the subject of this chapter. Works have *titles*, however, including "untitled," and of course words make many other obvious and subtle contributions to artists and audience alike. If works can be seen as independent it may in part be due to previous explanations of other works and their general setting. Therefore, looking to my own past for examples, the chapter closes with a discussion of the interdependence of these experiences — isolated aesthetic response and contextual learning — in the production and enjoyment of art.

If we ask painters, What does your creative enterprise consist of? What are its sources? What are the most fundamental intentions of your work and how do you realize them in paintings? I believe the first private response of those we tend to call artists, would be, I don't really know. Hiding in this thought or reply would be many different personal positions. One painter would suffer the familiar shock that an apparently necessary answer of greater weight was, once again, not forthcoming; another — or the same painter on a different occasion — would find some pride, justification, or glee in a fuller answer's absence; for another the reply would reflect exasperation at the complexity of any fairly complete or honest answer, or for yet another it would be a way of suggesting that these things cannot be fully known. However, all such attitudes seem based in one way or another in doubts about the necessity to verbalize, a respect for mystery, which Einstein claimed is the "source of all true art and science,"[1] and a consequent grave circumspection regarding both the facility and the imprecision of words. Artists have difficulty and doubts (and a tortured interest) in talking freely, accurately, and to the point about precisely what leads up to and goes on in producing their work.

Artists, like scientists, have usually seen their involvement as being with the primal or preverbal. The deeper and more integral their insights, the further from the reach of words and their connotations they see their work as being. Of course, no less than other human beings, artists are agents of language, and they are contributors, albeit peripheral ones, to the vast culture of words. However, they often disagree with scholars, critics, and academicians who assume that theirs is an antecedent process constituting a supreme court. An artist may feel that something fundamental to the inquiry is ignored when, for example, scholarship consists of rearranging the page sequence of one art historian's edition of Jacopo Bellini's books of drawings by subject matter, only to be questioned by another about the rearrangement's "repetition."[2] Another art historian writes, "As we must believe Wordsworth when he tells us how strongly . . . he felt the force of nature, so we must believe that art historian Bernard Berenson had an altogether exceptional response to painting and sculpture."[3] If this is true, the painter may wonder, how exceptional must be the response of the artist; and though paintings are in a way made to parallel the "force of nature" in this remark, a qualification may nevertheless be wished for. It may be all the more wished for because the primal position that Berenson gave to the painter is no longer taken for granted.

From high culture these verbal presumptions trickle down to the rest of society, where they are contradicted or unquestioningly accepted.

When Erich Segal, author of the best-selling novel *Love Story*, was asked if he had second thoughts about the unacknowledged use of Robert Indiana's popular *Love* painting idea for the book's jacket design, he is said to have replied, "The artist should feel honored."[4]

Among many artists, any combination of whatever words is too constricting before the implications of their work and the world it reflects. "I know that down to the last simple detail experience is totally mysterious," wrote Claes Oldenburg.[5] It is upon an ever closer approach to the mysterious, the unique forms in which it presents itself, and the overwhelming subtlety of matter — and matters — that the artist's medium is predicated. Aldous Huxley, arguing the crudeness of our expressions when set next to that subtlety, wrote, "The counterpoint of unique events is infinitely wide and their succession indefinitely long. That the purified language of science or even the richer purified language of literature should ever be adequate to the givenness of the world and of our experience is, in the very nature of things, impossible."[6] That art should be "adequate" is also impossible; however, artists will often assume that their art form's materiality and its possibilities for mimesis and representation more readily reflect our world and much of our reaction to it. To use Cézanne's phrase, they will feel that their plastic form constitutes at least a closer "parallel to nature."

The mistrust of words is a long artistic custom (honored in the breach *and* in the observance). Leonardo da Vinci rambunctiously dared any poet to set a description of the beauties of a lady next to the painter's portrait of her — obviously he had something of the caliber of his own work in mind here. "You will see," he writes, "wither nature will the more incline the enamored judge. . . . In Art we may be said to be grandsons of God."[7] In other words, the art of words cannot well match the delicate wiles of nature: as God made the world, so we, but twice removed, make another refined world in which we see ourselves, both worlds, and the many connections of all three. We are in the vicinity of Buddha's wordless lectures, in which a dandelion, like a picture, is held up as sufficient. (The grandchildren of God can be a testy and exclusive lot: the isolate Winslow Homer, a former illustrator who may have agreed with Leonardo about words, advised the would-be artist not even to look at pictures.)

The artist's sidelong glance at the confusions and ineffectualness of words continues, of course, into our own time. Wyndham Lewis was suspicious of the "word man" and felt that he could do painters "no good."[8] "Words are like the wind," chided Georgia O'Keeffe when she returned a questionnaire to a museum official.[9] She was passing along a comment by her Spanish gardener, who would have liked the old

English saying, "Words butter no parsnips." The critic John Russell received the following telegram from Balthus to whom he had written to request biographical information for the painter's retrospective in 1968: "No biographical details. Begin: Balthus is a painter of whom nothing is known. Now let us look at the pictures. Regards, B."[10] The telegram concisely demonstrates the point of view that even if there is to be a discussion, the brusqueness of visual rather than investigative verbal values should head the list of priorities. "The pictures" are not to be overly seasoned with words, and discussions of them based elsewhere, even in the artist's life, are tenuously founded.

Beyond the artist's less formalized concerns — and, ironically, while artists from cubism to the present were showing a mounting interest in at least the look if not other aspects of the word — the relationship of explanation and the arts, long a subject of specialists, became a somewhat more public and highly focused issue. This issue is exemplified by such books as Wyndham Lewis's *The Demon of Progress in the Arts* (1955); its heir and update, Tom Wolfe's *The Painted Word* (1975); sections of Harold Rosenberg's *Art on the Edge* (1975); Denis Donoghue's *The Arts without Mystery* (1983), and George Steiner's *Real Presences* (1989).

These concerns were, at any rate, present in my training as an artist. They may even have been underlined by my part of the unfortunate "legacy," discussed by Diana Korzenik, that separates the hand and mind and makes their interests mutually exclusive. I was the son of a family of "manual workers" and was around artists and craftspeople from an early age. Though modern educational discussions may emphasize the wrongheaded intellectual disdain of handiwork, the disdain flies in both directions. Though low-key and for the most part unarticulated, what might be called my "vocational mindset" as a young artist included a rather proud independence of the verbal. Had I known of it, Arthur Koestler's "true creativity often starts where language ends"[11] would have seemed a commonplace. As an excess of self-consciousness could hinder one's movements, so we thought too much discussion and analysis could reduce us as artists. One did not argue or read one's way to discoveries; one painted one's way to them. A judgment awaited those who strove, beyond a nebulous point, to articulate and philosophize and were too academically interested. Though many past examples of it were instructive, one could always count on injunctions against the vaguely described "illustrational," which I understood in terms of taste rather than purpose. To what degree one's painting was or was not "literary" could not always be clearly determined, but that it should not be was clearly deemed desirable. The poet and the novelist could occasionally be identified with, and their works even used, but the theorist's and commentator's contorted wrangles were found pathetically comic. This response was by no means always one of ignorance, and it was not intended as anti-intellectual; it merely presumed the flourishing of a kind of "naive wisdom." One trusted appearances. A book *could* be told by its cover. If, according to Shakespeare, there is no wisdom for reading the mind in the human face, perhaps the face was a revelation of which the mind was unaware. By and large, one trusted the palpable to yield up everything else. If one knew, sensed, understood — saw — then one's work would circumvent most verbiage and reveal that comprehension to another, perhaps unsuspectedly percipient eye.

In other words, it was the heyday of American expressionism and its effect on the painter's education. The postwar brilliance of American art had beamed across the Hudson River and into the plaster cast shadows of the hinterlands. It blended there with Zen koans, rock and roll, the first of the new grant monies, and the first bubbling springs of boundary-crashing (now "interdisciplinary") energies that would seem shortly to leak from artists (now "arts community") to the entire, would-be revolutionary society of the 1960s. Like the nonverbal artist, society-at-large, with its new television sets, music, and widescreen movies, was at every level beginning to loosen its binding connections with the word.

In the quietest moments, however, I harbored doubts. Matisse warned his students that if they wished to be painters "you must cut out your tongue because your decision has taken away from you the right to express yourself with anything but your brush."[12] The violence of this advice from the peaceful master of the Côte d'Azur was not lost on me. Neither was the irony. Matisse said this during one of two radio interviews in 1942 and was one of the very artists who had verbally illuminated the art of painting. In fact, most of the painters I knew were, if not always so illuminating, inveterate talkers. Although they often speak with uncanny accuracy, I have continued to learn more from the brushes than from the words of other artists; nevertheless, the loss of their tongues would also have been a loss to me as a painter. In the standard sententious manner of painters, de Kooning was appealing when he wrote that talking was what "put 'Art' into painting" and that "nothing is positive about art except that it is a word." Whoever was the first talker "must have intended it," for "right from there to here all art became literary." Many people who wanted to take talking out of painting did "nothing else but talk about it. That is no contradiction, however. The art in it is the forever mute part you can talk about forever."[13]

More frequently, my doubts left their harbor and sailed into plain view. Drawings and paintings had seemed perfectly complete and all-inclusive when I was a child, and I supplied them with, and derived from them, all manner of sound effects, verist links, conversations, and movements. Not until puberty did I give up or largely internalize the notion of such connections. Now, of course, I saw that if painting's simultaneous revelations from the infinite width of "unique events" were more distinct than the sequential revelations of other art forms, it seemed that its treatment of their "indefinitely long succession" was less so. At least, a more direct treatment of this was the interest of the temporal forms — music, film, dance, sculpture, architecture to a degree, and, until one can read hundreds of pages at a glance, literature.

Moreover, Leonardo observed that pictures can move us to laughter but not to tears, and I could remember being sorely moved as a child by Victor Hugo's *The Hunchback of Notre Dame* and, much later, Saul Bellow's novel *Augie March*. I would gladly swap tears for laughter, but there seemed to be a wider distribution of fundamental powers than was implied in Leonardo's challenge to the poet. Even painting's laughter could be but a smile beside Mark Twain's, James Thurber's, or Peter De Vries's. Not always so aware of it at the time, I was already beginning to steep myself in the contradictions that characterize the maker's life, finding my spirit in the artist's megalomania while developing intellectual and other checks on it; identifying with the artist's nonverbalism while doting on words from Picasso and de Kooning and reading da Vinci's notebook, Delacroix's *Journal*, Sir Joshua Reynolds's discourses to his students, Amedee Ozenfant's *Foundations of Modern Art*, Paul Klee's *Pedagogical Sketchbook*, Braque's *Notebook*, Cézanne's and van Gogh's letters, and other artists' writings.

I understood and identified with the artist's disregard for most chatter about art, but I also came to feel that it is easily misconstrued. If the poet frowns on translation within language it can hardly be surprising that a painter, in spite of attempts to merge them, sees little substantial connection between language and visual art. That does not mean, however, that artists are in the vanguard of those who disparage the word; or that the nonwriting artist is further evidence that art is responsible for the word's recent general loss of prestige. Shallow and commercialized attention to art may mirror that loss of prestige, but the loss does not originate solely in the habits or accomplishments of artists. Modern technology and certain responses to self-contained and deconstructionist philosophies seem to have been far more efficient in this respect.

Ours is becoming a panoptic society of vulgar-fantasy architecture and displays, covered with posters, photographic productions, omnipresent decoration, and omniform advertising, and agleam with color slides, movies, and television. An analysis of weekday evening newscasts reveals that in the twenty years after 1968, the length of political "sound bites" dropped from around forty-two to less than ten seconds, while the time given to wordless visuals of the candidates grew by more than three hundred percent.[14] The increased power and use of visual forms of communication, which glow at the heart of Huxley's and Orwell's frightening, best-known fictions, have concerned Jacques Ellul, Daniel Boorstin, Harold Innis, Neil Postman, and other critics for the last half century. I find much to agree with in Camille Paglia's justification for renewed expressions of the primacy of the "Western Eye," which, like the mute glories of Egyptian art as compared with word-wreathed Greek art, has lain for so long beneath the assumption that only words express intelligence.[15] The concern of the critics is also justified, however, insofar as these developments thrive on oppressive greed and thoughtlessness.

The artist's part in this turn of our society cannot be ignored, whether it was influenced by the early moderns' dreams of a transformed environment or by more recent reflections that seem to condone the hopelessness or confused jollity of it all. But it is a relatively small part, and the artist stands to lose as much as, if not more than, anyone else in an uncritically hypervisual society.

Even as the word itself was becoming a kind of image, important aspects of the image, too, were losing prestige. To the unsophisticated eye, surely, but to all eyes to some degree, the visual excitement of our society will seem a rising ante that artists cannot meet. It is the extensiveness of all "pop" or "mass" forms — and their political uses — that encourages some commentators to dub them, instead of "traditional" art forms, the so-called true art of our time. Still, there are artists who would not think of trying to meet that ante. Unlike those who proffer many of the daily stimuli, these artists are concerned with vision in both senses.

I do not question the primacy of the work of art in specifically relevant discussions consequent to it, but even that primacy takes place within a broad perceptual and cultural framework. Through that framework and its language both viewer and creator-to-be approach the work. Is there inherently enough in any visual work of art to insure not only its survival but the furthest impress of its powers if discovered, let us say, in a remote part of the globe by one who is utterly unfamiliar with such an object? If a Vermeer painting were found by a woman in the Maoke Mountains of New Guinea, she could no doubt find as good a use for it as Picasso did when he used his own painting as an umbrella in Montmarte. Like her neighbors who saw the overflights of our World War II airplanes as the visits of gods, she too would interpret it and find meanings in it. We are all involved in some such visual diagnosis every day, and one cannot firmly say that its subject is never of such alien character. Her community would, perhaps, eventually assign it a general classification of some sort and, within that, give it an interpretation and a vague or clear priority. Under notably different circumstances, we have done as much with the work of her people. However, may not a rewarding appreciation of the Vermeer and of Papuan commerorative poles — and their future physical condition — depend not only on the works but on conversations in the broadest sense? May not their revelations, particularly those intended by their makers, depend on the education of their discoverers, whether or not the discoverers are, or are to be, artists? Would not the education unavoidably depend in a finer than ordinary sense on the culture of words? Yes, I would say, to all three questions.

Rising from my discussion of creation, I hope, is the recognition that the dedication to making art will, of its own character, sooner or later find a way to place one's preconceptions in some doubt. The ensuing "internal creational argument" may strengthen or amplify as well as change preconceptions, but unless creation is understood as an extension of thinking processes into the rough realm of matter and experience, the understanding is false or narrow. More than other admonishments, it was the "arguments" between self and works that broke the youthfully proud and brittle professionalism of my "nonverbal stance." While a few painters were no doubt genuinely wordless, my experience suggested that many were so retroactively, hoping to enhance the pedigree of their work. This counterfeit consideration on behalf of romanticized unsophistication was offensive to me, and I finally admitted my differences with it and their bearing on my work. Unlike Euclid's geometry, which is ultimately based on a number of axioms, painting as an art may indeed float free of words, but the connections between language and the painter's personal, multifarious learning, however invisible and mysterious, are unavoidable and critical.

Neither reason nor any of its tools are in necessary opposition to creativity. The judgment that guides scholarly research is not greatly different from the judgment that guides the artist's daring and, ultimately, skill. The scholar's typically high interest in the truth and the preservation of memory against the fog of lies, myth, forgetfulness, and even the treachery of language strikes a responsive chord in me and is not, I think, foreign to the attitudes of the painter.

At certain key points, the artist's relation to language is also surprisingly similar to the philosopher's. Wittgenstein, for example, observed that philosophy was a "battle" against language's "bewitchment of our intelligence."[16] But of course it is a battle that can be carried full course only by language. Even though it can be carried out without words, making art, too, is an operation of our intelligence that, if not exactly a battle *against* language, is destabilized without independence from it. Similarly, however, the preparations for the operation and much that conditions the instruction and enjoyment of its results — not to mention the cultural judgments that will situate them among everything else of value and significance — are possible only through language.

A long Western philosophic tradition, deeply embedded in the everyday, is the assumption that the sensory circus of "mere" appearances is hopelessly undependable and properly diminished and controlled by the higher realm of ideas and abstractions. It contends with another, younger part of the tradition that puts it the other way round: the certainty of our ideas is finally based on "the certainty of perception."[17] As Hannah Arendt pointed out, the very fact that we are able to find revealing analogies, and that metaphor's relationships are not reversible, indicates "the absolute primacy of the world of appearances." By extension, that which deals more directly in appearance and the ways we apprehend it is a part of our most profound search and discovery. The traffic between the apparent and nonapparent "may be seen as a kind of 'proof' that mind and body, thinking and sense experience, the invisible and the visible, belong together, are 'made' for each other, as it were."[18]

Form and meaning, "whereness" and "whatness," are inseparable in the act of perceiving; in the written word, where abstraction permits such dualism, they are cut apart.[19] This is at the center of the artist's wariness — and the poet's challenge — of words. Add to this the fact that the artist is bent on the unique. Each work and each artist is unique, and singularities are indeed lost in the banalities of scholars. However, an insistence on uniqueness, a refusal of patterns, may stall understanding as much as extreme generalization does.[20] Even though writing cannot coherently present visual form and meaning at the same time, its abstractions and generalizations will one way or another be critical ingredients in the creative ferment of artists. The generalizations will qualify in numberless ways the viewer's encounter with art and are, anyway, inevitable. Between ignoring them as a painter, especially those concerning creation, and perhaps correcting them, given the opportunity, I prefer the latter.

Besides, I discovered that one's medium comes to mean both more and less as one goes along: more, in the sense that trustful, capable attention to it makes it "expand" to accommodate or infer ever more from outside it; less, in the sense that most of what one encounters, after a while, has already been intuitively "translated" into one's medium anyway. Furthermore, the simplicity of my youth was soon enough exchanged for the multiplicity of age. And O'Keeffe and all the others, including me, sent in their questionnaires, sat for the mystical interviews, and contributed to, as well as suffered, the word intensity of Public Relations. A picture is worth so many words—like its price, that number may also be inflated; the word is mightier than the sword, and so forth. But when it comes to parsnips, perhaps neither words nor paintings can butter them as well as a knife.

All of us work along spokes of specialization, but in strength we belong to a common hub. In times of utmost integrity a society can afford the emphasis of the spokes. In other times, under the stress of change or the need to grow and to elaborate our understanding, the wheel must be reinvented. I think such a time may be at hand.

I have considered the artist's aristocratic and other differences with words in order to review a frequently ignored aspect of the artist's growth and presence in the humanities. I wanted to alert the reader to the background against which a painter might feel it perilous to deal with creation at unaccustomed length and in an unaccustomed medium. In this discussion of "the creative enterprise," I often rely on the thinnest of the pronouns because I believe I can best serve the subject by relating my own substantiated thoughts, speculations, and procedures as they have risen from my painting and drawing since I was a child.

Creations do not easily reveal their true anatomy or even techniques. Indeed, the dream of many artists has been to make a work—and at times, apparently, a life—impervious to all such analysis. Given the complications at that level alone, the far more complex matters of an artist's general creation, sources, and methods are certain to be obscure and shrouded in speculation. The depth of the artist's origins in time, culture, and personality are such that explanations depend on sincerity and persuasion as much as rational argument. I am open to the latter, but am relying on the former.

I am aware that the sincerity of expression does not insure its credibility or acceptance. However, one could hardly offer these pages, much less confront the world with one's paintings, without a faith in enough moments of justifying reception. Meanwhile, I invoke for my protection a thought from Thoreau: "The word which is best said came nearest to not being spoken at all, for it is cousin to a deed which the speaker could have better done."[21]

NOTES

1. Albert Einstein, "What I Believe," *Forum*, October 1930, 194.

2. Charles Hope, review of *The Genius of Jacopo Bellini: The Complete Paintings and Drawings*, by Colin Eisler, *New York Review*, 19 July 1990, 28.

3. Kenneth Clark, *Moments of Vision* (New York: Harper & Row, 1981), 125.

4. Paul Taylor, "Love Story," *Connoisseur*, August 1991, 96.

5. Claes Oldenburg, *Store Days* (New York: Something Else Press, 1967), 49.

6. Aldous Huxley, "The Only Way to Write a Modern Poem about a Nightingale," *Harper's*, August 1963, 66.

7. Edward MacCurdy, trans., *The Notebooks of Leonardo da Vinci* (New York: George Braziller, 1956), 853.

8. Wyndham Lewis, *The Demon of Progress in the Arts* (Chicago: Henry Regnery Company, 1955), 48–49.

9. Jack Cowart and Juan Hamilton, *Georgia O'Keeffe* (Washington: National Gallery of Art, 1987), 267.

10. Stanislas Klossowski de Rola, *Balthus* (New York: Harper & Row, 1983), 7.

11. Arthur Koestler, *The Act of Creation* (New York: Macmillan, 1967), 177.

12. Jack D. Flam, *Matisse on Art* (New York: E. P. Dutton, 1978), 92.

13. Thomas B. Hess, *Willem de Kooning* (New York: Museum of Modern Art, 1968), 143.

14. Kiku Adatto, "The Incredible Shrinking Sound Bite," *New Republic*, 28 May 1990, 20.

15. Camille Paglia, *Sexual Personae* (New Haven: Yale University Press, 1990), 60–69.

16. Ludwig Wittgenstein, *Philosophical Investigations* (Oxford: Basil Blackwell, 1958), 47e.

17. Maurice Merleau-Ponty, *The Primacy of Perception and Other Essays*, ed. James M. Edie (Evanston: Northwestern University Press, 1964), 13.

18. Hannah Arendt, *The Life of the Mind: Thinking* (New York: Harcourt Brace Jovanovich, 1978), 109.

19. Hoyt L. Sherman, *Cézanne and Visual Form* (Columbus: Ohio State University, 1952), 3.

20. Tzvetan Todorov, review of *Modernity and the Holocaust*, by Zygmunt Bauman, *New Republic*, 19 March 1990, 30.

21. Henry David Thoreau, *A Week on the Concord* (Princeton: Princeton University Press, 1983), 105.

2

The Medium

At the heart of painting are the pleasures of handling paint, of cleanly overlapping one color, for example, with a sumptuous, sharply edged, knifed-on slab of another. Commendable works and the instruction that helps to bring them about do not come from those who dislike paint, who have not joyfully worked its subtle stages from water to clay, skin to bone, and thought of it as wine, plaster, cream, lava, and peanut butter. Taking this more or less for granted, I examine paint's properties in this chapter, but the real subject here is the direct flexibility of paint and the part its special character plays in the painter's creation. After making some comparisons with other media and discussing why introductions to paint, especially oil paint, are often troubled, I move on to some broader issues of its use — its ease in accommodating vision's "metaphorical quality," for example. The balance of the chapter deals mainly with an unforeseeable, existential factor in the act of painting and its significance. I close the chapter with a reminder of the large personal and cultural pattern in which that factor operates and how such considerations have figured in contemporary art.

The Beginning of something strikes me as a troublesome notion, maybe an impossibility in the strictest sense. If I think of it at all, I can best start something — a journey, a painting, or a conversation — not as A Beginning, but only as a lowercase, commonsensical beginning. However, beginning in that plain, technical sense often seems to me "after the fact," after the real Beginning. Real Beginnings, the auspicious, creative kind, are more seamlessly connected to what has gone before. That is why only they and the momentum they represent can herald something genuinely new and valuable. Identifying the ordinary beginning is a relatively simple matter, but the artist often develops a keener than usual sense of the governing, uppercase Beginning. Therefore, creation may involve a strong fundamental or anterior awareness that, though more personally than impersonally oriented, may be easily encouraged to include a historical sense. (It seems appropriate that a sixteenth-century artist, Giorgio Vasari, set the history of art in motion.)[1]

It is an awareness engendered, however, by the present. Even so, a *full* grasp of now includes *then*. There is no glory at the moment (if there is any at all, that too is earlier or later); likewise, no moment can in that moment be called A Beginning. A Beginning is discovered only afterward to have been one.

Such thinking is strongly influenced by my years as a painter; by the transitive nature of paint, particularly oil paint, and the fluctuant nature of picture making. Ideas, presuppositions, and theories are important, and some aspects of creativity are no doubt shared among artists and everyone else, but a more specific understanding of the painter's creation begins here, with the medium.

The literal and figurative fluidity, and perhaps my unsimple views about beginnings, is based in the medium's preeminent material characteristics: oil paint remains workable for two or more days, in most situations, and can be purposely kept so for a bit longer; in any case, its drying is usually gradual and not without warning, and in most cases it may be painted over when dry. This means, as a student once put it, "there are no excuses." More positively, it means that at any time, while the painting is wet or dry, a new conception can either sweep everything before it or insinuate itself into the previous beginning.

Therefore, though often originating in insights, thoughts, drawings, and studies well before the first stroke, The Beginning of a painted image may indeed turn out to have been the first touch of color or, rather, decisions on top of it after a month's work (and the changeable extent of The Beginning's impact may lie well into the future). The commonsense beginning and end may be directly linked, conceivably fused almost as one, or, as with some of Albert P. Ryder's work, years apart. There may be no uppercase End (a goal, yes, but not conclusively attained in a single, "masterpiece" canvas), which is what Camille Pissarro had in mind when he said Cézanne had all his life been working on the same painting.

The medium's mutability embarrasses simple description. Having started in any way, one can end in any way. Quickly and easily, even with considerations for the painting's durability, one is free to start and end with a plan; to junk the plan on a whim and entertain several other entirely different possibilities; and then junk *them* to realize either something new or one's initial objective in a version perhaps superior to the plan. For those, like the novelist, playwright, or composer, who barely employ materiality or do so for the sake of another kind of form, this is not a description of anything unusual. For those who work with concrete form, it is. With such protean means, the concept "mistake" is diminished, taking on a different meaning than it has when it hovers over the splitting of a diamond.

If one begins a sculpture in stone by chiseling away several large fragments, a world enough of possibilities remain, but none of them can include the missing, once continuous mass. One may happily attend to the remaining possibilities instead of regretting the cavity, but a decisive beginning has been made all the same, consciously or not, whether or not there was a plan. After the choice of canvas or support (no smaller a matter than the choice of stone) such *physically* determining acts in a painting are either nonexistent or far less exclusionary, particularly in the first hours. One does not discover that a critical point has passed, leaving one on the brink of a waterfall, so to speak, helplessly on the way downstream. There is such a thing as going with the flow, painting ever more heavily after losing the sparseness of the first applications, for example, but one can always revolve in midfalls and head back upstream. That is, paint can be wiped or scraped away to thinness, allowing, among other things, more or less simple changes from opacity to transparency. The same can be said for changes in color, contrast, brilliance, intricacy, and almost any other visual quality. Physically or aesthetically, one can alter ever so subtly or radically. One can add and subtract. Mediation is always possible. For the painter, "beginning again" is not an overly problematical or hypothetical dream, but a continual option.

Such means are open to quite different purposes and frames of mind during the development of a painting. Let us imagine that when Rembrandt stepped out for a glass of ale, a young Mondrian, stopping by for a visit and moved by the hazy beginning he found on the stout easel, might have worked it in the direction of a smaller piece he had been painting, *Mill by the Water* (figure 1). Delacroix, enjoying his dream of being in what seemed to be Rembrandt's studio were it not for the crude canvas, might have idly brushed its wet paint into forms that, when he was awake, would become the basis for his *Women of Algiers* (figure 2). Picasso, always drawn to the mixed, might have dropped by, and being so intrigued by how like Delacroix's harem were the smudges he found, might have been compelled to vary them until they called up yet another of his favorites, *Maids of Honor*, by Velázquez (figure 3). When Rembrandt returned, astonished by what he saw and resolving to drink no more ale, he might have wiped it out a bit and gone on to complete *The Wife of Tobias with the Goat* (figure 4), benefitting in some ways no longer apparent from vestiges of all these artists' colors and shapes. Although a principled mind may see the various costs of these digressions as outweighing their contributions, the painter in any particular instance may welcome (or at least accept) such "waste" if it yields special qualities or helps to secure an

Figure 1. *Mill by the Water*, Mondrian

Figure 2. *Women of Algiers*, Delacroix

Figure 3. *Maids of Honor*, Picasso

Figure 4. *Wife of Tobias with the Goat*, Rembrandt

objective. Consider further that several tubes of certain colors of paint in the hands of only a moderately skilled painter with a fan brush may yield a relatively low-cost, large-size, subtly graded range of hues (and intensities within hues) that is available no other way.

What all of this comes down to is an unworldy amplitude and compliance in the medium that may be either marvelous or maddening. It is surely closer to maddening for many who take it up for the first time. Except for intuition and a healthy unconcern for the outcome of the first fifty or so hours of painting, nothing seems to prepare us for such freedom. Though ultimately beneficial, drawing skills may at first hinder as well as help. Notwithstanding their welcome rigor and anesthetic effects, prematurely definite aims usually make matters worse. Most people in their first hours with the medium are as humanly alert as ever to the "path of least resistance," but instead of being drawn as one might think to the casual, free-fall exploration of its properties, their worldly conditioning draws them to a defensive struggle with "inconvenient" nonwater solvency and slow-drying "goo," the exact source of the medium's permissive elasticity.

A part of the creation and enjoyment or understanding of painting, as of every art, is the evaluation of what is important and what is trivial. One major reason for the earliest possible practice of the art is to inculcate a sense of how importance and triviality are identified differently in art than in life. Art may be the expression of an underlying human conviction that nothing is trivial. In any event, such appraisal is not always easy or simply intellectual. It reaches widely and involves not only disciplinary or cultural formations, but the breadth of individual sensitivity. Learning to play poker, a painter may ruin a straight flush by relieving all that black with a bit of color. The imposition of rules in this case does no harm to the "artistic instinct" (if anything, the rules will in some way become a part of it). However, the poker player, learning to paint, is faced with quite another game, if you will, one in which crisp rules are nonexistent and categorical judgments ("muddy" as a pejorative, for example) may constantly shift and change their value.

The trivial-important evaluation should not be isolated in thought. It must continue through works, where it can more undeniably lead and mislead, elate and disappoint. It is as though everyone had a certain number of bad paintings to do before they could get to the good ones, and the number could not be reduced by taking longer to do them. Later, we must be torn even from that mooring as subsequent work reveals our judgments of the first "good ones" as premature and shifting. Growth is not only toward new categorical judgments and their confirmation by the work; growth is also signaled by the work's tendency to bring any of the judgments into question.

Meanwhile, beginners may grumble about what the paint and appliances prevent, as if they could have their way with jackhammers and granite, a loom and basketfuls of yarn, or a coarse chunk of black chalk. In a sense they are right, for we are used to counteraction and interferences — so much so that we may not acknowledge them until they are removed. We are used to planting little more than hints of full possibility in the small patch between iron restrictions; used to exerting our preconception and will to overcome inertia. We come to expect and then to rely on friction and resistance in our actions. (Pilots report that beginning flyers, accustomed to automobiles and terrestrial assumptions, commonly "overcontrol" a plane in flight.) Emptily or with purpose, we are not practiced in cooperating with a forgiving medium that can simultaneously ramify so widely, simply and quickly, respond so directly and immediately, and constantly permit easy change.

The difficulty is that beginners are not so much prevented as allowed. They are far more familiar with materials that strongly delimit use at the outset. The "jackhammer" would relievingly coarsen expectations and bring them into line with its operation. If a tube of cadmium red were literally the price of gold, if all paint were workable only at a narrow range of temperature, if it dried uniformly in an hour and could never be painted over — or could be applied only through *in*direct and "high-tech" means — then, notwithstanding another set of more common complaints, beginners would be more comfortable. Out of the close, arbitrary limits and the overcoming of a lower grade of obstacles, a certain charm would appear. After all, a bare canvas or sheet of paper has little inherent value or physical presence. Only ability or artistic discrimination can bring to these surfaces a value and presence that surpasses the appeal of a silver doorplate or the cannon in the courtyard. With my fanciful restrictions, more of the responsibility for the character of the beginner's first work would be wrested from them and shared with unchangeable circumstance. They would be in the familiar atmosphere of all those who deal with more instrumental, intractable, or unforgiving substances and processes; who are more in competition with reluctant material conditions than involved with immediately summoned content and references. It is often the setting in which the dog in Samuel Johnson's quip walks on its hind legs: judgments of how well something is done are belittled by its having been done at all.

Similarly, if the most informative and evocative level of *reference* were the point, even such exemplary works as the delightful early sixteenth-century tapestry *Hunt of the Unicorn* would fall short of, say, Raphael's *Alba Madonna* (figure 5), painted at about the same time. Reason and the senses pick out and applaud the tapestry's daunting labor, technique, and cunning in a quicker and more conscious way than with the painting. If we ever do the same with the painting, it is after a telling period in which our ordinary sympathies have first been given play; "air" is breathed and "flesh" is sensed, if only for seconds, before we admit "paint." The threads, conspiring intricately, amazingly to suggest "flowers," remain threads (figure 6). In spite of such impressive and traditionally woven contemporary examples as Pamela Topham's realistic landscape tapestries, one doubts that such media could ever have the descriptive ease of Georges de la Tour's *The Fortune Teller*, in which the tapestried garment of one of the figures is clearly distinguished.

Painterly chauvinism — if that is what it is — may start early. As a child, I was once among a group of other children who examined a cowhide on which a rustic scene had been tooled. I silently decided that the *picture* might have been done by the same hand to much better effect with pencil and poster paints, and probably in half the time. Untouched, the *cowhide* would still have been beautiful. Therefore, the exact purpose of what we beheld, and a few of the others admired, puzzled me.

No, "content and reference," and their meaning, are of course not alone in their appeal to viewers, even viewers of pictures, and especially nowadays. The profoundly or completely representational, although the modernists who abandoned it once assumed it to be the ideal of the unschooled, is not and rarely ever was the only "point." Our attention and curiosity are also drawn to the struggle with obstruction and our clever stamp on the obdurate. Contention with matter intrigues us, and there are many confusions in appropriating, translating, or replacing this interest in the aesthetic. Michelangelo's hours of work on his back in painting the Sistine Chapel will usually arouse as much interest as the artistic scope of the murals. Anyone who regularly frequents museums can recall the hushed praise, How *long* that must have taken! The lifetimes required to erect them figure largely in the ordinary appreciation of medieval cathedrals. Therefore, it was often its impudence as much as its assault on realism that raised resentment against modernism: nothing so unexhausting and immaterial as Malevich's square or Matisse's linear squiggle could inspire awe.

By now, impudence of some kind is almost a given, and mere impertinence has been made to seem quaint; but if our sense of toil is engaged, if in a work or deed we can read cost, hazard, signs of labor, or elaborate

Figure 5. *Alba Madonna,* Raphael

Figure 6. *The Hunt of the Unicorn* (detail), late fifteenth-century French or Flemish

preparation, we will tolerate and rationalize even more of it than usual. Throughout Japan and the west coast of the United States, as I write, the Bulgarian artist Christo is having large, fabricated blue and yellow umbrellas temporarily installed to symbolize the interdependence of those regions. As with his twenty-four-mile "Running Fence" (1976) in the hills of California, television and other commentators, attracted by the enormity of the undertaking, are usually unwilling either to compare it with, say, the region's more enormous freeway system or to say very much about its existence as art. They usually report such things as the time and effort involved in seeking permission and materials for the installation, the coordination of technicians, and engineering problems. Of course, many regard all of this as much a part of the piece as its blueprints. If so, one might as well include the fabrication and transportation of materials, the newscasts, the inevitable photographs, the later disassembly, and so on. The umbrella project's intent is laudable, but its seriousness in the public eye is increased primarily by its dangerous, expensive rigors of agreements, construction, and the like. Symbolizing the same message by pushing carved bamboo and redwood poles into the ground would not only be less technologically consumptive, hence "old-fashioned," but also too easy.

In any case, as painters and students of art, we are the heirs of deeply embedded cultural and physical responses that may at times hamper our practical and aesthetic access to the medium and our valuation of what it can do. The medium itself is not about resistance, but susceptibility. This is not to say it has no physical or customary limits. Many painters, such as Braque, carried into modernism a classical wisdom that still, if barely, survives: it is in limitation, not extensiveness, that mastery is first revealed. Like Delacroix, an experienced painter may even occasionally growl about the "confounded facility" and, as a temporary corrective, wish for the strictures of marble.[2] Nonetheless, the fundamental means of the painter readily lead to unbounded play, improvisation, variation, and correction.

In order that they be optimally exploited and guided, something of this central nature of painting must be experienced by the novice, the sooner the better. Something of the breadth and speed of the means — and their often surprizing relation to end product — must be felt; something of their tonal capacity, which rivals nature's, must be sensed before they are applied to more ambitious objectives. Otherwise, if such resources are too quickly turned to the narrowing purposes of, for example, the flagrant masterpiece, therapeutic compulsiveness, or the reach for a "style," it is like using a Rolls Royce to take the garbage to the street. It is like insisting on learning how to play the piano by playing only Ellen Taaffe Zwilich's Piano Concerto no. 1 — no scales, exercises, or fooling around.

One finally learns to extrapolate from *every* move, including those in the completion of the narrowest objectives. One learns how the medium accommodates vision's "metaphorical" quality: the mind sees and retains a little self-contained abstraction or landscape in its treatment of a ballerina's skirt. More than is commonly realized, painting anything may be but a short step from painting anything else, which is why Degas could say he did as he pleased and only at the last moment added the signifying accent. One sees the presence of water in a treatment of sky, a core of hardness in softness, the brush's wantonness at the center of high control, submerged description in stray components, or a possible grace in the most awkward gesture.

However, unless there is some care in the beginning, it will be assumed that all such transient phenomena, if noticed, are either irrelevant tendencies or are meant to serve the painting's subject. The beginner must be urged to see it the other way round: the subject is a pretext for entertaining the transience. If the fluency of the medium is to serve concentration instead of scattered distractions, it must in part be controlled by acceding to it. If the "Old Masters" were able to start and end with a subject, it was, in addition to their unrelenting purpose and ability to draw, because they had first understood and become proficient with this sequence.

In exploiting or responding to the transience, the painter's grasp of the work at hand alternately tightens and loosens, both within seconds and across hours. It is a critical experience for the student. The painter may experience such alternations with pleasure or foreboding; however, the pleasure may not be an introduction to things finally kept, and the foreboding may lead to distinctive work. "Tighten" does not always mean "capture," and "loosen" may not mean "loss of control." The actions and their results are interchangeable, that is, letting the painting "get away from you" may mean just that, or it may help to secure an effect; tightening or bearing down may at first promise but finally spoil a painting, or it may provide the needed quality. The key is the alternation itself: the artist rather continuously gives way to the one in order to know best how to take advantage of the other.

It may be impossible now to spend more than several hours in any of this country's art schools without hearing, from students themselves or their teachers, that one must "loosen up." An interchange between the technical and the sociopsychological implications of this advice seems easily, almost eagerly made. Unfortunately, interchanges between "tight" and "loose" are not as easily recognized. I suppose no more harm comes from this than if "tighten up" were the more frequent bywords, but, more important, no great benefits can come from doing either one until they are seen as relatively linked and technically, aesthetically necessary to one another.

Not much reflection is required, then, to see how a painting, although accomplished with the most direct actions, is the result of countless midcourse corrections — "course" referring here either to a single gesture or the painting in general. Most students paint almost exclusively with a final "look" in mind and with inferences drawn from finished, more proficient works. While this end-first view will eventually serve them, they should be helped instead to experience and understand how the pursuit of unpredictable, irregular developments in at least the first stages of a painting enriches their ability and improves the work without canceling their objective. They must be helped to reveal to themselves the extemporaneous, the makeshift, and even the capricious, not as threats to plans or necessarily as ends, but as fundamental to the art. Nature, according to Dante, is a great workman whose hand trembles.[3] Although many will either prize or negate the trembling and therefore separate it from the workman's basic intention, the best painters reveal how inseparable they are. The makeshift and impromptu are the trembling and as such belong among the rudiments of painting with the clearest of ideas and purposes.

The painting's appearance is achieved crabwise, through a sidling, shifting, sliding accumulation of plans, revoked decisions, reaffirmations, and rejected and accepted happenings. Clearest at the beginning and end, it is a process often blind and chancy in the middle. Having no sufficient way to generalize this path, I turn to figures of speech. The painting's progress is often the tacking and trimming of a sailing ship at sea, not only the straight advance of a machine on land. Or, to mix metaphors as painting mixes all of its elements, it is the simultaneous coordination of the edgeless force fields of quantum theory more than the building of a wall, one brick at a time. Two forward steps may sometimes be gained by sliding back one. In short, it is lifelike in the sense meant by Justice Oliver Wendell Holmes when he said life was painting a picture, not doing a sum.

In saying that the unrehearsed is fundamental to painting, I mean no less than that. My comments may seem to address only one part of the spectrum. To bring up "Old Masters" with "transience" may seem to look at Titian but away from Piero della Francesca. And talk of mutability, play, midcourse corrections, mixed elements, unpredictability, and the like may be fairly taken for ways to imply romanticism, expressionism, abstract expressionism, neo-expressionism, and so-called painterly or heavy surfaces in general. Though I do not mean to exclude these, I have in mind another, broader purpose. My remarks are directed to the broader foundations of any endeavor in painting, even to those where mercurial properties may not be celebrated but are essentially present and dealt with in a significant manner.

Clearly, the works and procedures of certain painters — Fragonard, Monet, Soutine, Hans Hoffman, Susan Rothenberg, Alice Neel, and Anselm Kiefer, for example — more or less obviously demonstrate the characteristics discussed above, while others, like Jacques Louis David, Mondrian, Roy Lichtenstein, Agnes Martin, Philip Pearlstein, and Robert Mangold, do so less obviously. The traits I have touched on are, nevertheless, significantly present in the works or procedures of them all — and of any number of others, wherever they may fit in groupings made for different reasons. The significance lies in an aspect of every painting experience so common as to seem — or actually be — beneath the painter's conscious notice.

The standard notion about painting of any kind is that it is made from two sources. The first is the subject, however widely or narrowly defined. Directly observed, remembered, invented, or a combination of these, it is evoked, wholly or partially, clearly or clumsily, according to the skills, techniques, and intentions of the painter. The second source is, for lack of a better single term, the painter. That is, paintings are seen as reflecting the painter's emotions, thoughts, messages, moods, attitudes, and artistic purposes. Painters paint paintings about something, if only about the painting itself, and in doing so reveal themselves and their subjects. With that curious need to believe that the inspiration and the end-product are identical, anything not traceable to subject or intention is put down to insurmountable conditions, weak talent, or misreadings of the subject. Understandably, this is thought to account for a painting's ingredients and general import.

However, both the directness of the personal revelation and the treatment of the subject are affected at the root by a third source. One might well propose here the *viewer's* inevitable contribution, a deserving topic in itself, but I have in mind something else more critical to the making of the painting, or at least something that will already have had its effect by the time the viewer sees the painting. Broadly speaking, I have in mind the very act of making as the third source; however, I wish to be more specific about one of its prime, though fleet, factors.

I think of this agent, common to every painting experience, as small and ever present. One might simply and imprecisely call it the operation of fate or chance. It is beyond control, except by a coarsening decision that permits its constant refinements to flow unnoticed by the painter; or reactively, following acceptance or notice of it to some greater degree. One could use jargon to say it occurs between "input" and "feedback," being infallibly born of the former and a denied or accepted part of the latter. I refer to the existential fact that even in the most careful, well-planned work of the most talented, premeditative painter, a good deal of what happens, on the whole or stroke by stroke, is *unforeseen.*

Some may paint expressly for this experience; others, like the late Ad Reinhardt, an advocate of rigorous, minimal form, may strain to escape as much of it as possible. Now and then, what happens is treated as if hoped for or expected, but perhaps not in the way in which it came about. However, one might as well say that none of it, what exactly happens or the way it happens, is or can be completely envisioned.

It does not amaze me that, like the work of every other painter, Reinhardt's exclusions and insistent preconception nevertheless required development over time and, for all we know, *within* each work. If he was not satisfied with the very first stark painting after his "classical" ideas were already clear, was it purely because of faulty *conception?* I believe, instead, that minute qualities joined throughout the *making* of the works, confirming and replacing, proving and disproving, derailing and retracking his ideas.

He may have called this "discovery," "experiment," or "technical problems"; I doubt that his anti-romantic program dignified the inclusion of "accident," but it might as well have. What we designate as accident is but a cruder, more intrusive version of what is continually going on and being disposed of without name or especially demanding notice. What the artist allows to stand as finished work, and what is taken, usually absolutely, as an embodiment of the artist's intention, includes an inestimable trade in this conscious and subconscious experience. There may be no way to analyze it, but I believe this experience is at the core of much that is enigmatic in art. The enigmatic is an ingredient, not the motive of my work; however, I believe this "accident digestion" is one of mystery's locations and is not too rarefied to be considered as an important element in the act of making paintings, and therefore in teaching and considering the subject.

As a way of introducing some of its implications, I will give a typical instance of what I mean by the existential factor — or E Factor, as we may facetiously call it. Let us suppose that I paint a streak of earthy yellow on the canvas. Immediately, I begin adjustments between what I *see* and what was to have happened, or might have happened, and now may (should, can) happen next. As usual, enough of what has just occurred is so unpresumable that adjustments are all but automatically begun. The adjustments are between the whole work, as affected by everything about the new yellow, and what an instant before I had expected; or between the actuality as I now see it and prospects, subliminal expectations, and memories flicked into consciousness by the actuality. In either case, the painting is dramatically or infinitesimally budged from its previous course, actually and in my thinking about it.

The general range of such adjustments may be, (1) to take measures that further suppress conscious control — a more awkward tool, greater speed, suspended judgment, and so on; (2) to leave, wipe out, or alter the last touch, each of which is a positive act, requiring further adjustments both there and throughout the painting; (3) to take measures that may further extend conscious control — renewed discipline at every point in the process, slower and more calculated steps toward a preconceived objective, refusal of unexpected charms in favor of preliminary work or ideas, and so forth.

The first kind of adjustment allows the E Factor, at least for the meantime, a greater role in the appearance of the painting. The third kind seeks, at least for the meantime, to minimize it. Ingenuity makes its most obvious appearance in the second kind, demonstrating the ability to connect the purpose, whatever it is, with the most unruly mishap or even the weakest hints of the E Factor. Moreover, the second kind of adjustment — and I suspect the more usual, even in many works appearing to consist mainly of the third kind — also more easily represents the constant discovery and compromise of artistic work. It represents the attainment of a somewhat loosely sought end while rolling, as it were, with every little punch.

The key points of my earthy yellow instance and the operation of the E Factor are these. First, I imagine everything in my instance as taking place in a few seconds. Second, regardless of the kinds of adjustments, the E Factor is *continuous* to a considerable and important degree, for it is nothing less than the boundary between the unknown and the realization of art, the heart of every idea having to do with the manipulation of a medium, something instrumental. Third, regardless of the "type" or "look" of the finished work, the same painter will have responded for some length of time in all the ways discussed above, not only within the whole painting but in quick succession after a single swath of color.

Teaching and painting are not exactly analogous, of course, but they have many parallels. One is between the E Factor and the importance Diana Korzenik gives to the teacher. She stresses, I think correctly, the importance of the teacher beyond abstract "educational authorities" (see chapter 13). The importance lies in the teacher's background and intention coming together under specific circumstances with the skills, personalities, and demands of specific students. Only the teacher, not the theorist, meets the actual test and opportunity of given moments in a given classroom. The painter's most distinctive interaction with the "authority" of previous work, influences, intentions, and so forth, also depends on non-doctrinaire, direct, momentary performance at certain points of the unforeseen in a given work. In neither case can the distant authority's or one's own plan be sacred. In both, a sensitivity to the immediate actuality leads the way, whether in execution or departure from plans.

They may be the narrow pass through which everything must go, but of course no number of discrete, five-second instances of "action-adjustment-reaction" on the canvas accounts for the whole history and configuration of a painting. For one thing, smooth or abrupt coordinations also take place on the palette or with various adjunct operations and materials in nearby locations. Surrounding shapes and colors may also become absorbed in the reactions. Elusively or definitely, the E Factor is present in the selection of colors and their amounts, the selection and use of brushes, the arrangements of light, and many other considerations that move directly through the image and beyond, on to "clean up" and the next day.

In addition, though imagination is involved in the action-adjustment-reaction of making, something like these hyphenated transactions may also occur wholly within the imagination, like a "ghost painting" or hidden pulse throughout the work. Some experience is needed, of course, before most students can concentrate on a work well enough to have something left over, but they should think of this "extra" imagination as a source, not as superfluous. Both feeding and feeding on the work at hand, such proposed but unapplied imagination may be directed toward a future work or call up options unsensed during a past work.

Added to the countless chance perusals and observations of any single day, all of this qualifies — and will in turn be qualified by — the work in the studio or classroom. It is from the larger patterns of all of this that one comes to and carries through with one's work. Because most students will be "aiming at their work," instructional considerations should always include this broader pattern and its bearing on individual selection and operation. As the brushstroke is couched in the painting, so the painting and its origins are couched in a range of real and often arbitrary decisions. Their work often advances when certain students are made conscious of the wider artistic, personal, and physical matrix from which it rises. Ironically, a painting achieves a brilliant autonomy through the artist's fidelity to a larger fabric. The artist may choose to attend closely to as much of that fabric as possible or to acknowledge it only above a certain high threshold, but being an artist, as well as being a teacher, is knowing that it is always potently there.

A considerable part of artistic discernment is involved in the disposition of the unforeseen. When they are made, the next moves can produce important qualities that no degree of experience or commitment to purpose could prevent or prearrange. When skill is unmechanical it is guided by sensitiveness to these qualities and the everchanging reality of the work *as* it progresses. Whether I generally exert control or consign the character of my work to the contingencies of each move, the effort soon takes on an unavoidable texture of variably demanding judgment that continually revises my purpose or reconnects it to what I have done. If there is a "probity in art," to quibble with Ingres, it is this all-inclusive texture, not only "drawing."[4]

The texture has to do not so much with the overlapping abstractions of "expression" or "subject" as with what is *now* explicitly taking place. Thus the many aphorisms about the painting "painting itself"; thus Matisse's need, like that of so many before and since him, to spend time with the finished painting, acquainting himself with it almost as if it had been done by someone else; thus the difference between the artist's and the public's attitude to the work. The public's attitude, especially as most exhibitions have an advisory atmosphere, is This is definitive, while the artist's is more like, Look what happened. "How, then," Matisse asked, "do you expect an amateur to understand that which the artist does not yet comprehend?"[5] Neither Matisse's making himself acquainted, Reinhardt's studious pose in the famous photograph of him framed in silhouette by his studio window, nor Jackson Pollock's vigils over the day's results would make much sense if the work were only the product of unsurprised craft.

An old Chinese military maxim may be pertinent here: no plan survives contact with the enemy. As one cannot tell the future in convincing detail (and no one is "ahead of" his or her time), there is no such thing as carrying off a conception in every particular, and art is very much a matter of particular as well as general reckoning. Depending fully on neither the making nor the planning, the painter "leads and follows him or herself" to the fullest deliverances of art, whether in Periclean Athens, the Royal Academy, Lascaux, or Soho.

We take the view that artistic intelligence and intention are well in advance of the work, even cynically in the case of those who disavow it; that the artist, however loosely, guides the work. This is obvious, of course. We are not so considerate of the ways in which intelligence and intention are called up by and through the working, of the ways in which the work guides the artist. This too is supportable and applies to conceptual artists and to Franz Kline; to Seurat and to automatists; to minimalists and maximalists. This too should figure in any consideration of creation.

Of course, changeability can be mockingly demonstrated for its own sake (there being no other objective). It can supposedly be avoided by merely occupying the format as the only move whatsoever (blank, dadaist canvases) or churlishly stopping with the first move. One may certainly make a show of obviously shunning not only the work's guidance, but any notion that there is or should be a "work." One may radically simplify processes to the point that they are, or seem to be, controllable and hence a perfect match of intentions. As if to announce a magical, breakthrough disposal of the process, along with "sensitivity" and the rest of its throwbacks, one may *displace* the process by prefabricators, assistants, or robots, or by studies, trials, and experiments that supposedly leach out the unexpected until a moribund result can be presented as the work.

These were among the ascendant strategies and provocations of the past two or so decades of American art. They refute and refine the developments of at least seven or eight prior decades of modern art. They have shaken the social and aesthetic enterprise of art and made many inroads on education; but, though it may seem of little consequence, the quintessence of creating and sensing remains the same. On the one hand, the wildest, most nihilistic or sensual work will not preclude judgment or second thoughts; on the other, Mondrian's neoplastic ideal of excluding the senses from the mind's creation, even if such a thing were possible more than once, will not hold.

With the simplifying gesture that painters often make (and others often call oversimplifying), Monet is supposed to have said that all painters are impressionists. I sympathize with this eye for the continuous and an aesthetic sense of the One in the Many. I gladly exchange all the small coins of the "isms" for larger currency, for although there are differences among painters, they are both fewer and more profound than fashion, art journalism, and the Market of Newness would lead us to believe. The viewer is now meant to reel before each invention as if before a change in mode, like moving from a panel by Jan van Eyck to, let us say, baseball, instead of from one painting to another. But artists know better. Instead of the Million Uniquenesses, the student, too, must be given the common bases. One-of-a-kind pretensions make better theater and far more copy, but that is different from making paintings.

I join with the painter and art historian John Golding in his acclaim for the Museum of Modern Art's memorable exhibit Picasso and Braque: Pioneering Cubism.[6] Because I also sense in it a somewhat mutual approach to painting, I would like to quote his praise of famous and seminal creativity in order to make an observation about the painter's creation in general.

Having also touched on the belief of some of us that "pictorial meaning and linguistic meaning are two different things," he goes on to describe how the paintings and the way they were shown in New York reminded him of how "the highest moments of art are often held in precarious balance." He feels that Braque's 1913 painting *Pedestal Table* shows the beginnings of what Braque described as "perpetual revelation," an awareness in which the painter later said that objects existed for him only insofar as there was a "rapport" between him and them. He describes how, for at least two key years, the painters were "carried by forces beyond their own control." Their accomplishments were begun as "voyages . . . the final destinations of which were not known or appreciated until they had been reached."

Without tarnishing Golding's estimates of Braque and Picasso, I believe much of what he writes may, with considerable dilution, be said of painting in general. "Precarious balance" is imminent throughout the act, even though the results are not high moments that eventually overshadow the low. As with Cézanne's fabled rapport, the "perpetual revelation" of Braque's rapport is a more dramatic and more literate description of the painter's "action-adjustment-reaction": the rapport between painter and tabletop objects passes through the *medium* in both directions. That is, the rapport is with the medium, as influenced by the objects, as much as with the objects, which are studied not only abstractly but in terms of the medium and its possibilities. Though the consequences may never weigh as greatly as those brought about by the two famous friends and collaborators, it is in the nature of painting that painters are liable to somewhat uncontrollable energies that can help to take them on voyages to places nonexistent and unappreciated until after they are there.

The blend of purpose and responses to the unforeseen informs all characteristic appearances in painting. For example, I sense its conscious presence in the supposed subconscious of surrealism and, as I have noted, Cézanne's *petite sensation*. It is alive in Marcel Duchamp's "art coefficient"—the differences between "the unexpressed but intended and the unintentionally expressed."[7] In prehistoric cave paintings, one sees in the delicate realism of the animals the artist's momentary, useful responses to and cooperation with the rugged walls.

However, instead of dealing in greater detail with this aspect of painting, I would like now to examine a few more standard aspects, namely, style, impulse, eclecticism, and color.

NOTES

1. E. H. Gombrich, *Meditations on a Hobby Horse and Other Essays* (New York: Phaidon, 1971), 108.

2. Walter Pach, trans., *The Journal of Eugene Delacroix* (New York: Viking Press, 1972), 99.

3. Dante Alighieri, Paradiso, Canto XIII, v. 76.

4. Jack D. Flam, *Matisse on Art* (New York: E. P. Dutton, 1978), 76.

5. "Matisse Speaks," *Art News*, 3 June 1933, 8.

6. John Golding, "Two Who Made a Revolution," *New York Review*, 31 May 1990, 8–11.

7. Kim Levin, *Beyond Modernism* (New York: Harper & Row, 1988), 22.

3

Some Other Factors: Style, Impulse, Eclecticism, Color

From the medium and its specific character, we move in this chapter to the consideration of four general art making constituents that either impinge on its use or reveal it in ways not yet mentioned. In each case, these are considered more abstractly than my examination of the medium.

Two kinds of style are reviewed, but I have given more attention to the organic kind that emerges unattended, so to speak, while its producer is otherwise involved. The section on impulse provides an opportunity to touch also on spontaneity, premeditation, and inspiration and their place in making art. What has often been given a bad name, eclecticism, I attempt to show as an expected part not only of the artist's growth and interest in making art but of our seeing and enjoying art. A discussion of color closes the chapter. Using the remarks of two painters and a recently published book about one kind of painting, I argue that instead of being one of several "elements" of visual experience, color is more practically understood as a word for the indivisible unity of that experience.

Notions of style are very elusive, and many artists rightly regard the word with suspicion. Style is still too often understood only as a garnish, a personal quirk, something added or done to a work to give it flair and specialness, much as one who "has style" might wear *anything* a certain way. It is also often understood as a kind of index, a preexistent look or idea that guides the making of a new work, much as one might wear *certain* clothes a certain way in order to be "in" style.

In this sense, being "in" style is somewhat similar to working in a particular, broadly recognized mode. Although the individual's own touch, materials, and ideas are represented in the work, they are subordinated to the predetermined qualities of the style. Judgments that dwell on how such works are aligned with a style can have the effect of de-individualizing "topical concerns" and disowning content. Superficial resolutions and "anti-style" statements, such as derisive or heavy-handed blendings of contemporary with older manners, are current ways of refusing the implications of traditional stylistic development.

A painter's "having" style is a more complex matter. "Having" style points more directly to the individual than to the recognized style in which he or she works. It points in the direction of such adages as Georges Buffon's "Style is the man" (and, for what it is worth, the art critic Emily Genauer's reversal of that). Because of their recognition of style's intrinsic origins, I believe such views are more in harmony with the larger concerns of creation, not only because they make style "natural" but because they make it the result of something more important than style.

In the same vein, I would make style that which is irreducible and individually persistent beneath either the least or most effective efforts, in the way that no facial expression can for long hide the true structure of a face. Mozart, who said he neither studied nor aimed at originality, believed his music's particular form and style were probably due to "the same cause which renders my nose so large or so aquiline, or, in short, makes it Mozart's, and different from those of other people."[1]

One does not, therefore, "whip up" a truly personal, durable style. Such styles are the result of artists' having worked at great and knowing lengths, honestly, confidently, and with no vital concern for style per se, down through every kind of superficiality to a solid ground plane, one below which, given their medium, intent, personality, historical milieu, and so forth, they *cannot* go. As with every accomplished artist, Picasso's style, for example, is what is ineluctably present, no matter the kind or number of liberties usually regarded as his "changes in style" — what Picasso himself referred to as his having "no style."[2]

The stressing of style in the act of creation is therefore one of the less helpful forms of self-consciousness in art education. The "look" or general identification of the product is more convincingly distinctive when, instead of paying short-cut attention to it, the artist ignores it and takes the longer way around, concentrating on the subjects, conceptions, meanings, influences, and actual satisfactions that motivate it.

"Inspiration" has largely lost not only its connotations of the divine, but in many respects its sense of a high, overarching drive that guides one through any number of works and their conflicts. Its use is increasingly interchangeable with "impulse." In a decidedly secular way, and with either condescension or approval, a painter may say of one of his or her works, "Something came over me."

No one can doubt the strong presence of impulse in American art of the past fifty years. Even when it is not really there, we seem to prefer the thought that it is. Therefore, some of the most careful planning and thinking in our art is dressed and staged as impulse. Perhaps the same may be said for much in our entertainment and general public communications. This preference is part of an outlook that equates spontaneity with "the good, the true, and the beautiful" — and with art per se. As such, it may also represent nostalgia in technologized circumstances that, all advertisements to the contrary, increasingly limit impulse. Conversely, the far reaches of premeditation (the nearer, such as stretching a canvas, we concede) are often thought to be a zone of intellect that is cold and hostile to art.

There is still, nevertheless, a lingering mistrust of spontaneity, even though it may surface as no more than a mildly practical caution, as in the phrase "impulse buying." A climate of financial risk or impending epidemic may deepen but does not necessarily cause it. Such mistrust can simply be the perennial, stoical doubt of anything as effusive, flighty, and hopeful as impulse. Or it can represent another kind of insight. For although "premeditation" may first imply "the planning thoughts of a murderer," the word, especially in art, is not and can never be fully eclipsed. In spite of all pretenses to the contrary, art houses all of its fickle, changeable spirit in premeditation. That which is "freely" or thoughtlessly obtained is meditated, once it is recognized, judged, retained, and then built upon. It is then included in subsequent expressions of a particular, premeditated form and its history and traditions.

Impulse, then, is one way the form may be still further revealed. Whatever its general moral reputation, Yeats's "lonely impulse of delight" is another matter in painting. The two, impulse and painting, are practically inseparable. I can more easily imagine approaching a canvas without inspiration than completing one without once being goaded or giving in to impulse. As we have seen, the medium allows it to be taken back or followed, and the integrity of one's search may demand it.

Many painters have spoken of the futility of beginning without emotion, plans, enthusiasm, or other would-be determiners that can be understood as "inspiration." However, I have begun simply out of routine, and once the E and other factors set in, the most lethargic beginning can turn or return to inspiration. There is little chance of excellence in trying to work exclusively from either inspiration *or* knowledge. I believe the two are combined at their highest levels, and the fulcrum between the two is often impulse. What impulse is based in are the reactions begun by the kind of "enclosed randomness" I emphasized in the preceding chapter. Even when it seems merely to strike out at tedium, impulse — the sudden trying or overruling of conceptions — can be a sign of contact with something larger.

Therefore, before pronouncing the painter "self-indulgent," "inconsistent," or "directionless" on the basis of half a dozen examples, the viewer should see another thirty or so works from before and after the half dozen. Patience is due the gifted or formerly involved student who seems suddenly to have "lost interest," to be unable to "settle down" and "concentrate," who leaves work unfinished, or "spoils" work and departs from a cogent series of previous achievements.

"Eclecticism," stemming from the Greek word for "to select" or "to pick out," was originally a disparaging reference by classical scholars to the mixing of philosophies that for about four hundred years followed the singularity of Plato and Aristotle. Though highly regarded as a philosophical approach in the seventeenth and eighteenth centuries, eclecticism of other kinds have most usually been cast in an unfavorable light. In art, the Eclectics were late sixteenth- and early seventeenth-century Italian painters who hoped to imitate the grandeur and vitality of the Renaissance masters, Michelangelo, Raphael, and Titian; but, according to two well-known authorities of the 1940s, "the result . . . was only facility, superficiality, and eclecticism."[3] Allegiance to European themes and treatments among contemporary American painters in that energetic postwar period was also denounced as eclecticism by certain other painters and New York critics.[4] The art critic Robert Hughes refers to the "numbed eclecticism" of 1980s art.[5]

In all three examples, the subjects of the charge may not have *redeemed* what they took, but then being influenced and failing the influence are quite different. After all, the "Renaissance" of the titans means rebirth. As with style, we have here another case of difference between the generic and individual values of a term. For the spirit of wide selection, picking out, and gathering from past or present is something without which it is difficult to imagine the nourishment and growth of an artist. As the painter might qualify them, the atelier and other teaching methods, apprenticeship, and the general development of one's art may in many respects merge to the point of hazy practical distinction with eclecticism.

Viewers more widely acquainted with art in general are more likely to sense its multifarious effects, generally or in any given work. Whether they describe the work as eclectic, which is more often justifiable than we might think, depends not so much on the number or range of influences as on the way they are resolved.

In any event, the postures and practices that earn the eclectic label are to some extent inherent in the making and seeing of art. No matter how knowledgeable and empathic, someone looking at a two-hundred-year-old painting can be expected to see it, in some degree, in relation to personal, artistic, and other issues and events that could not have had a part in its creation. No matter how distinctive an artist may be, the lengthy and populous existence of the art will work against the purity of the distinction. To think otherwise is, at worst, to accept the impossible exaggeration that creators can be so uneclectic as to "reinvent the art"; or, at best, to see greatness in the most exclusive rather than the most inclusive creation.

Relatively recent and special needs for "the exclusive" have driven some to a sophisticated version of Charlie Chaplin's hallucination that his shoes were steak: connections leading to and from a kind of work are overlooked in declaring it a new kind. However, in art one is subject to more or less constant influence, even in the philosophical games with its permeable boundaries. The force of both detail and design decree it: anything may be grist for the creative mill, which may grind it coarse or exceedingly fine. Whether the invention of collage; or the flagrant mimicry of others' art now in vogue; whether Manet's use of third-century A.D. Roman sculpture, by way of Raphael's *The Judgment of Paris*, for his *Luncheon on the Grass*; or the general attitude of Michelangelo as he sought inspiration for Saint Peter's Church in the Coliseum, it is all the same. The painter's often unpresuming eye is voracious, easily attracted, yet independent.

Sir Joshua Reynolds wrote that a great portion of the painter's life "must be employed in collecting materials for the exercise of genius. Invention, strictly speaking, is little more than a new combination of those images which have been previously gathered and deposited in the memory: nothing can come of nothing; he who has laid up no materials can produce no combinations."[6] Although it was not clearly his intention, I take his "materials" to include not only the copious art of one's formal or informal education, but something from everything else.

In other words, I do not believe that art is exclusively born, either of life or of other art. The notion that "nature copies art" — that we often see life as art, or see it to the extent that artists have defined it — by itself rightly confuses the matter. So does our momentary reading of art as life, which is not in itself naive. But even without these ideas, it should be obvious that between the lengthy preparation of the painter from a stock of past and present accomplishments and his or her trained and innate sensitiveness, many moments of creation with an always newly arrayed medium are bound to be a blend of phantoms, reminders, conscious models, subconscious references, odd allusions, surplus possibilities, and borrowed traits; bound also to be a refinement involving more than art.

The connection between eclectic tendencies and the viewpoint I have been pursuing, and perhaps other aspects of creation, may be further clarified by considering originals and reproductions of paintings. In the time before great paintings needed armed surveillance, I recall standing as close to the canvases of Rosa Bonheur, Velázquez, Constable, and Manet as they must have done in painting them. This callow habit alone, this "becoming them," was often enough to change my thoughts and feelings and hence the painting. In nearly empty galleries I would raise my hand as if it held a brush and "paint" the paths of colors and decisions that coursed through satin, porcelain, blood, and vegetables. Doing so was a form of homage, I suppose, but it also made more vivid the enormous pull between the beauties and necessities of making and those of the whole conception and completed picture. Actual works fleshed out the other generality, which had been made more categorizable and artificially intensified by being reduced in reproductions. I discovered in them a web of fractional relations (including relations to my own work) that were opposed or missing altogether in theory and reproductions.

More to the point, habitual reflections, pigeonholing, and both the picture's authentic and mechanically generated aura are dissolved in the more comprehensive *sum* of the real thing's qualities instead of being reinforced by those that are more photographically reproducible. Replicas may be a godsend at other stages, but the serious maker sooner or later needs vital meetings with the reality — the mixed reality — of what has been made. At such meetings the reality has time and again forced me to revise estimates and assumptions insecurely founded on simulacra — and the opinions of others. At a few paces, those of Elena Sisto's paintings based on "Nancy," Ernie Bushmiller's comic strip, are not a reprise of Philip Guston's gnomic work; El Greco's *The Expulsion of the Money Changers* is not still another swashbuckling half-wall, but a Prodigious Gem, a class more numerous than recognized in an age of giantism. The examples are almost as numerous as the exposures to the real.

Only the direct company of art's reality can properly nurture and cleanse creation. I may breeze through several downtown galleries and uptown collections and, once again in the studio, find that I have chocolate indigestion (to paraphrase Picasso) — the square-foot patch of varicolored, Miro–Donald Sultan–Joan Snyder–Van Dyck browns over black lines to which some of the day's art is reduced. Or, unlike the prim divisions of explanation and the condensed reproduction, the real thing may bestow the Poussin-like passage in Rubens; Charles Burchfield's sprightliness in Paul Nash's war scenes; the feel of Japan's Kamakura period in works by Ben Shahn, Lucas Samaras, and de Kooning; the presentiment of Walt Disney in Boucher; the California nexus in pieces by Richard Diebenkorn and Wayne Thiebaud, and the unmistakable similarity between the bread truck, parked outside, and that particular Frank Stella.

With enough time and faith and regular work, real things bestow on the painter a sense of his or her place. What one has seen of different times, places, and methods is gradually unifiable, thenceforth to be seriously subdivided only along lines of quality or practical operations. This comes about with the same management of momentary impulses as between palette and canvas, with something like the teeming adjustments of perception. As one demands the whole delightful list of ice creams, but prefers pistachio and tastes flavors beyond those implied by the names, so one respects intellectual sorting without surrending one's own practical, aesthetic, and personal connections between a Sean Scully painting and windows, playing fields, Amish blankets, highway signs, one's own woodcut, and the art of Piero della Francesca.

The anathema of overly revered and piled up art is by now an old artistic cliché. For more than a century some of its most vigorous producers have questioned Art and its entire social superstructure. Despite (or perhaps because of) part of the art world's debunking of earlier bohemian attitudes and its careerist embrace of "the system," skepticism about art's establishment may still be expected of the artist as a proof of his or her authenticity. In any case, the motivation lies one layer deeper than the anarchy or the "networking" of the person who makes effective art. It is one more example of the tensions of creation that the artist eventually acknowledges the origins of that motivation in the work of others and not only in the supposedly whole cloth of the self. Artistic egos must support the fact that the most bodacious innovators of any period are more like than unlike their peers (a distinction more difficult to make as we approach our own time).

As a painter, one of my most fervent wishes is for the actual—I want almost to say animistic—presence of enough first-rate realizations to weaken the hold of generalizations on me and encourage my own accomplishment. In this light, the artist's relations with the conserving establishment, though never without strife, are subversively favored with benefits.

With reason, some would say that color, not paint, is the painter's medium. Clay, too, is changeable, and one may add and subtract in working with it over a long period of time; therefore, if I have made transitivity, fluctuation, mutability, and amplitude the soul of painting, it was because I had far more in mind than the slow-drying fluid or pasty vehicle, however enabling it is. It is the powerful phenomenon of *directly managed color* that compounds everything I have written or implied about "speed," "reference," the "E Factor," and the general erraticism of the painter's process.

Although the paint is certainly tangible and its substance can be of great significance, it can obviously be used for the sake of "another kind of form," as was noted earlier of the composer's and writer's use of the tangible. As a painted surface can appear to be textured without being so, and vice versa, so the gathering of colors and its effects have no necessary proportional relation to the amount, kind, or general nature of the paint. As with musical harmony, the effect of union among colors can seem greater than the sum of its parts, however defined. Together, though, the characteristics of the paint and the behavior of color create a quality that slips free in every physical setting to affect a work's stability, intellectual proposition, accepted meaning, and gross as well as delicate performance with its changes: nuance.

It is difficult to make even cursory remarks about color without becoming a part of one of art's longest-running family squabbles: line, drawing, or black-and-white, *as opposed* to color. Perhaps the issue has rankled in some form from the beginning, for it is a part of the old and fundamental arguments of differing philosophies. It was present at the outset of our era when, discussing church decoration, Leon Battista Alberti looked back to Plato, Cicero, and the origins of our civilization for the authority of white (color's supposed absence) as a symbol of purity.[7] Whether from Plato's cave or the earlier ones at Altamira, one might follow color's wavering but rising fortunes through all the divorces and reconciliations of Western art and sensual appeal, past one of the more famous of the issue's clashes between Ingres's neoclassicism and Delacroix's romanticism, and up to impressionism's deliverance of color and its fruition in the modernism of Matisse and Picasso. Almost no development of consequence in painting leaves the discussion unruffled. Even the recent cleaning of the Sistine murals, for example, awoke those who saw either welcome or regrettable changes due to the rejuvenated, or at any rate different, color; and those who felt the same ways, but due instead to the loss of sfumato and consequent light-dark changes.

Another chance for gauging the hardiness of this issue is offered by a recent publication of broad interest. In discussing a painting by Caravaggio, the art historians David Robb and J. J. Garrison wrote in 1942 that it "presents as skillful a handling of light as one could find in any expert Hollywood movie."[8] As if fired by this observation, Anne Hollander has dichotomized painting in new but still recognizable ways in her ingenious *Moving Pictures.* Her thesis is that yet another aspect of contemporary life, motion pictures, was prefigured by painting. This time, it was by a kind of "proto-cinematic" painting, which in turn had absorbed certain emotional effects from black-and-white print reproductions and graphic illustrations. While color is not her subject, her careful handling of it (in a way an extension of established distinctions between Northern and Southern European art) is quite necessary to the explanation of her idea.

"Color proves the painter," she writes. "It definitively separates him from the workaday graphic practitioner and raises his efforts into the sphere of arcane understanding. The alleged 'secrets of the Old Masters' were all about the control of color, which meant the control of natural forces, and color supported the idea of the artist as analogue of a divine creator."[9] Therefore, she continues, when the impressionists once again desired the "autonomous sovereignty of the painter's art, they naturally used color." However, a number of contemporaries, such as Manet, Degas, and Fantin-Latour, forsook this "divine prerogative," choosing instead the "dialectic of light and shade," as had Vermeer, Velázquez, Van Dyck, Rembrandt, Goya, Caravaggio, and history's host of movie signifiers.

Hollander effectively strives to moderate the division, referring to color that is "potent" as the "servant of tone" in many works of the latter group. Nevertheless, well before the end of the book, even though raised on behalf of insights into the painting-movie connection, the old, familiar issue is upon us. Color is "the basic sign of the superior" film artist who, like avant-garde twentieth-century painters, seizes color's new cinematic role and "transcends narrative and illustrative goals."[10] Throughout a well-detailed discussion, color has to do with "beauty" and the "abstract," creates "independent responses of mood," contributes "pleasure" but no meaning to visual narrative, and is "celestial," meaning irrelevant. Black and white, the "vehicle of truthfulness," brings us the "comedy, sex, violence and sentiment" of photography and popular commercial art, and stands for the "mundane," meaning the real.

These valuations of her division (some work as well for color as for black and white) concern me less than the dividing itself, for I cannot see the elements as truly separate. In fact, as in many other moments while writing here, I can barely keep from hanging quotation marks around "color," "drawing," "black and white," and "line" as a signal of their divergence from a more cohesive experience. I know this contradicts an earlier statement that a refusal of generalization may hinder understanding, but surely color is a subject that begs the greatest possible patience with the singular.

Hollander's association of movies and painting is understandable and appealing; if one stays away from a worrisome middle zone, one can make sense with this customary branching of the visual experience. I believe, however, that if we were to study the many originals of paintings among the book's 301 fittingly black-and-white reproductions, we might find the dichotomy less tenable. Color is not without substantial, even contradictory effect in her tonal, proto-movie examples, any more than "colorizing" leaves movies unaffected. She claims that such films "just look more lush, delicious, and expensive," but that the color has little other impact.[11] The point, however, should be not only the effect of the "colorization" now deemed commercially acceptable, but the impact that color *could* be made to have on such films.

My differences here stem from my *use* of color, which has left me with a greater respect for its capacity to break containments than I have for explanation's capacity to fashion them. To spell out my view a bit further, let us look at quotes from two artists with extreme and opposing attitudes about color. First, Ad Reinhardt: "There is something wrong, irresponsible and mindless about color, something impossible to control. Control and rationality are part of any morality."[12] Ergo, color is immoral? Cut off the offending part? Hollander would perhaps not go as far as this in elucidating her theme, but the ease of the dichotomy seems basic to both. Reaching back as far as 450 b.c., when Democritus thought color a subjective effect of the objective atoms of existence, and to the Puritan's rationale in the seventeenth century for "colorless" dress, one hears in Reinhardt's remark the endless rift and the mood of all those who, unable to deny the fact of color, seek to regulate it by regarding it as detachable from the rest of visual perception.

Second, Matisse: "What counts most with colors are relationships. Thanks to them and them alone a drawing can be intensely colored without there being any need for actual color. . . . It is not possible to separate drawing and color."[13] I recognize the linguistic pitfalls here, the sensual extremity, and that Matisse drives us to technical, perhaps physiological concerns, but I am more sympathetic with this statement, which is similar to those by Cézanne, Delacroix, Paul Klee, and others on the identity of light-shade, drawing, and color. I am sympathetic, for that matter, with Reinhardt's remarks. Things would be simpler if they reflected the obvious truth. However, I cannot ignore my experience as a painter, suggestions of which I see in Matisse's words. Both, as I noted, are extreme — Reinhardt in a general direction, Matisse in the direction of particular instance; even so, the older master allows for the actual characteristics of sight.

It is not color but *vision* that is impossible to "control." Having reached a conclusion on its role in the senses, and the demands of the senses on life and our knowledge of it, vision would still present us with intriguing difficulties, as long as we closely attended it. Anyway, after the relativity with which we conditionally take in what we see and, through confusion and peculiarity, make art, come the inevitable impositions on it from the forceful experience of others.

Visual effects continually strain simultaneously toward *and* against control, which can neutralize any plan or envisagement and make every painting more improvisational than we tend to admit. Any rule concerning color will contend unsuccessfully with necessity, nature's tricks with the observer, and informed or uninformed personal inclinations. The nature of color is best understood by accentuating one aspect of what is obvious in any act, even if such emphasis is at the disorienting expense of its other aspects: however mechanical or technically governed the execution of a plan or idea, submitting it to the quirks of time and realization-in-color makes the act an especially unpredictable, adjudicative performance.

Therefore, realizations having the full potential of color at their heart are apt to have grown from protracted, diffident processes. An intelligent carpenter places the piece to be secured, nails in a strategic few nails to hold it, but drives them in only halfway; then, when all seems well, nails all of them home and completes the job. In a similar way, it is color more than anything else that in painting often demands (of taste as well as intelligence) that things first be introduced "halfway" and, if need be, concluded only after first and subsequent "placements" seem right. The only other option, if it is color's full potential that truly integrates the work, is to proceed toward realization through a series of completions and destructions. It is paint, more than any other medium, that most ably allows either one of these approaches to the full extent of color's powers.

The vagaries of color (including the efficiency of tone) or tone (which includes the powers of color) cooperate in making and seeing art. Chiaroscuro, size, shape, composition, and the character of the actual surface are basic to the way we see, understand, and, especially, talk about painting; but they are in reality interdependent. More significantly, they and color are interdependent. To mention any of them is to bring up the others. Together, they generate associations, projections, modulations, and the actuality of color, and there can be no hue, brilliance, or color relationships without them.

Strolling renewed from the integrity of the studio and into the noises surrounding art, which lately are grumbles and uproars superimposed on art, I often feel that "color *versus* . . ." is emblematic of every misunderstanding of the act of painting and seeing, and is something of the magnitude and obstinance of the mind-body dualism in philosophy. In any case, we seem driven to the wall of major changes and poised, hopefully or in fact, for a giant turn of events, a rumbling, ultramodernist revision in which every tenet in the art of painting, and therefore necessarily color, would be resophisticated and redisposed.

We will look into one part of that revision in chapter 5, but for now let us consider another important part of art making, the studio.

NOTES

1. Mozart's letter is quoted in Brewster Ghiselin, ed., *The Creative Process* (Berkeley: University of California Press, 1952), 35.

2. Dore Ashton, ed., *Picasso on Art: A Selection of Views* (New York: Viking Press, 1972), 96.

3. David M. Robb and J. J. Garrison, *Art in the Western World* (New York: Harper & Brothers, 1942), 714.

4. Albert Boime, *Franz Kline: The Early Works as Signals* (Purchase, N.Y.: Neuberger Museum, State University of New York, 1977), 15.

5. Robert Hughes, *Nothing if Not Critical* (New York: Alfred A. Knopf, 1990), 15.

6. Sir Joshua Reynolds, *Discourse in Art* (New Haven: Yale University Press, 1975), 27.

7. Alberti's *De Re Aedificatoria*, bk. 7, chap. 7, quoted in E. H. Gombrich, *Meditations on a Hobby Horse and Other Essays* (New York: Phaidon, 1971), 16.

8. Robb and Garrison, *Art in the Western World*, 715-16.

9. Anne Hollander, *Moving Pictures* (New York: Alfred A. Knopf, 1989), 37.

10. Ibid., 48

11. Ibid., 46.

12. Lucy Lippard, *Ad Reinhardt* (New York: Harry N. Abrams, 1981), 147.

13. Jack D. Flam, *Matisse on Art* (New York: E. P. Dutton, 1978), 99.

4

The Studio

I am happy with my picture that returns me to the middle of
all these movements of my mind.

— Matisse

In the middle of these chapters, I too return in this one to "my
picture." More precisely, I return first to the studio, where not only
pictures come together but also many of the habits, attitudes, and
ponderings that lead to them. Then, after considering the importance
of the site of art making, the chapter further examines the making itself.
In considering the source of ideas, the priorities among them, and the
actual process of making images, I have been necessarily drawn to some
of the most personal reflections of this commentary. Though particular,
they nevertheless point, I believe, toward the creation of "makers" in
general and the variety of its groundings. Following a definition of
the "crossroads" of my essay's title, the chapter ends with a discussion
of how and why I try to reconcile the extremes of art's "culture" and
processes.

The matters I have examined thus far are by no means an always
conscious part of my work. My work is perhaps based in them and,
as I have tried to show, they condition what I do, but they are not
the only sources from which the work flows.

The flow is easy, by and large. It is arranging one's life to produce
it that is more difficult. I can imagine no situation that would find
me empty or "blocked" in the way so notorious among writers. If
anything, it is the continual attraction of the studio and the overwhelming abundance of possibilities and my desire to pursue them that have
occasionally given me pause.

The flow itself (I mean its ease, not its amount) has at times led
me to question the value of what I have chosen to complete from what
cries out to be done. A consideration of what I should do sometimes
rises in conflict with what I have been doing. When it does, it has the
ring of conscience, not missed opportunity, an urge to return or stay

nearer to the center of my deepest intentions than to what I could otherwise easily do. Curiosity steers, but is also steered, and my expansive leanings are monitored. I am reminded that ability or the mere readiness and capacity to do are not always enough. The unexamined painting was not always worth painting. I must provide more tests and confrontations of my own methods and purposes than anyone else. After many years, I can see that a steady and at times disheartening ratio is always in effect. That is, what I might present as "my work" is actually the half of it that gains its height from standing on the submerged ruins, doodles, jokes, dead ends, and failures of the other half. I am spared from always knowing exactly which is which.

Otherwise, the prospects can often be an embarrassment of riches. More than I could possibly investigate streams with little provocation from these sources: the serendipity of the process; the wish to see something not yet existent; the wish to play with, correct, or affirm what already exists; the engrossing momentum of what is, by now, a dialectical process whose directions, terms, and demands keep changing and beckoning, compelling and rewarding.

If I express sureness, which is too often taken as greenhorn egotism, it is because the process has come in a curious way to represent any ability I may have; consequently, in regard to retrieving something valuable from the studio's profusive search, I have the sense, not at all brash but as with a foregone conclusion, that ultimately I cannot miss. I have come to believe that by the time I find myself at the threshold of something different or exacting, I will have been prepared to carry it out. There is always a proviso, and the one here is large and serious: I must arrange the life, ward off any overtures of futility, and be present for the work.

I often have, then, two similar but contrary experiences. A new force, in spite of attempts to engage it, is helplessly dissipated, leaving behind, however, a fertilized version of recent work; or, less often, a fresh, new development rises more or less unannounced from otherwise ordinary approaches. Therefore, if not curiosity, dormant concerns, or my ideas, beliefs, and associations, then the flexibility of the means will rescue any failed flight for one of the half dozen or so themes among which my work seems to circulate.

I almost never angle diligently toward the themes. They are simply there, and have been for a long time, like a forgotten safety net beneath the effort toward any other objective. And below and around them, the reassuring ambience of the studio.

I have had seven studios, private places in which to keep the supplies and do the work. Only in two of them did I remain for less than a year, and I worked in one for a decade. Spacious, cold-water, no-water, optimum — they have differed in many ways; however, in one important respect they have been the same, as I now see any studio would be for me. Each began as a no-nonsense place that permitted full focus on the work but became much more, a palladium, a lectern, a hideout, an arena, both the placid wherewithal and the site of hurricanes. They became intergrown with the work, the one at times an extension of the other. Sometimes, seeing how diminished my works seemed outside it — rarely has anything I have done looked better than in the studio — I have allowed myself the thought that it, the studio, is the work.

Two opposing extremes strike me as foolish. One is the assumption that the studio's character and location can have little or no effect on the work. We may not share Leonardo's preference for small rooms, but his awareness of the room as a factor at all should not be ignored. The other extreme is the fastidious fussing to make a studio conform with untried ideals of how a studio should be, as if by some window-dressing magic the seriousness of the paintings to be made in it is enhanced.

The rightness of a studio, which takes time to find and is often the unnoticed barometer of the rightness of the paintings, lies in its honest, direct externalization of the habits and needs of the person(s) who occupies it. If the two-way influences of public and architecture can be claimed, something like the same principle may be at work in the triad of painter, painting, and studio.

The jumbled scene of work energizes. It is an atmosphere that I breathe in differently than any other. "In the presence of extraordinary actuality," wrote Wallace Stevens, "consciousness takes the place of imagination."[1] This could be taken by some as a compelling reason for their studio's isolation from such actuality, and yet, my room's own raw, kaleidoscopic actuality, surely not what Stevens had in mind, often brings about in me a stern and fuller consciousness. The room holds clutter, juxtapositions, and chance geometries (figure 7) that serve as chorus to the main scene and the stuff of meditation. A pressure-chamber between the work and the world, its disorder is a necessary continuance of the disorder another poet, Paul Valéry, said was "the condition of the mind's fertility."[2] In some cases, of course, the disorder may be another form of order, or the order we were not looking for.

Painting is a visual art; therefore, the visual character of what is nearby when we paint, as when we see a painting, is apt to become part of it and its meanings in conscious and subconscious ways. The studio walls need not be iridescent green for the painter to know this. I take it for granted, even though the work I am doing has little or

Figure 7. Studio interior

nothing to do with the obvious qualities of the surroundings. One might argue that artistic intentions create the studio surroundings, not the other way around. While this is of course basically the case, the reality, I would say, is that after a while there is permeation in both directions, as analysis of the work and environments of James Rosenquist, Louise Nevelson, Mondrian, Picasso, and Alberto Giacometti, for example, might suggest.

In the direct, eastern light of morning, a painting can be reduced to a puny surface brushed over with colors at once pale and gaudy. The physical nature of wood, cloth, nailheads, and each square inch of paint are stripped of all illusion and stand out as what they are, after all — simply more of the infinite rubble of the world. The meanings of any human-made surface are put to the test in that glare. Even in the last decade of the twentieth century a generous amount of constant, temperate north light is still desirable in a painting studio. For me, however, the optimum space also receives some of that lively and leveling first eastern light. It is harshly revealing and contemptuous of illusions, and I have always felt closer to the truth in it. But above all there is the satisfaction of daring to work on the artificial in its presence.

The effects of anger and outrage, as in Picasso's *Guernica*, are well scattered throughout art, but they are a prominent part of our time's, from Otto Dix and David Sequeiros to Sue Coe and Robert Morris. How, I have wondered, do we explain the *enjoyment* of transforming those effects? How do we account for whatever *pleasure* there was in painting all those crucifixions, drawing *The Disasters of War*, or "disrupting the pleasure of a spiritually comforting image"[3] (one critic's sign of postmodernity)? One way is to propose that however contradictory or shameful it may seem, the artist's truth dwells in the paintings; that as long as the joy even barely surpasses the outrage, the artist will paint them, rationalizing the cohesion of pleasure-outrage instead of fully venting the outrage any other, more direct way.

However disatisfied with it I may be, I have always enjoyed my work, but I have also struggled and felt exalted, which took me beyond enjoyment to different kinds of alertness. It is a troublesome admission, but even frustration and dejection have seemed *afterward* to be involved in the enjoyment. But any emotion in the inconstancy that is painting may also prove a chameleon, for both depend on what happens next. And in painting, far short of the technical excesses of a Ryder or a Reynolds, there is great and easy latitude for many "nexts."

As any site may become revered in some way, the studio takes on the overtones of countless gratifying rides on this bucking surfboard, countless wipe-outs, recoveries, acknowledgments, and satisfactions. It is there that one finds the pleasure of moving-thinking inside the medium's vast, colored tent, the confidence to impose one's purpose, and the wonder of finding purpose. Simply to step into it can bring about a powerful clarity.

As there have been times, of course, when I was brought up short by difficulty or the gradual revelation of the wrongness of what I was doing, there have also been times when I was moved by what had all along been flirting just behind appearance and now stood successfully before me. The former, the moments of disappointment, always seem due to my stupidity; the latter often seem to be the visitation of a kind of grace. I use religious terms here to accentuate the sense of elevation in the experience: I brought about what is moving me, and not solely by chance, but only up to the point at which it could go on to reveal or demonstrate standards I had not known I incorporated, directions I had not fully known I sought, and forces seemingly beyond absolute manipulation. Although I had begun privately and alone, and will return to that mode as the only one in which I know how to operate, I am startled at suddenly having joined, at least temporarily, an archaic but progressively complex undertaking. Only then do I feel a peculiar sense of responsibility. Only then does "Art" and my association with it have a full enough credence not only to withstand but to turn back the more sardonic assaults of doubt, dissatisfaction, and an increasingly confrontational society.

Much of the time I go about my work as by second nature, a ritual as personal and unremarkable as brushing my teeth. On any given day it may seem mercifully removed from purposes beyond the room, and for the meantime what is right under my nose commands who I am. Left to my own pace and preferences, certainly after many years of such rhythms, I work as if it were as plain and normal as breathing and well within my or anyone else's comprehension. I have learned, here and there, that my motives and procedures, unextraordinary and demonstrable as they are, seem by many to be puzzling, amusing, or incoherent. But theirs is not the perspective in which I work. The center from which I work was formed early and is so intact and precedential as to make these descriptions of it seem to me like a schizoid riddle. I have learned that I depend on solitude, that there is no durable benefit from looking into the daily changing versions of the public eye, that I stare and reflect at length and am subject to bouts of not always "productive" labor; but in the studio all of it passes as benign necessity. I go for days at a time, thinking that *everyone*, of course, has a studio and that I am not really alone.

But where do the ideas come from, and why is *that* idea selected for elaboration from among the others? Here, we encounter more chance, mystery, and general lack of knowledge.

To answer the latter question, there are times when an idea seems in various ways to select itself. For example, I have decided to work on an idea, only to have another one elbow its way into the proceedings — and sometimes out again. However, the key word here is "seems," for in almost every case these are subsidiary ideas that I am willing to consign to the functioning of chance or materials because I have long before taken stricter measures in a broad but specific direction. The "blue" out of which so many receive so much is bountiful for me only after I have provided something fundamental on my own.

I may have, then, (at least until this thought) a peculiar approach to the notion of ideas. The making of a single painting may call up many quite different subjects and compositions, and although I think of and refer to them as "ideas," they and most of the paintings they lead to are really in the service of only two or three ideas in the usual sense of the word. I will address these later in discussing my themes.

Again, concerning the reasons (excepting commissions) for selecting one from among other ideas to work on, not only my private, arbitrary reasons, but even the artistic reasons are often lost in the strange inevitability of the accomplished work. The selection can be affected by wanting to "paint that way today." Practicality, for example, the coincidence of the right kind of time or the presence of the right materials or light, dictates a great deal. In allowing such practicality as great a scope as the priorities of ideas is, I admit, an indulgence or a compulsion that only dwindling time has corrected.

On the other hand, I have learned that a degree of faith in these matters is necessary. If the work will not wholly work them out, neither will dogged mental insistence. As with the disorder that is another form of order, the apparently vagrant paths of my work have found their way to premeditated goals that were long before pronounced lost.

As to the source of ideas in the first place, I can offer but three personal, seemingly flippant answers that explain, at least logically, any given instance: I do not know; primarily from the work itself; anywhere else.

"Primarily from the work" means that the work seems, at those times, to stir, dictate, or temporarily direct my knowledge, memories, wishes, and so on, prompting an idea and eliciting a certain appearance before "handing back" the painting to me. Preceded by a coercive phase in which the painting refuses any longer to be put off or prepared for, it is as though the painting briefly becomes my brain; as if I, not the paint and tools, were the medium. This points, among other things, to the duality that painters can feel in respect to their work. Speaking with the man who arranged a large exhibition of his paintings in 1966, and mixing the duality with the heightened, perhaps emotional viewpoint of advanced age, Picasso said, "it's the inventory of someone with the same name as mine."[4]

"Anywhere else" is a very large category. Nothing less will do. A large part of it is the inferential "visual life," as some might call it, which includes not only the Ideal derived from and applied to "nature," but sheer dailiness — the highway, the grocery, trees, tabletops, water and sky, people and the shining face of the world. (Renoir, I think, when asked how he chose what to paint, said that he turned his head, turned his head . . .) A large portion of the traditions, including the work of my peers, and the hapless and other overlappings of the feverishly expanding class of objects and acts known as art, is also a major part of it. Obviously, it includes the full extent of my thought and belief, concerning art and whatever else. In a sense, all of my work, even that of uncommon origins, is ultimately shaped by various combinations of the traditions and visual observations of life. Several years ago,

Figure 8. "Macondo" drawing, M. Brown

following a series of doodles and drawings that were unusual and perplexing in their mixture and general feeling (figure 8), I decided that ever since traveling through Spain I had been wanting to paint palm trees and that they were sprouting up in this form because there was no room for them in my painting at the time. Only a week or so later did I finally grasp the obvious: I had just read consecutively three novels by Gabriel García Márquez. Their flooding Latin-American images had merged with the old interest in palm trees and were breaking out in these casual pieces. The connections between my work, my thoughts, and my imagination are not usually so hidden, and except for Icarus, *Don Quixote,* and some treatments of Ovid, biblical subjects, and perhaps a few other things, I have not often worked from literature. Nevertheless, the pieces of which figure 8 is an example are more like than unlike the rest of my work: though "imaginary" they rely on my observations of the real world and easily fit into various modern niches of the tradition. They also exemplify the belief that one reason for working from models is to be able to work to similar ends without them.

Much the same can be said of *Travels* (figure 9), a piece I worked on while listening to music. On the rare occasions I work to music, its separation from my work is usually maintained with no conscious

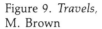
Figure 9. *Travels,*
M. Brown

effort. This time, however, for reasons that are lost in the normal tumble and mystery of the everyday, Schubert's Ninth Symphony, immediately following a string of pieces by the Neville Brothers, became a definite and positive determinant. The music did not intrude upon so much as coincide with the general thinking behind the work. The painting made a single flow of the two kinds of music. My hammering on the collage wood seemed directed and absorbed by the flow. Although I was more intent on certain formal properties than on making visible the mood-thought with which I started, I was struck (and assisted) by how easily my notions of travel were reflected in the music. Like travel's abrupt dislocations of mind and belongings against the three-part symmetry of home and nature in the painting, the symphony rolled in a horse-and-landau passage across underlying continuity. Again, though unusually produced, the work relies on the instructive blend of previous artistic standards and, less strongly, my work from life.

Less directly arrived at works are especially difficult to describe. To avoid the tedium of detailed accounts and the confusions they may add to the subject, most painters skip to overgeneralization and aphorisms. I am no different. More than an entire work of architecture or a literary epic, a painting, though complete in its way, is to me like a densely packed atom, a fable, a very rich musical phrase, or a paragraph-long story by Kafka. Whether "masterpiece" or parts and slivers, and apart from the real time of production, I identify with a "brevity" in all of them. Therefore, to the extent that I am conditioned by my work, my language and general manner are apt to be parenthetical and have the abrupt junctions of collage. As paintings may fit into a kind of narrative, so may a painter's truncated "stanzas" of thought and activity form in the aggregate a continuous and, in its way, organized pattern. Anyway, I must trust that approach in this discussion of my work.

For now, I will offer as examples of "less directly arrived at" the work that is puzzling because its "essence" suddenly and inexplicably appears after a long period in which, though known, it was completely forgotten; work whose origins and development overlap or are the same, but which end up with opposite effects; works with quite different origins, but that are nonetheless alike; works that are abandoned for a time (often as if never to be finished), then suddenly taken up with an urgency that is obscured by its calm conclusion; formerly straightforward works that are nudged and chipped at until they are destroyed (becoming the base for another painting) or reach another conclusion.

I should say that I see nothing unfathomable in all of this. Perhaps if an accountant (preferably invisible) had kept strict, chronological track of every single surface and every moment I worked on them since high school, I am sure their entanglements, developments, and multiple relations, though something on the order of a week's worth of big-city traffic jams, would yield a taxing but intelligible picture. Incidentally, chronological accounts, even if not so all-inclusive as this, would still reveal more about creativity than the usual "editing" and compartmenting of painters' work. Many people, artists among them, prefer magical to probable explanations, but this is not my attitude. As I have tried to make clear, there are zones of quirkiness and mystery both in producing and apprehending images, but those of intellect, skill, and reason are not completely overwhelmed.

Having said this, though, I will balance it by adding that while painters often see order, connections, and meaning where others do not, it is also painters who, in some respects or at certain times of concentration, are most addled by the traffic's potentialities and least conscious of the full extent of their own matter-of-factness. The eye of the hurricane is not always placid. The confusion is necessary, however, and clearing it up, if it were possible, would help neither work nor painter.

Instances of the most straightforwardly achieved work are the easiest to describe.

An idea is held loosely in my mind, where it undergoes ungovernable and seemingly pointless changes, as well as the purposeful kind, for days, sometimes weeks, and in a few cases, years.

Because I know it may be both muddled and clarified by the act of realizing it, I have learned to be relaxed in making ready for the idea's appearance. I test the idea's force by allowing it first to emerge as it will before pulling on it. A rigor of carelessness sets in right away.

Beyond an intuitively definite point, I think of any further thought or scattered drawing as delaying, for there is little one can do before the painting that one cannot do during the painting. I rarely make studies or drawings that propose an entire composition. I move at that point to the canvas, not through anxiety, to insure the informal, or to subvert craft, and so on, but to make sure that the preparation steals nothing from the fulfillment. I do it with the same mind as Montaigne in feeling that "the very fact of being bound to what I have to say is enough to break my grip on it"; besides, as he wrote, "Often a man stupidly strips to his doublet only to jump no better than he would in a cloak."[5]

To the canvas I jump, then, cloak and all. I may even begin on two or more surfaces at once, pulling out a sheaf of likable but only vaguely related drawings and hanging them about on the off-chance that they may spark a development or themselves be further revealed. If I cool, am unsteady, or *too* open-minded, other ideas apply to claim precedence or as more reasonably meant for *that* size, proportion, texture, and so forth.

Except for murals, a few early tempera panels, and other special pieces, I cannot recall making a complete drawing on the surface beforehand. When I uncharacteristically press toward such a completeness, I often discover that my idea does not permit or will not survive such reduction. The purpose, time, and place for drawing are not only to set something now and beneath, but to correct and sharpen something later and through.

With no warning at all or no sense of having begun, as when we find ourselves "there" instead of "arriving"; with a few general charcoal or painted lines, some of them quite exact, depending; with a rashly gambled blocking in and half-polish of an important area that is meant either to guide the rest to conclusion (the tail wagging the dog), or to yank the painting to life in being destroyed; or with large, overlapping gulfs of color that, though evoking the general spirit of the idea, are thought of as expendable (they may not last the trip), the painting begins.

However straightforward, and whether or not the painting goes on to easy resolution, I come in the majority of cases to a crossroads, a hiatus that I have grown to expect and accept. There can be dirty work at this crossroads.

Any worthwhile idea, and any worthwhile effort to realize it, has more in it than the mind can use right away. Fruitful ideas threaten, excite, intrigue, and clarify. They propogate and mutate, and are often first disguised as "the obvious." For the most part, they are, for a while, in advance of my judgment. They must be given every opportunity to emerge completely and with all of their baggage. To do this, one must go with them, be dragged anywhere by them, help them even to come apart or to form other or opposing ideas. One does not, at first, really have ideas. They are fully gotten only through the work, and not unless the work toward them is allowed to have its say can one have them. The idea's proof is not only how deep but how far afield of its center it can carry. To be made effective, the idea must early on be taken to the edges of what surrounds it. It may need to be risked and endangered in order to be fully known.

In other words, it is precisely the good painting that sooner or later poses the question to the painter: Shall we finish what you thought we started, or shall we look further into what I've shown you?

Whatever the answer, the question annoys only those who cannot arrange their lives to suit the consequences. It aggravates those who cannot trust their means or their answer's connection to their past and future work.

I believe it is at that crossroads that the painter's skill (and wisdom, such as it is) is most surely tried and fed. There the painter receives the first warm flirtations of stylization and the coldest profitability of his or her craft.

Making their first practical appearance there may be the painter's corollary to F. Scott Fitzgerald's "two opposed ideas," the holding in the mind and functioning with which were his "test of a first-rate intelligence."[6] Not only must this be preceded by having one idea, but the "first-rate" intelligence may in fact be the one that is able to distill one idea again from this opposition of two.

It is there that the painter begins to confront time and movement in a static art form; where theme and variation, the spine of the art, becomes truly apparent, from inside out, not only as play or experiment, but as necessity. There the painter chooses to finish what was started, noting future possibilities along the same lines, or chooses instead to follow new developments and perhaps try another time for what is being left behind. In either case, it is there that the cake that is eaten but still had is first positively tasted. The painter's energy and self-trust are most consequentially rationed or freely expended for this task at that crossroads.

If it is ever to be accomplished, it is there that intuition and the subrational or suprarational begin to contribute without obstructing conscious purpose. The most difficult but highest achievements sometimes require the softening of these boundaries and their ocassional operation almost as one.

Having worked oneself to that crossroads, whose revelation is a good view in several directions, one must not only accept but act on the consequences. Among these is using some but not all of the effects, sequences, occurences, and insights that will never again arrange themselves in quite the same way. In other words, among the inevitable consequences is loss.

Whatever the answer there, art lies beyond that crossroads.

Though not all, much of my work circulates, as I have noted, among several themes. It is impractical to examine all of them here, but I will discuss a few and allude to others. Some of them overlap. For example, a conscious cruciform tendency, if not theme, steals through some paintings (for example, figure 9), rising more obviously in others. I cannot avoid the historical, even specifically religious connotations of the Latin cross, but the cruciform in general has always had for me the stronger and more formal implications of my use of it in explorations bordering on the golden section, the proportional key first worked out in Greek geometry of the fifth century B.C.

This measure or proportion informs many of my compositions and treatments of certain themes, particularly one concerning trucks (figure 10). Although I was not aware of it at the beginning, the trucks had, among other associations, a vague connection with the human face, torso, or general presence. This was particularly true of their frontality, but also of their symmetry, the very basis of which I take to be the frontal human face: we tend to think of symmetry as a left-right, not a top-bottom or near-far balance. The trucks carried less historical freight than the human face, but they brought new dimensions to it. Though related in my mind to countenance, the truck permitted more direct use of the life around me and was a way of entertaining both a kind of planar abstraction or design and various senses of space

Figure 10. *Green Truck*, M. Brown

and volume. Also, it readily enabled the use of collage, legends, and decorative insignia, was even faintly hieratic, and eventually became an unsentimental pathway to landscape.

Shortly after the period during which these works began to cluster as themes, I sat on Rhode Island's southern shore, near Jerusalem, watching a group of women who were wading and clamming in the bright sun during low tide. Most of them wore bathing suits and stood quietly for long minutes, digging with their feet, bending over into the water and strolling about in the thigh-deep Atlantic. The drawings I made then, and on many similar occassions in other locations, gradually coalesced and underwent various transformations as yet another sub-unit of my work, another springboard to more elaborate works, and a consciously examined end in itself.

Once more, the female, truncal forms, abbreviated by water, were obviously drawn from my direct observations but have an equally obvious, though not for the most part deliberate, connection to tradition, from classical and classically derived modern sculpture to contemporary painting. As with the truck theme, this one offered a number of variations through its universal air, the reflections in the water, the position of head and arms, front and back views, and the range between more and less idealized versions.

One variation, almost completed before I saw it as such, was painted after a trip through the Southwest. As I worked on a landscape (from

memory and a few watercolor notes), I lost interest in the challenge
of such stereotyped wastelands and began to insert doodled vignettes
of the nude torsos. As they accumulated, and the tone of one of them,
a backview, worked nicely with that of the terrain, I saw the opportunity for the kind of stolid, single-figure landscape I had long wanted
to paint. I returned to my first effort, realizing just as I finished it that
it was also another "wading woman" (figure 11). Casually assuming
that the painting is a "comment" on any number of current social issues,
viewers are sometimes doubtful that although I do not exclude the
influence by such issues, the work is actually rooted in the kind of
thematic searches described above.

I can do little better at describing the larger idea or ideas beneath
these themes and the rest of my work than to mumble a few possibly
contradictory words — humorous, noble, current, timeless. It is uncomfortable to say them of my own work, but they are appropriate words
for what I generally prefer *later* to see in it, regardless of what urged
me at the time the work was done. These qualities are not necessarily
or easily available in any given painting, for I am not purposeful about
them. They are attitudes with which I anticipate and make the paintings,
not always applications from the outside. Also, they are often emphasized or blended according to the circumstances of the work. The
Roman poet Catullus, I think, said the Muse is at her best when she
is laughing, and it is both this lightness and the seriousness that Plato
imputed to the smile that I mean by humor. Reinhardt had hold of
a paradoxical truth: "Art is too serious to be taken seriously."[7] The
dignity or eminence implied by "noble" seems ultimately based more
in the static art form of painting itself than any subject or pretention.
I sense and work toward connections of the two, however, contrasting
and gently playing off one against the other. I see even the most detailed
and particular contemporary references in my painting as removed to
a level of general or contemplative significance. The art's own vener-
ability may, again, be responsible for this, but then I find myself doing
the same thing as I watch television. My work now and then seems
to slip into the costume of the comedian or journalist, but I suspect
it was wearing the timeless garb of the art form all along.

The flame of a candle has been called "the simplest example of an
open system.'"[8] The way a flame constantly exchanges its materials
while preserving a stable shape is similar to the way a painting may
undergo considerable change while remaining essentially the same. All
painters deal with the prematurely precious, but it is the inexperienced
in particular whose efforts are often wasted or cramped because they

Figure 11. Untitled landscape, M. Brown

are overestimated. They are late in perceiving a general pattern or stability or, having perceived one, presume that it is so fragile that it must be protected from every decision. Experience means in part having learned how much things can change and remain the same; how unity need not prevent variety. As the flame's stabilized form is also change, without having to be blown out, so the stabilized form of a painting in process may greatly change without undergoing wholesale conversions.

An ignorance of this coolness around the flame causes many of the difficulties in learning to paint. Among most students, general absence of preparation is now the style, but for technical reasons, at least, I feel this is better than too much preparation. Reasonable preparations are always in order, but when they are inordinate, too many of the benefits of what is yet to come are unwittingly shut out. The overcareful beginning spreads its hope to the four corners of the canvas. The shapes and colors are ordered up and dryly executed to fit the hope. A bald expedition begins to scratch unreflectively toward the desired end, which is thought to be close at hand. For a while, what needs to be done is precisely known; therefore, it feels good.

To the uninitiated, the march from Idea — the more suddenly and entirely inspired, the better — to this more or less comfortable point is what painting is. It either did or did not work. A century of hair-raising developments may have changed certain notions, but not this one, except for the aforementioned, who translate those developments to mean freedom from any preparation at all. To them, their problem is simply that they have no talent in the first place, or their ideas are bad, things which they seem to know without having to waste time with strenuous trials. How unfortunate that Picasso's cult of instinctively accomplished genius took him at his word, turned its back on his actual practice, and gave such a bad name to experiments.

That a final, willed image results does not mean there was no ambivalence, doubt, stress, or even temporary loss of purpose on the way to its completion. Why else would discipline, skill, judgment, and a prevailing sense of accepted or repugnant standards be necessary? The "crossroads" is a preeminent example of countervailing, contradictory tendencies and pressures that occur throughout the art. For example, both detail and the universal, novelty and sameness beg attention, and neither is convincing unless all gaps between them are genuinely filled. One frequently faces a range of choices that eludes full comprehension but that nevertheless offers shadowy promise. One learns another reality besides the amorous one behind the old Latin proverb, *festina lente* — "make haste slowly." Even in a stately procession toward a familiar end, distinctions among the elements deviate and change. Two areas of the same work, or two or more related works, cannot be completely seen at the same time, and so quickness, memory, intuition, and a trustful generalizing are always being depended on. The painter's famous squint and tilt of the head are among a number of ways the shift in distinctions are freshly seen, tested, and tended. They are an attempt to modify, for a balancing moment or two, the methods to which the painter immediately returns. Simply the stepping back several paces to a more distant vantage point than the one in which the work is made speaks volumes about the mixture of thought and action and the artist's broadest relations to potentially ambiguous work.

In December 1904, Cézanne wrote in a letter to Emile Bernard, "we turn to the admirable works handed down to us . . . in which we find comfort and support, like a plank to the swimmer." Ten months later, to the day, he wrote another letter to Bernard, telling him that "we have to render what we actually see, forgetting everything that appeared before our own time."[9] Poor Bernard; on the plank, off the plank. But as a painter, he too may have been vacillating and contradicting to little perceptible effect in his finished work. In this connection, Courbet's populous *The Studio of the Painter* always seemed to me something of an inside joke about the to-and-fro I and others have known, concerning the isolation of the studio: the work requires it, but one can tire of it — why not keep working and invite society *here?*

I do not wish to overstate the wavering or paradoxical swings and gyrations, but I would be remiss in playing down such lateral movement. Although the extent of the swings may not be great, they take place at every level, technical and otherwise.

As rock lyrics and the partisan press preach, the middle is no place to be, especially in a society that fancies itself neatly divided between problem makers and problem solvers. And yet, the middle is where the work is done, as Matisse's remark implies, the "true one in all things," as Mozart wrote.[10]

Our word "medium" is based in the Latin for "in the middle" and "in between." The self-appointed wings can be counted on to remind us that "mediocre" is also one of its cousins; closer to the source, however, is a more important word, "mediation." Artistic mediation is responsible for much of the still popular, romanticized notion of the painter as fickle, inconsistent, and strange. In this light, and in general ignorance of the background against which he or she mediates, the artist is a "character," one whose vulnerability or general commitment to experiment, the senses, aesthetic or other ideals, heroic realization or consummation—to anything that threatens pre-cut social and ideological standards—renders him or her undependable. From mediation also spring many of the art process's paradoxes. The certainty and unequivocal confidence of the art, for example, are often the results of the artist's doubtful, dualist methods and feelings. A painter is a *medium* artist, a moderator and mediator of images and ideas, intellect and sensation, beauty and ugliness, formless enthusiasm and objectification, and all such contention as regular-irregular, geometric-organic, conscious-subconscious, analytic-intuitive, artificial-natural, manifest-latent, flat-spatial, and so on.

I am artistically situated, every day and painting by painting, between opposed cultural positions. At one extreme, the paroxysms of emotion, desperate novelty, and savage rebellion; at the other, fixed and anemic attitudes frozen in formulae, unexperienced rules and conventions, and narrow, shallow depth. Interesting, debatable, sometimes only awkwardly identified, these "positions" matter to me primarily as reminders of my own extremes, which, though similar, are not as far apart. They require close attention and conciliation if my intent is to be significantly realized. It is an attention that heightens my awareness of both individuality and the necessity of a common sense. Art that lasts does so in part by *including* along the broadest base as well as the newest extensions of the culture. This requires artistic mediation of every kind, for the extremes cannot provide something enduringly provocative or consoling. And if the consolations of art are not among its reasons for being, then why the choice of such a trammeled means for incitement? Or are we finally losing "art" in the consolatory sense, tossing aside mitigating and other former "artistic" effects because they blur and restrain incitement? Are we simply gaining a new parlor more wholeheartedly for politics, business, social therapy, and "show-biz" that is no more or less "artistic" than their other rooms?

The attempt to comprehend, and the mediation that goes with it, is no longer taken to be a vital part of artistry or the education and training from which it grows. The prevailing mode, lasting by excluding, seems to assume that one is an artist (or is "behaving artistically," if there are no longer to be such distinct persons) to the extent one highlights an extremity within a small, rather fashionably defined generality, whatever the cost to wider artistic explorations and the strictly personal. Like a professional athlete or party worker, the artist and, in schools, the art student are therefore too often expected to wear one color, to have one approach or answer, whether or not the answer and the consistency are the results of broad cultivation. Picasso may have been the last painter of great consequence whose most varied personal abilities and private wishes, affections, interests, and compulsions coincided so well with his own "historical moment"—if his aggressive personalism did not in fact define that moment. Now, oddly, when selfishness is rank, the very notion of what an artist is tends to minimize the deepest, most thoroughgoing "personal" in favor of the watchful, only supposedly eccentric reflection of "the moment." The necessarily long preparation and comprehensive blend of the personal *with* a continuous commonality may already have passed from our time's art.

It is the agents and attendants of art, not the artist, who are thought to provide such comprehensiveness as we are to have. The creative sorting and predigestion of middle-person managers now stand between the viewer and the raw creation of the artist. They presumably resolve the parts, however whole, in larger, more "timely," entertaining, and digestible wholes.

When something especially interesting is going on in the studio, I am continually in and out, looking at it before I go to bed to see if it is as good as I thought it was, gloating, and finding it different the next morning. There are other times, however, when I walk into the studio routinely and blankly, without a definite purpose, allowing whatever is there to reassert itself. On one of these days I once stood over my drawing table and looked around at some traces of the week before. I could not recall their direction. There were small drawings from Daumier's seated figures and a drawing pad I had been carrying around, opened on seated figures from life. It was when I saw the reproduction of Dürer's engraving, *Knight, Death, and Devil* (figure 12) that I remembered.

I had been interrupted as I nibbled at a possibility drifting amid the slouched Victorians, my preoccupied diners, truckdrivers, musicians,

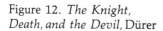

Figure 12. *The Knight, Death, and the Devil,* Dürer

and other folk, and the tensed "rider" (as Dürer referred to the print). I subdued my interest, wishing instead to work on something else, but I looked below the rider to the dog, "Veritas." I thought of the dogs in Rembrandt's prints and of the same little one that shows up in Titian's *Last Supper, Danae, The Flaying of Marsyas,* and others. I was taken for a moment at how dogs were scattered throughout art, from Egypt, through their prominence in English art, to our time. The hound in Tintoretto's *Washing the Feet of Christ* is central, and the foreground placement of one in Veronese's *Christ in the House of Levi* helped to put the painter at odds with the Inquisition. As I pondered the range of implications in art's "ordination" of animals (Robert Beauchamp's exciting canvases came to mind), all of the materials on the table gave way to one specific image in my mind: an old man, sitting next to his hound in the dappled shade of an alleyway.

When I was a boy, I once talked with that man, an old neighborhood gentleman who said he had, with the same watery eyes I gazed into, seen Abraham Lincoln. If everyone who claimed to have seen Wild Bill Hickock had in fact seen him, my grandfather once told me, Wild Bill must have lived out his entire life in the saddle. But even if the old man in the alley lied, which of course I prefer not to think, his story was possible. If, when he saw Lincoln, he had been about my age at the time, he would have been around eighty-seven years old as he spoke of seeing the president loom above the crowd at some distance. (I found this remarkable at the time also because he resembled Lincoln, particularly toward the end of his story, and now because of their resemblance with the Knight.)

A few years later, stuffed with dates and intellectual boundaries and checking my math over and over, I could hardly believe it. It was a period of interminable length for an adolescent: had the man not seen Lincoln in another *century?*

Now, closer to what would then have been a science fictional 2000 A.D., I find it quite real and steadying to know and think of in this way: separating me from Lincoln, the Civil War, and the rest of those times around the world, were only the days of that one old man, who once sat with his dog beside me and still bucolically sits in my memory. If we use lifespans of slightly more than seventy-nine years and put them end to end, birth to death, only *six people* are needed to reach from today to 1513, the year of Dürer's engraving near the summit of the High Renaissance. If we expand those lives to the old man's age of eighty-seven, they overlap and, like my old acquaintance, each could pass along something to the next one in his or her own voice.

Studying the old man's likeness in the Knight — Lincolnesque tophats in Daumier! — and the hourglass in Dürer's *Melancolia*, I felt in greater than intellectual proximity to all of it. Michelangelo in the quarries of Carrara, Leonardo toying with a scaffold, Bosch's barely noted death in the Netherlands, and the Ming dynasty master painter Shen Chou's unprecedented refusal of his government's support — I decided that it makes an important difference to think of it all as taking place six persons instead of a colder "480 years" ago. "Gauguin was eating canned food in paradise less than two persons ago."

I left the table and went to work on the other project. I remember being stunned that I had never before made *any* of the above connections with it. It was yet another variation on a theme that I have not mentioned, "man with dogs."

NOTES

1. Quoted by Joyce Carol Oates, "Against Nature," in *The Contemporary Essay*, ed. Donald Hall (New York: St. Martin's Press, 1989), 364.

2. Paul Valéry, *A Course in Poetics*, quoted in *The Creative Process*, ed. Brewster Ghiselin (Berkeley: University of California Press, 1952), 105.

3. Lucy Lippard, "Andreas Serrano: The Spirit and the Letter," *Art in America*, April 1990, 239.

4. William Rubin, ed., *Pablo Picasso: A Retrospective* (New York: Museum of Modern Art, 1980), 8.

5. Donald M. Frame, trans., *The Complete Works of Montaigne* (Stanford: Stanford University Press, 1967), 761.

6. F. Scott Fitzgerald, *The Crack-Up* (New York: New Directions Books, 1945), 69.

7. Lucy Lippard, *Ad Reinhardt* (New York: Harry N. Abrams, 1981), 124.

8. Arthur Koestler, *Ghost in the Machine* (London: Hutchinson and Company, 1967), 220.

9. Richard Friedenthal, ed., *Letters of the Great Artists* (New York: Random House, 1963), 184, 185.

10. From a letter Mozart wrote to his father, quoted in E. H. Gombrich, *Sense of Order* (Ithaca: Cornell University Press, 1979), 303. Mozart's complaint that such a middle position was "no longer esteemed" was a premonition. He felt that one had to "do things which are so easy to understand that any coachman could sing them at once, or so unintelligible that they please precisely because no sensible person can understand them" (ibid.).

5

Creativity

You whose speech is made in the image of God's speech . . .
Be easy on us when you are comparing
Us and those who were the perfection of order
Us looking all around for adventure . . .
Us not your enemy
Who want to present you strange mighty lands
Where flowering mystery surrenders itself to the taker
  Where new fires are and colors unseen
Phantasms by the thousands weightless
Which need to be given reality . . .
Pity us battling always at the limits
Of limitlessness and tomorrow
Pity our errors pity our sins

— Guillaume Apollinaire (1918)

Having dealt with the medium and the act of creating with it, I move in this chapter to more general considerations of creativity itself. I seek to cultivate the ground between two major current contentions about creativity. Although both are discussed in some detail, I give more time to one of them, the sophisticated "anti-creativity" viewpoint. I do so not only because it is complex but also because I approach it from a broad direction less often taken in considerations of its separate examples.

I begin, however, with my reaction to the whole debate. The two "caricatures" of that reaction, though in some respects similar to the above two contentions, are meant to remind the reader that creativity is ultimately conveyed not by groups and theories but by individuals. More important, such individuals demonstrate the volatile, contradictory nature of creativity.

The last part of the chapter discusses some of the results and issues that follow upon the advance of the "anti-creativity" view and its combination with other social forces. The chapter ends with my thoughts on why art must be protected in the classroom from the extremes of both contentions; why the hand's training and creativity are necessary.

Perhaps all frontiers have a few things in common. When entertainers failed to show up, were tardy, or not up to par in the old American West, the theater itself was sometimes shot full of holes — "deconstructed" one might say — in the rowdy, agitated misunderstanding and impatience of the moment. Whether one sees ultimate loss or gain in it, there is reason to think that we too are on a frontier of sorts and that the "theater" is under fire.

A noisy and burning spirit of revision and revenge, loosed at every level of our society, is coming quickly to characterize what one thinker has called the "baffled sense of drift"[1] that closes this century. There is no period in American history when the cement between any two formerly grouped stones of meaning has been, or would be, so avidly blasted away. In a relentless cultural subdividing that tightens the "radius of trust,"[2] any criterion is quickly strained, strategically shifted, or refuted. The overt scrambling of politics with entertainment, and art with both, causes and represents more confusion. The significance and definition of opposites (fake and authentic, for example)[3] are purposely merged. As all kinds of old and new sequences of order collide, being chronologically out of place is (except technologically), by turns, more prevalent and impossible. Any ideas of propriety become steadily less supportable. The general crumbling of the terms and rules by which it might be conducted threatens all debate. "There is nothing left to ground ourselves on," cries a fashionable savant. "All that is left is theoretical violence . . . radicalization of all hypotheses."[4]

Owing to a multitude of interests, friendly and unfriendly, major cultural institutions and conventions and their imperatives stand weakened or, like science, the "last redoubt of impersonal reason,"[5] as candidates for dismantling critique. As the other arts disperse, architecture, "the last bulwark of a consciousness of the real world," buckles and joins them, forming, among other sculpture-based phenomena, a "kinetic theory" with "explosion as a strategy."[6] Writing on the "intellectual climate" of our "postmodern" time, a historian notes its declining impulse toward the objective, its unruly "blurring of fact and fiction," and the cyclone of skepticism about the grounds of our knowledge that is blowing through "every humanistic discipline."[7] The heroines, heroes, and the great, along with those words and their accomplishments, are commonly associated with only instrumental power and are lined up as far as the mind can think to receive their feet of clay. In a society in which motherhood is technically no longer easily defined, it should be no surprise that "creativity" has fallen on hard times.

I am curiously put off by most discussions of creativity. The very sounds of the overly repeated word amuse and embarrass me. My tangled inner reactions are perhaps best stated as two broad caricatures.

One caricature is that of a forthrightly hard-nosed, unpoetic man. "Coming from a family of farmers, coal miners, and carpenters may have something to do with it," he says, "but in the gushing talk of inspiration that comes with such discussions, practicality focuses my attention on personal skills, social connections, and hard work. I see a futile yearning for the mystical in what plainly has to do instead with experience and information, surrounding cultural tides, a tested sense of qualities, and opportunity." This is the mood of one who uncynically believes that he and the technicians of, say, *Life* magazine would be able to provide images for a billboard campaign, a record-album cover, and at least one "creative" photograph—recognized as such when shown at the Museum of Modern Art over a properly luminescent name—from a roll of film exposed on an arbitrary schedule in the cheapest of cameras by any ten-year-old.

"Besides, creation is a rare and supreme activity. It is uninducible and renders humbling, long-reaching, and impersonal judgments. Titian created. The great Persian court painter Bihzad and Giotto and Rembrandt created. Joachim Patinir, Hieronymous Bosch, Goya, Constable —all of these gave to us what had not so invaluably existed before. Surely, if I am creative it is euphemistically or in the murkiest of contemporary senses. In any case, they were not (in some respects could not have been) mindful of all that would make them singular, and neither very gainfully can anyone else.

"Furthermore," says the worldly one, "such creators are diminished and we are freed in the fullness of ourselves only after their work and conditions have been absorbed with a respectful understanding that will be repaid tenfold in the strength of our own work.[8] To behave as if this were not the case may yield a few *frissons* each gallery season, but the cost of these little thrills is stupendous when measured for what they place ahead of the growth and eventual gifts of the artist—and therefore ahead of the possible benefits to all of us. If your diminutive position on the 'shoulders of giants' is sobering, it is hardly to be improved by imagining that you alone have both feet on the ground. You have two choices: enjoying the ride and learning from (which includes changing) the view—as good a working definition of 'tradition' as I can think of—or refusing to do either. If you refuse either but insist on painting, you will fool no one who might otherwise have nurtured your work."

The other caricature is an unworldly, somewhat beatific being. His tolerant, smiling response to most talk of creativity is like his response to children earnestly playing grown-up. "They examine the reality from too far outside it," he says. "They would first have to have been there. Along with the serenity of the workshop and much else, these talkers are blind to the 'shock of recognition' that Melville thought would pass through an assembly of all the world's ingenious.[9] Therefore, not knowing wherein they would recognize each other, and having no substantial experience of the work or the assurance it requires of its creators, their discussions lack a vital core.

"Like all categories and truisms," he continues, "the notion of the artist as an indefinably unique or perceptive human has undergone the divesting rituals of our day. When they served us, the rare gift and quixotic idealism of the artist were found everywhere, past and present; lately, however, especially since the early 1980s, all we seem to find, from the wall painters of Pompeii to Mark Kostabi's production lines, are shrewd and calculating businesspeople. But long before they were everyman, media stars, and entrepreneurs, before they were romantic greathearts, bohemians or prophets, artisans or slaves, those in the caves who first drew images and thus beauty and meaning from themselves and the materials of the earth knew a strange, still unexplained, and still effective confidence. Their special, already developed trust in the hand and the eye must also have included the fitness of their implements for reflecting (and reflecting on) their world. A clear and bouyant sureness seems to have driven them.

"The satisfactions and broader mysteries and implications of such practices already brought honor and entitlement to the practitioners, for they were in league with a kind of magic. Memory, dreams, and knowledge were illuminated by what Lewis Mumford called 'the memorial arts of sculpture and painting.'[10] But their effects echo through all that came afterward. In them lay future realizations of form (functional and otherwise), the bases of writing, and subsequent visual representation. Could *any* one of its inhabitants have produced the paintings in Altamira's caves, or were they the work of a few 'gifted' and perhaps delegated individuals? We cannot know for sure, but if a few did them, they and their counterparts among the music makers, dance-actors, and storytellers would have been the few who tended the soul and all that distinguished humans from all else. And if those in their long lineage could explain the spell — who else can? — they would no longer be in it."

Caricatures: overdrawn and quaint. The first tries to shrug off any view that would separate the joyful blending of mind and hand from plain life. Uneasy with obliging gossamer and unctuous spiritualism, it regards creativity as mainly a random, external matter, or at least as inseparable from the puzzles of social and coincidental flux. The second speaks (always at greater length) from the beleaguered but persistent individual center, where the most personal and idiosyncratic of insights and affinities grow. It presumes creativity to be special and primarily an internal matter, an issue of the "transcendent, inviolable" self. Though opposed and questionable, such responses to chatter about creativity are in varied measure common, I suspect, among those who bring a full range of thought and emotion to the long practice of something with as many impinging factors, and as vast a history and array of possibilities, as art.

The ambivalent self-possession *and* exuberance characteristic of making and enjoying art seem for me to counter almost any assertion leading too briskly toward a supposedly prime mover. The ambivalence may have many roots. However, I see it as but yet another part of the "internal creational argument"—a stringency that works toward but questions *theoretical* resolution; the kind of uncertainty that, as well as certainty, creation can foster. I admit to many moments when the work seems to emanate from the inner, preeminent, and unmannered center of the second caricature. But more often I am the mundane practitioner, although my work may suddenly contradict me, however cunning and made-up my mind had been.

The caricatures are of my dissent from unseasoned views on creativity, not of my refusal to recognize it in fact. Though expressed in some of the same terms, the ambiguity that now generally surrounds creativity *is* about its acknowledgment. Instead of the personal entanglements of individual expression or making, it has to do with doubts about creativity itself, its identifiability and veneration; or, contrarily, about its compromise by lesser forces. As part of a larger sociopolitical debate, the ambiguity boils with many currents and is a perplexed issue that includes the continuing implications of Freud and other developments that argue the incidental character of artistic, if not all personal life. I have neither the room nor the inclination to pursue that perplexity to great depths. Even so, because I believe anyone's understanding of art is improved by real efforts to produce art, I would like to review enough of the issue to distinguish the productive experience against the background of current doubts about the notion of creativity.

In however high regard they may once have held it, some reject the term "creative" because it has become meaningless, randomly applied to anyone doing anything, however well (the poorer the performance, in fact, the more applicable it may seem to become), and to any end. Meanings it could or should have are deformed, they would say, by our reluctance to make distinctions and face their possibly far-reaching and unwanted implications. As the glory and the name of art are borrowed for meaner tasks, so "creative" is preempted for general use. "Words that were meant to describe and encourage Beethoven and Goethe are now applied to every schoolchild."[11] The mountain now comes not only to the prophet, but to everyone.

In a recent essay on creativity, Jacques Barzun traces the burgeoning use and devaluation of the word, examines the importance of the shift from "having" to "being" a genius, and urges that the "at least four layers of meaning" suggested by "creativity" be seen, privately and publicly, as a hierarchy. The "layers" begin at the bottom with "the commonplace quality of initiative." "Next comes the . . . widespread knack of drawing . . . and versifying, modestly kept for private use. Above this . . . the trained professional artist, including the commercial [*sic*] who supplies the market with the products in vogue. At the top is the rare bird . . . whose works first suggested the idea that a human being could be called a creator." The rare bird is a "phoenix," "making something new and out of little or nothing" and, in the case of our future, "rebuilding" out of the destruction and "glutted" world in which everyone has been persuaded "that creative power is within the reach of all by natural right, like political power."[12]

Recalling some of the more famous explanations of creativity, Barzun doubts that its "specific traits" can be made certain, once and for all. The broken and reforged linkage of creativity and mental instability, first made by Plato, is an example of why such doubt may be justified. For centuries, what Shelley called "harmonious madness"[13] was a staple of reflections on the creator. In the nineteenth century, Cesare Lombroso argued a special but definite relation between "the genius" or creative type and insanity, in which he included categories of degeneracy from "Vagabondage," "Rickets," and "Sterility" to "Amnesia" and "Double Personality."[14] With the further spread of science and less general conceptions came different and opposed arguments (Barzun mentions Francis Galton's normalizing findings). The unbalanced van Goghs were not more numerous than the highly organized Hiroshiges or commen-sensical Rubenses. By the 1950s, Lawrence S. Kubie's conclusion was, with technical qualifications, representative of this changed approach: such instability, far from being its agent, "corrupts, mars, distorts, and blocks creativeness."[15] Now, alas, a recent investigator, aligning the newest findings, sees the broth as convincingly stirred anew. In support of the link between creativity and madness, "there has been no good research until very recently. Indeed, until the mid-1980s it was possible for some authorities on creativity to deny that the link exists." However,

he says, "five new studies . . . should now lay most doubts to rest."[16]
The argument about "traits" continues.

In the decades of its ascendancy, "creativity" has spawned mountain ranges of scientific and unscientific studies, and yet it is my unspecialized but not so cursory impression that they say (in different language and more bewildering detail) what may be inferred from opinion and studies before this century: strong, original, and highly influential works can rise from practically any personal or collective condition. Only qualities as abstract and question-begging as creativity itself (intelligence, for example) seem everywhere present. Teasingly, as it were, and for no universally dependable reasons, the brilliance migrates from its preponderance in one place and time to another; shines only from the backbreaking labor of one and the apparent effortlessness of another; appears now on demand, now uninvited. Reading that creativity occurs after the "boundaries of the known" are "mastered . . . through convergent processes, and then extended . . . by the application of divergent processes,"[17] one imagines creativity as the Scarlet Pimpernel, suddenly appearing in disguise to confound the theorist: in quick succession and in the same town, the Pimpernel gives us, first, divergence that leads to control of the heretofore only subliminally known, and *hence* convergence; then, on the other side of the tracks, convergence and divergence in such speedy alternation that it would be scientifically tricky to separate, identify, and trail them.

In his magnification of its mystery, Barzun typifies those who regret the pollution of the language by misuses of "creation." Taking aim at the matter-of-fact phrase, "creative process," he argues that if there were such a thing, by now "its operation would have been reduced to formulas, recipes, which intelligence and method could apply" to great works. But aside from the inheritance of "technique," that is not what happens, because "creation does not proceed, it occurs," and the occurrence "defies analysis."[18]

Others reject the word for different reasons. Some believe that creativity's mystique is unfounded, that it follows natural laws, as Aristotle argues in his *Metaphysics*, and that the glow of the nimbus is really due to labor, learning, loving care, careful accumulations, patience, and other extraordinary amounts of the ordinary. With scientific perseverance, some remain open on the question and continue to consult their own or others' research. For some, a sophisticated cynicism leaves no room for creativity. According to the artist Robert Smithson, for example, the "existence of self" is at the heart of art's "expressive fallacy." He felt that "As long as art is thought of as creation, it will be the same old story. Here we go again, creating objects, creating systems, building a better tomorrow. . . . there is no tomorrow, nothing but a . . . yawning gap. . . . There is no point in trying to come up with the right answer because it is inevitably wrong."[19] Creating an "answer" that might be the galvanizing premise of at least a few years' work by an individual or a generation had already become untenable.

As an avant-gardist maker of "earthworks" (notably *Spiral Jetty* on the edge of the Great Salt Lake, Utah, in 1970), Smithson was also bemoaning an inflexible, object-oriented, metropolitanized atmosphere in which the rigor of earlier artistic groundbreakers was no longer possible. Without question, attempting a "right answer" in what had become, and still is, a thoroughly commercialized "artworld" bore directly on creativity. The painter Romare Bearden once said, "I don't believe in goals; goals are for a football team. An artist is just seeking what he may find."[20] The time when many widely noted modern artists could say this while working productively for a broad, contemporary audience had gone or was quickly passing. The sardonically cranked out repetition, not "seeking," was late 1960s vogue. Later, the painter Red Grooms would say, "Half my time is spent with my career, just kind of curating and monitoring it, and the rest of the time I try to be as I used to be."[21] (Therefore, others believe, the present "system" works toward keeping artists "in the same slot. . . . One is encouraged to repeat, discouraged to explore and radically shift the nature of his terrain and viewpoint.")[22]

However, Smithson's remarks relate to even deeper moods and attitudes that bear on the idea of creation. His belief in the possibilities of an "art against itself," one that "always returns to essential contradiction," is born out in a highly publicized portion of our day's art that is studiously contradictory and self-canceling.

After the collapse (or was it abandonment?) in the 1970s of both a critically viable, progress-promising "mainstream" *and* the avant-garde, one could fairly think the 1980s would consist of recycled efforts at continuity: the prefix "neo" figured understandably often in the art press's treatment of the constructivist, geometric, expressionist, and figural works of the decade's opening years. In the old attempt to override style's inevitabilities and the meaning behind André Malraux's observation that "a clumsy style does not exist," some painters tried purposely to cultivate what Berenson once termed the "originality of incompetence."[23] Others, like the painter-critic Suzi Gablik, called for the "reenchantment," "remythologizing," and general resacralization of the realm of art as more than a bazaar of commodities.[24] More prevalent, however, though mixed with these directions, has been the effort to reawaken and extend the same line as first established by an older avant-garde and later urged by Smithson and others.

For example, Allan Kaprow recently speaks of the "un-artist," who is not "the artist but the artist emptied of art" and who "makes no real art but does . . . lifelike art, art that reminds us mainly of the rest of our lives. . . . They find meaning in picking a thread from someone's collar . . . in just making sure the dishes are washed."[25]

This is the weak echo of World War I Europe, where bitterly iconoclastic futurism and anti-art dada flourished, where Picabia pointedly hung an empty picture frame in the air, and where Malevich, among others, declared painting forever dead. The echo, grandly renewed in the 1960s and now intoned daily, is also from Marcel Duchamp, who supposedly gave up painting in 1920 and told an interviewer in 1966, "I would have wanted to work, but deep down I'm enormously lazy. I like living, breathing, better than working. I don't think that the work I've done can have any social importance whatsoever in the future. Therefore . . . my art would be that of living: each second, each breath is a work which is inscribed nowhere, which is neither visual nor cerebral. It's a sort of constant euphoria."[26]

Not only was Duchamp's social prophecy wrong—if, in accordance with fashion, we qualify his not working as his work—but we found upon his death in 1966 that his "constant euphoria" had, after all, allowed him the secret completion of a work of the other kind, *Etant Données*, 1946–66.

The echo might be said to come from sources even farther afield, of course, not only from Oscar Wilde, an admirer of the "art of doing absolutely nothing,"[27] or from Jean Jacques Rousseau or Plato, but from, say, the Chinese philosopher Chuang Tzu, who lived until about 300 B.C. Chuang Tzu wrote, "In the days of perfect nature, man lived together with birds and beasts, and there was no distinction of their kind. . . . they were in a state of natural integrity. . . . And then when Sages appeared . . . they said they must make merry by means of music and enforce distinctions . . . and the empire became divided against itself. . . . Destruction of the natural integrity of these things for the production of articles of various kinds—this is the fault of the artisan."[28]

Chuang Tzu, however, seems to be on firmer (if slippery) ground. When he asked an unwanted governmental visitor if a tortoise would rather be alive, wagging its tail in the mud, or enclosed in an ancestral temple, the envoy said it would rather be in the mud. Then Chuang Tzu cried, "Begone! I too will wag my tail in the mud."[29] By all accounts, he and his followers secluded themselves from society and its governers, practicing what they preached. But many others since, professing to wash dishes, play chess, and otherwise wag about in a state of natural integrity, have in fact been hanging around the ancestral temples, painting moustaches on the icons.

In other words, we live in an atmosphere that is uncomfortable with any grounds for making binding connections, for linking *this* with *that.* Bred on oxymorons, many of us are burning our candles at both ends, which is one result of an increasing impatience with *any* framing conceptions of art and related terms, including "creativity." From the earlier difficulties of an art that would be "conceptual" but also marketable, to current urges for the aboriginal with all the advantages of inheritance, a significant segment of contemporary art seeks to have it both ways. As Duchamp could be attracted by the idea of the artist as craftsperson while dismissing the hand's role, a critic can write of an artist's work that it "challenges the boundaries formed by . . . belief and disbelief."[30] (This recalls the anarchical author Alfred Jarry's early-century "identity of opposites," which equated such concepts as darkness and light, day and night, good and evil.)[31] Jean Dubuffet, one of the louder exponents of anonymity, can exhibit his work in the Guggenheim Museum in tandem with his opposition to institutional culture. One can, like Rimbaud, renounce art and become a gunrunner in Abyssinia but, unlike Rimbaud, have the trading there regarded as art. One can strike the characteristic pose against art with actions and productions, but refuse any implications of their being anything else.

This ambiguity has complex origins deriving from every corner of our age's and modern art's development. I will discuss one source because of its relation to my closing remarks on creation: the desperate attempt to revive a century-old avant-garde thrust in art — or at least one issuing from the customary regions of that category.

The upward incline of art's "progress," or, if you prefer, major changes and originalities, had gotten steadily steeper since cubism, particularly since the New York of the forties, fifties, and sixties. From assaults on its pitch we slid back into a predicament created by three things: (1) art's having already made its historic passage from symbolic to ideal, to realistic, to abstract; (2) a worldwide awareness (augmented and spread by growing communicational media) of obsolescing fashions and frantically elaborate analysis, identification, and valuation of art; (3) a distorted emphasis of old cultural expectations of progress, represented by the marketplace's control and insatiable hunger for novelty. What was "innovational" became more and more particular — "wall-size linoleum prints," for example. To see The New as new depended increasingly on a short memory. That Picasso made purposeful and original advances while painting what he wanted to paint is not only a mark of his genius, but also of his place on the edge of epochal changes and of his relatively traditional creative temperament. That he was later reproved for not having forged beyond cubism to the "next step," like meeting a contract or choosing "fundable venues of research," was one of the surest early signs of the theoretical mania now in full sway. (There are many such signs: with no evidence of sophisticated humor, a journal speaks of Van Dyck as being "unlucky" and having "bad timing" because of his relative ranking and chronological proximity to Rubens; "content" is described in the same issue as having been "re-discovered.")[32] However, in spite of countless forays to stake out a disappearing inch or two at the forwardmost edge, the movements, "isms," and brain trusts directly or indirectly enabled by cubist formalism and twentieth-century nostalgia, nihilism, and materials had, in at least a token sense, exhausted practically every vein by the 1970s.

Therefore, if the heady spirit of wholesale replacement were to be kept alive, drastic measures would be necessary. Aspects of many contemporary works had helped to keep alive the avant-garde venture, particularly those of the painter Robert Rauschenberg's that seemed to reach out beyond art. His telegram, "This is a portrait of Iris Clert if I say so," may recall, but significantly raises the stakes beyond, René Magritte's 1928 painting *The Treason of Images*, in which a pipe is painted above the sentence "This is not a pipe." The rush toward the absurd would soon be on, and no motive would prove stronger than to be the first to make any motive pointless. However, even Rauschenberg's "portrait" telegram and his erasure of a de Kooning drawing as an act of creation have an artistic center of gravity. With the rest of his work in place, they seemed then to be part of the perennial in-house rough-house and cross-talk among artists. But art was becoming a free-fire zone that could drift anywhere. Anything not firmly fixed in the convulsions of change (and sometimes even if it was) could be claimed for it.

With the likes of Smithson and single-minded others, some of whom saw art as, above all, an embodiment of a "right answer," the center of gravity shifted. There would no longer be a "house of art," or rather, as with the German artist Joseph Beuys, *all* of life would be art; "artist" would apply to everyone; "art would be *any kind of being or doing*"[33] (my emphasis).

The motives that compelled Chris Burden to be nailed to an automobile or to fire a pistol at an airliner as it took off from Los Angeles must have had a force only slightly greater than the motives of those who considered it as art.[34] Strong among these not necessarily conspiring motives was to identify this new, unshackled, mainly intellectual energy more obviously with social and political goals and possibilities; to replace or more obviously mix its fading formal involvement with other urgencies.

A principal argument in this endeavor, allying it with the momentum and freedom of modern art where it might otherwise meet more resistance, is the enlargement of a characteristic but heretofore limited, romantic-modernist attitude to the definition of art itself: art is trouble. If it is not ominous or disturbing, it is not really art. "Art is nothing in itself," wrote one critic in 1974, "the only purpose . . . that can be assigned to it is to oppose society," all "academic and museographical seriousness" to the contrary.[35] But a "premier curator," no stranger to museums, also recently said that art's "very reason for being demands that it engender controversy."[36] It is up to "those who make . . . and finance art to seek more trouble," writes a battler, not as a dadaist trying to outrage a complacent power but as an instrument of power. "Artists belong out front . . . they have no other job. . . . Let us learn to jump into a nasty political fight and . . . get on with our work."[37] And if the work leads away from the fight, which is to be followed?

Usually left unclear are the levels and kinds of controversy the prohibiter has in mind. Even more misleading is the simplifying of the artist's relation to controversy. If, as Samuel Butler wrote, genius has the "capacity for getting its possesor into trouble,"[38] the trouble cannot always be presumed to have been the point of the ingenuity. Braque observed in his *Pensées* that "art upsets, science reassures." Braque means that if one does it right it will alter, if not upset, as will anything so thoroughly, even bittersweetly remindful of life's chanciness and constant touch-and-go as art; but this directs one's instincts toward the necessities of one's art, not toward directly insuring an upset. Older and more numerously significant than intended conflict, and perhaps more disruptive, are instances of creative involvement that are innocently begun but which for that reason are able later to spread out more troublesomely or in directions other than the creator might have expected. But again those of the new ambitendency would have, to absolute degrees, both the activist's immediacy *and* creative detachment, at the same time or whichever is momentarily most advantageous.

Such Making it New does not consist of a new act in the same play but of abolishing first the play, then the "theater itself." Not the alienated work of a small band of bohemian malcontents, this newness is organized at the heart of the art establishment and comes by way of healthy hordes and intellectual stripminers in almost every segment of society. The newness is in the identification of art with everything — the "highness" of art is leveled; the "lowness" of anything is dignified. The newness is in the mockery, demolition, and reconstitution of art itself, its history, cultural roles, customs, spaces, and curricular and other classifications, *but* under the protection of its ancient reputation. This vanguardism is not revealed in works or ideas so much as in feints and fronts, the selection and combination of stances, actions, images, and phrases meant "to represent forward movement" and ritually "function as symbols of advance or of the will to advance."[39] Old wine in *no* bottles.

As in most operations that now swap fundamental methods with the contemporized "artworld," such motives sweep aside considerations that might slow the breakneck angling for jarring juxtapositions. Purporting progress and enlightenmnent, they and ever-converted newness drive us in all categorical and emotional directions and come to be expected within ever-decreasing segments of time. Some may see cynicism, confirmation of the Show Biz Society, or even hope in the ironic fact that if substantial newness is proposed in a field that is thought, like education or medicine, to be more sensitively situated than some, there is often an equally exaggerated effort to appear *customary*. For example, the company proposing to revitalize American education with in-school, commercial television will be headquartered in a "Georgian-style campus," with "schoolhouse light fixtures" and an "instant," hauled-in environment of forty-foot oak trees.[40] In most cases, however, the need for the appearance of newness is greater, and it exhausts the patience required to obtain newness as a product of genuinely, closely linked developments.

In his preface to *Roderick Hudson* (1876), Henry James refers to an absolute continuum and the artist's perhaps instructive courage and ability to deal with it: "Really, universally, relations stop nowhere, and the exquisite problem of the artist is eternally but to draw, by a geometry of his own, the circle within which they shall happily *appear* to do so."[41] Of course, this immemorial "problem" is radically solved by denying all conventions about the circle and simply equating art and everything else in life. Art's *license* is still useful, but the encumbrance of art itself is thrown off (Nietzsche spoke of poetry as a dance in chains). The specifically artistic skills of drawing that circle, as well as the imagination's ability to find completeness within it, are lost in an unmeasurable scope. "When" is art, not "what" is art, becomes the contextually defined question. Art is extinguished in its liberation. Its motives find accomplishment the same ways any other motives are realized in a real, economic, political world.

Bueys's tag, "Social Sculpture," suggests that it is toward social reform instead of artistic or "formalistic" changes that there is to be "forward movement," really or ritually. Therefore, if, as he announced, "art is a basic metaphor for all social freedoms,"[42] it does not follow that everything once connected to "art" is to be included. Restored, as it were, to real life, art would no longer include aesthetic classifications or any hint of hierarchies, either among objects or their makers. No more "fine" as compared to any kind of art. No art separate from its social philosophy, causes, and effects. No James Joycean artist god or goddess off to one side, cleaning his or her fingernails. In fact, no more diplomatic immunity for "art" or "artist."

Finally, no more "creativity," with its "elitist" privacy and presumptions, special objects, and mystic arcanum. If, as a recent investigator writes, "a product or idea is creative to the extent that expert observers agree it is creative,"[43] then in the absence of inherent quality in the work or generally shared conceptions and cultural agreement, it is inevitable that we begin the bickering hunt for *who* agrees that they are experts, *why*, and how *they* got there, the better to control, defuse, or replace the power thought to reside in the label. This hunt, not the practice or even the examination of creativity, becomes paramount.

Between the time that Hegel announced God's death in the nineteenth century and John Brockman, at least, announced humankind's death in the 1960s,[44] Art too supposedly died. It may have been a tradition instead of art that died. Or it may have been the first of many death throes that, through lingering hopes and new expectations, go on for many years before the realization in the twenty-first century that something else profoundly vital had indeed ended some time ago. In any case, art will not be as it has been, in some fundamental respects, through even the most fractuous times of it history. The divide stretches between us and sailing ships, horse and landau, and old masters.

Not even the not-so-old "masters" would any longer be at home. From here, Melville's "mystic" but traditionally persistent wrestle with "angelic art" and Apollinaire's modernist battle on the edge for our sake look very much alike. It is we, who are neither the "perfection of order" nor the devoted makers and givers of realization, who are different; whose roots run so shallow that we see the "flowering mystery" as wilted delusion. For us, the "limitlessness" no longer has enabling limits, and instead of "pity" for the necessary "sins" and "errors" of noble "adventure," we seek immediate rewards for pallid, clever displacements of that other seriousness.

Yet, I am not as sure that all of those who survive these conceptual deaths will have undergone basic change. It is for this reason that I believe the educational category creation — "create-activity" or art making, the ineffable, lively contact and cooperation with physical, especially extensional properties — must be protected from the extremities of *both* of the positions I have written about. The idea that such "activity" may sully the word "creation" and the good name of art with tawdry, inexpert efforts, better spent on more obvious priorities, ignores the depths of those very priorities. And in regarding such creation as only therapy, recreation, or an educationally unjustifiable rearguard of advanced art, "basic" learning is made not more but less flexible and comprehensive. Therefore, the constant intrusion in the classroom-studio of even the highest, well-meaning standards will be no less ruinous of creativity whether they are translations of exclusively social or artistically technical objectives.

Maurice Friedman described the existential temper as "a reaction against the static, the abstract, the purely rational, the merely irrational, in favor of . . . concrete, personal involvement . . . action, choice, and commitment."[45] This is a partial but fair description of our beginnings as students, long before we might read his list more abstractly (as "commitment to values," and so forth). Then, we are more literally of this temper. The root of creation, and the model of much later development, is the manifold way we are drawn to doodle, play, experiment, assert, examine, rearrange, copy, destroy, reflect, fantasize, remake, and invent with what are, at those moments, extensions of both ourselves and the universe.

It seems clear to me that amplification of this kind of activity will favorably condition *and* profit from an atmosphere of learning — even though creation in some form or other will of course take place without it. Creation is neither a completely personal possession spread onto works nor impersonal decrees that have found individuated points of friction. It occurs in the most diverse alliance of individuals with a medium in a broad tradition. The exact, not general nature of that alliance, its character, and points of contact, is the base of any broader generalizations about "creation," "creator," and "creativity."

"For the things we have to learn before we can do them," according to Aristotle, "we learn by doing them."[46] In regard to painting and drawing (if not, in some degree, art in general), such learning may seem to have been compromised. The realm of modern technology extends well beyond what we can hear, touch, and see. The camera and the computer in particular would seem (especially in regard to representation) to have stolen the hand's supremacy with their convenience and speed and their substitution of the more remote air of efficiency, uniformity, and empirical accuracy. These tools can make the hand's mastery so seemingly subordinate that we are mildly shocked at remembering that they were, of course, made by hand; that in their first development and "co-conception" they sprang from the hand, "the human organ of culture."[47] And may not the relatively recent and explosive popularity of organized sports and the performing arts be due in part to the waning evidence elsewhere of such sovereign human presence?

Furthermore, as we have seen, an intense intellectuality has by turns playfully and combatively increased its control over the creativity of which it is a part, over physical and "manual culture," and especially over the standards by which works are championed. Having redefined art and artist, and having questioned the bases of any supposedly non-social standards by which the works of these "outmoded" estates might be judged, this intellectuality then asks, "What's to be learned? What we want or need can be deemed rather than done," as with "found objects" and grafitti, or the consideration of the museum's firehose as another work of art. For plodding city shoppers to become consummate dancers it is sufficient only that they be so considered. "And anyway," it adds, "if it needs to be done we are, all of us, by ignoring harsh and ultimately oppressive standards, *already* capable at any state of age, ability, or experience."

Such a temporary divestiture of skill, knowledge, experience, and art has always been a stock in trade of the artist. Its benefits, however, are in ratio to the opposite on which it depends; that is, the investiture of the same things culturally or by the same artist at deeper levels. For cooperation with a medium sooner or later brings out the choices, qualities, and unsuspected capacities that, even in their momentary denial, become in time the skill and authority that permits such regressive wandering. For the artist who understands the difference between the authority and the wandering, who sees the latter as enabled by the former, not as its absolute replacement, such experience is informative. It exhilarates and fortifies the querulous, ambivalent nature at the center of our being as artists. (As much as anything else, it is something about being a painter that makes me contrarily, stubbornly think of Piero di Cosimo when pomp and dignity are invoked, Grunewald's *The Isenheim Altarpiece* when "play" is made to explain all, Frank Auerbach's slovenly power when "craft" is stressed, Egyptian murals when I hear "expressivity," and so forth.) For those who do not accept the relation between authority and "wandering," the latter becomes simply another instance of the exploitation of the world's resources by the free but feckless, impatient modern ego.

Moreover, the hand's training, its inclusion in the intellect's training, remains necessary. The top floor of the highest skyscraper stands nevertheless on the ground. However far robots, electronics, boredom, fashion, or weightless ambition may take us from the hand, someone will always have to subject ideas to form and be commanded by the Muse of Realization,[48] who over and over keeps murmuring as we are tempted only mentally to make things work, that it is still harder than we thought.

NOTES

1. Christopher Lasch, *The True and Only Heaven* (New York: W. W. Norton & Compnay, 1991), 22.

2. James Fallows, *More Like Us* (Boston: Houghton Mifflin, 1989), 25.

3. Susan Tallman, "Faking it," *Art in America,* November 1990, 75.

4. Arthur C. Danto, review of Jean Baudrillard, *Selected Writings* and *America;* Douglas Kellner, review of *Jean Baudrillard: From Marxism to Postmodernism and Beyond, New Republic,* 10 September 1990, 46.

5. Clifford Geertz, "A Lab of One's Own," *New York Review,* 8 November 1990, 19.

6. Aaron Betsky, *Violated Perfection* (New York: Rizzoli, 1990), 30–31, 109.

7. Gordon S. Wood, review of Simon Schama, *Dead Certainties (Unwarranted Speculations), New York Review,* 27 June 1991, 12.

8. Those familiar with Sir James Frazier's *The Golden Bough* (New York: Macmillan, 1963) may recognize here a version of our forebear's more literal and symbolic absorption of gods and paragons as discussed in chapters 24 and 50.

9. Raymond W. Weaver, ed., *Billy Budd and Other Prose Pieces by Herman Melville* (London: Constable and Company, 1924), 137.

10. Lewis Mumford, *The Myth of the Machine* (New York: Harcourt, Brace & World, Inc., 1966), 118.

11. Allan Bloom, *The Closing of the American Mind* (New York: Simon and Schuster, 1987), 183.

12. Jacques Barzun, "The Paradoxes of Creativity," *American Scholar,* Summer 1989, 337–51.

13. Percy Bysshe Shelley, *To a Skylark,* stanza 21.

14. Cesare Lombroso, *The Man of Genius* (London: Charles Scribner's Sons, 1895).

15. Albert Rothenberg and Carl R. Hausman, eds., *The Creativity Question* (Durham, N.C.: Duke University Press, 1976), 148.

16. Melvin Konner, "The Art of Darkness," *Why the Reckless Survive* (New York: Viking, 1990), 241.

17. A. J. Copley, *Creativity* (London: Longman Group, 1967), 29.

18. Barzun, "Paradoxes of Creativity," 349.

19. Lucy Lippard, ed., *Six Years: The Dematerialization of the Art Object* (New York: Praeger Publishers, 1973), 90.

20. Harriet Welchel, ed., *Artists Observed* (New York: Harry Abrams, 1986), 146.

21. Ibid., 114.

22. Ibid., 152.

23. Renato Pogglioli, *The Theory of the Avant-Garde* (New York: Harper & Row, 1971), 177.

24. Suzi Gablik, "The Reenchantment of Art," *New Art Examiner*, December 1987, 30.

25. Allan Kaprow, "The Meaning of Life," *Artforum*, Summer 1990, 145–46.

26. Pierre Cabanne, *Dialogues with Marcel Duchamp* (New York: Viking Press, 1971), 72.

27. Quoted in Camille Paglia, *Sexual Personae* (New Haven: Yale University Press, 1990), 531.

28. Lin Yutang, ed., *The Wisdon of China and India* (New York: Random House, 1942), 670.

29. Ibid., 690.

30. Lucy Lippard, "Andreas Serrano: The Spirit and the Letter," *Art in America*, April 1990, 239.

31. John Richardson, *A Life of Picasso, Volume I: 1881–1906* (New York: Random House, 1991), 366.

32. Leonard J. Slatkes, "Anthony Van Dyck: The Bad Timing of a Good Painter," *View* magazine, *Journal of Art*, November 1990, 21.

33. Robert Hughes, *The Shock of the New* (New York: Alfred A. Knopf, 1982), 381.

34. Even nihilism cannot quite escape precedence: Burden can be said to have actualized an old avant-garde metaphor, as used in the title of the futurist poet G. P. Lucini's *Revolverate* ("revolver shots") and symbolized in Alfred Jarry's pistol, which Jarry bequeathed to Picasso. Of course, pistols served defensive and other than avant-garde ends in the dangerous Montmarte of that period. (See Richard Dorment, "Lautrec's Bitter Theatre," *New York Review*, 19 December 1991, 16.)

35. Alain Jouffroy, *Miro Sculptures* (New York: Leon Amiel Publishers, 1974), 54.

36. Carol Lutfy, "Fumio Nanjo: Japan's Premier Curator of Contemporary Art," *Journal of Art*, January 1991, 24.

37. Charles L. Mee, Jr., "When in Trouble, Start More," *New York Times*, Sunday, 8 July 1990, C11.

38. *The Notebooks of Samuel Butler* (New York: AMC Press, 1968), 173.

39. Harold Rosenberg, *Art on the Edge* (New York: Macmillan, 1975), 251.

40. Barbara Aston-Wash, "The Schoolhouse that Whittle Built," *Knoxville News-Sentinel*, 30 June 1991, E1.

41. Henry James, *Roderick Hudson* (London: John Lehman, 1947), viii.

42. Hughes, *Shock of the New*, 381.

43. Robert J. Sternberg, ed., *The Nature of Creativity* (Cambridge: Cambridge University Press, 1988), 14.

44. John Brockman, *The Late John Brockman* (New York: Macmillan,

1969), 1. For Hegel's description, see "Beliefs and Knowledge," in *Works* (1802; reprint Frankfurt, 1970), 2:432, quoted in Hannah Arendt, *The Life of the Mind: Thinking* (New York: Harcourt Brace Jovanovich, 1978), 9.

45. Maurice Friedman, *The Worlds of Existentialism* (New York: Random House, 1964), 3.

46. Aristotle, *Nicomachean Ethics*, bk. 2, ch. 1.

47. Otto Rank, *Art and Artist* (New York: Tudor Publishing Company, 1936), 247.

48. Bill McKibben, "Prophet in Kentucky," *New York Review*, 14 June 1990, 33.

6

The Classroom

From Picasso, Arshile Gorky learned above all, keep at it. . . .
If there is shooting outside the window, go on drawing. For
the artist, there is only one real situation, and only one salvation: art.

— Harold Rosenberg

I begin my last chapter with some of my experiences as a student,
which are intended to lend yet another context to all that I have written
and offer a further basis for the more important remainder of the
chapter. Next, I touch on the issue of education's uneasiness with the
artist and art making and how that uneasiness may overlook, among
other things, a broader import in the above quotation from Rosenberg.
I conclude with some suggestions for emphasis in the classroom.

The trite and corny are tied at some length to the truth. In spite
of the new urge to end the romanticization of artists, the threadbare
trail of anecdotes continues. Even as the line grows dimmer between
the life of the general populace and its notions of the life of the artist,
that trail is identified and examined for many reasons, including what
it may tell us about creation. I have witnessed this around the lives
of my painter friends and can attest to it in my own experience.

With perhaps excusable exaggeration, my mother informs me that
I drew before I walked, and I overheard many other such probable
exaggerations as I grew up. I was prone to alarming feats of comatose
attention, "hiding" in open places (atop a mantelpiece, say) and poring
for long periods over a single object. In circumstances of whatever
duration, my behavior was safely predictable if I was given pencil and
paper. As a schoolboy, I "lived alone on a raft in the river," as rumor
had it, and "papered my hut with drawings." This report from concerned
adults scandalized the household, although it was acquainted with such
tales, some of which it may have originated. (I am told, for example,
that at age six I presented an elaborate drawing of a "living room" as
a "picture" of her family to the visiting mother of a numerous, somewhat

lethargic clan from down the street, and when she asked where the family members were, I explained, "Asleep upstairs.")

Whether they are evidence of society's need—different in many ways from the artist's need—to dramatize or revere art, or of more obvious social impulses, these stories are lesser examples of the well-stretched yarns that seem to crop up around artists, particularly their beginnings. They exemplify a small way in which society may be in greater need of art than the artist. And it is, after all, a situation ripe for entertainments: those who in some respect are thought to be precocious or adultlike as children are, once adult, often called childlike.

My introduction to the "will of the medium" was in the first grade of public school. I was given the task of illustrating a pamphlet, but with a ridiculuous, round-tipped mimeograph tool that had none of the grandeur of pencils. The fragile film fought me literally at every turn, and none of the praise heaped on it eased my disappointment with the outcome. I would copy and revel in comics (carefully saving "funnies" with out-of-register color) and absorb the wealth of newspaper illustrations, signs, and "commercial art" in general, but my preference for the singular as against the mass produced may have been sealed with my first commission. Sensing my disatisfaction, my teacher allowed me to color and rework every copy I could lay my hands on.

In fact, I should stress my good fortune concerning art teachers. In recollection, at any rate, none were remiss, bland, too skimpy in their support, or too positively intrusive. As if by a shared and uncanny grasp of my interests, all of them made timely contributions to my awareness. Their instruction seemed a lucky blend of all four of the teaching traditions outlined in Diana Korzenik's third chapter. Under strictly honor-bound conditions, I was entrusted at the age of eight with a supply-room key and the private, lunch-hour use of the room's contents. I became acquainted there with india ink, pastels, scratchboard, and other new and exciting materials. It is interesting now to imagine the rationale for giving a boy such leeway, but the privilege was worth any amount of responsibility, and it was in order to protect my benefactor's semi-secret trust in spite of an obstreperous classmate that I was involved in my first out-and-out brawl.

A year later, another teacher showed reproductions to us. They were the largest and greatest in number I had ever seen. Here and there I mistakenly thought I caught glimpses of N. C. Wyeth, Frederick Remington, and others with whose work (not names) I had become familiar. Many of the reproductions were urgently different, however, and some were awesome. They were my first exposure to the premodern achievements of the world's painting. I found them complicated and serious, like newsreels. As I stared at them, I thought I understood my teacher's gentle but persistent disregard for my tour de force copies of educational materials, my cartoons, or my absurd room decorations (the turkeys with hats and blunderbusses, the squatting pilgrims with feathers and wattles). After a weekend's work at home, I won her approval with my most ambitious project to date, a dense, full-bore version of Emanuel Leutze's *Washington Crossing the Delaware,* including updated details from the atmosphere of war around me—a horrific explosion on the horizon, a few small P-38s and other "air support," several contemporary marines in the back of the boat, and one in front, melting the ice with a flame thrower. It was glued flat to a piece of blue-gray pasteboard, just like the reproductions.

Independently, but under the strong influence of Marguerite Alexander, my sixth-grade teacher, I first painted in oils when I was thirteen. One day long before this, however, she asked me if I would help her after school. Shyly uncomfortable and ignorant of our destination, I found it more difficult to talk to her outside school and riding in her car across town to a complex of large, churchlike buildings. Walking toward one, I saw the only landmark I recognized, the football stadium. We were at the university. I entered a massive stone portal and, expecting a chore ahead of me, walked behind her down a dim hallway. She disappeared into a dark, echoing space and invited me to enter. Numerous clicks: at first weak, then progressively bright explosions of light filled the room, almost as large and empty as a gymnasium. Now she was beaming, looking directly at me. Only after several long moments did I understand that the paintings on the walls, about forty of them and surrounded by matts and stately spaces, were mine. She had quietly saved the watercolors and temperas I had painted, and now they hung before me, framed and transformed. I was, of course, dumbfounded. It was what she called my first "one man show" at age twelve, but more important, it was the occasion of my first shaky comprehension of the objective, formal, social aspects of such things. It was where I first felt the disturbances and nearly ungovernable excitement before the demanding imposition and seductiveness of having made such things.

My high school art teacher was a formidable lady, Virginia Parker, who had studied art, dramatics, and stagecraft at Black Mountain College, Traphagean, Columbia, and the University of Tennessee and had taught English, history, and Latin. She signaled the change of seasons by wearing a series of splendid hats, and the clear expression of her sharp critical judgment was personally tailored and to the point. Her contrasting introduction to modern architecture and its promise was a long, silent slide show of the false fronts, lame references, and grotesqueries of recent national building, followed by two lethal, heartfelt words: "Sham and pretense."

It was under her guidance that at sixteen I made my first formal studies of anatomy, joining with a group of older painters who met on weekends to work from models. She also introduced me to C. K. Ewing, with whom I would work through the next four years, and obtained a small university grant for me. With it, I bought my first large bundles of personal art supplies. As I worked my way to the present, Ewing trained me in fairly classical representation and drilled me in drawing, printmaking, and a variety of mediums for three years before I became his mural assistant. He encouraged my first submissions to national, juried exhibitions and was responsible for my nomination to a National Woodrow Wilson Fellowship, which I was the first painter to receive.

Perhaps due in part to the intervening 80,000 miles at sea with the navy and the accumulation of wider experience, it was not until graduate school that loose strands began to weave together. The principal factor, however, was Hoyt Sherman, my last formal teacher. He was a defiantly complex but highly efficient blend of the pragmatical and the abstract. He was a Master of the Right Question and the Opaque Gesture, to understand which invariably took one through ignored but critical territory. His confident direction, visual sensitivity, wit, and insight into painting and the productive personality were the legendary stuff that, however camouflaged, was once so routinely treasured and transmitted among artists.

As our youth may seem to have passed in special times and places, regardless of all subsequent verdicts, we should expect the period in which our work gathers or seems to gather its first cosmopolitan strength to be of special, perhaps distorted importance for the artist. My time with Sherman was such a "second adolescence," a time of broadly informed works and an incredible range of new and reinforced insights.

But then I have been able to isolate my work's fortunes from those of the times in which it took place only with difficulty. Promising times and a run of good paintings seem always to coincide, as do hard times and not so good paintings. I have never said, "Those were happy, positive years, but my work was lousy," or "Grim were the times, but at least my work was going well." Instead, I hear myself saying that regardless of objective evidence to the contrary, and apparently *because* my paintings were healthy, smiling, and pregnant, I find in the time all sorts of falsely labeled good, hidden significance, and hope. And if the studio is barren, so is the time, no matter the "upturn in the economy," a "new human solidarity," or what have you. I am rationally appalled. What kind of introversion or superstition is this? I jeer the thought, but nevertheless have it: "Just as I could 'see air' and change things merely by staring at them when I was a boy, all of life will be better if I can make better paintings."

We still do not quite accept as a rich and equal educational source the actual processes of the artist, with their possibly childish, even sordid turns and confusions. Although we are reluctant to associate our most serious enterprises with those of the artist, we seize the artist's product, capitalize it (in every sense), and ponder its utility and what it implies about our condition, past and present. But the studio, like the workshop, laboratory, or library, is among society's soulful repositories, not an "ivory tower." The artist in Harold Rosenberg's remark is not of another planet. It is indeed an individual who continues while shots ring outside, but it is also a culture whose "salvation" lies in the continuity of that and similar processes. A society unable to recognize itself or find value in the *making* must question the depth of its judgment about the *work* of art.

I am addressing, of course, the usual separation of more or less sanitized art and its more or less problematic makers and making. "Learning about art," says a commentator, "is entirely different from learning to make or experience it. There is . . . some tension between the two activities."[1] I agree, although it is important that the two can strongly augment, if not call for, each other; that there is little reason so quickly to interrupt the early, generally productive cohesion of the two with that later, more sophistical "tension." There can be reason and integrity in approaches to learning that genuinely, fully include or definitely exclude the "hands-on" or experiential. The difficulties begin when the inclusion is only weak or nominal. Unless educational access to the fullest, most serious levels of these phenomena is as usefully prized as it is anywhere else, "making and experiencing" in particular will yield fewer relations to other disciplines and confirm either their relative insignificance or sphinxlike isolation.

I do not mean to suggest that correction of this "usual separation" necessarily depends on Artists-in-the-Schools programs, especially as they have come to be known over the past two or more decades. One of the worst of many bad things about such programs was the whisper within the phrase itself: two alien forces joined! Many have noted with amusement that during that time everyone became an "artist," but only the very specially prepared can be teachers. Even so, "artists," why-ever they are so called by whomever, are no more certain than "accredited teachers" to handle "making and experiencing" in such a way that creation and its interrelations with other disciplines are of a high, syncretic quality. In the terms in which this issue is most often examined, my view poses difficulties, no doubt, but I identify rather than isolate "artist" and "teacher," at least insofar as together they form a "middle entity" on which the highest, long-term functions of both art and education have always depended.

Argument on these matters seems to boil down to two broad approaches. One is based in the belief that art in the schools is best used frankly and directly as an instrument in establishing certain values; the other is based in the belief that these and other values are eventually best served when art itself—its craft, unpredictable creation, and apprehension—is given priority. Although the two approaches may not seem necessarily to exclude each other, in practice the wilder, disinterested spirit and helpful insights of art are more often lost to the first approach than social or other concerns are ignored in the second.

If, as I believe, it is the artist who encounters the whole of human history in his or her lifetime, it follows that anything having to do with the serious transmission of art's information, practices, or values will be a many-particle fusion. It will include the craft of making and making as expressing that which "cannot be put in harness to any but spiritual uses."[2] It will include or be directly informed by its many aspects, aesthetic, psychological, historical, and otherwise. However anomalous their preparation, however many hyphens in their titles, the individuals who present "making and experiencing" in this light will be comfortably, prolifically, and contemporarily based in it.

We may all be regarded as having at least a logical affect on the future. But it is the broader, somewhat less uncertain significance of it that Henry Adams had in mind in his famous speculation that the teacher's effect is infinite.[3] If this is correct, then even an art teacher's technical concentration cannot be separated from potential personal, intellectual, or social significance. Enlightenment through creation is universal currency. To assist in it, the teacher, like the artist, may choose from the full scope of human learning and employ whatever subversion or elaboration of theoretical programs is necessary. Both may control as well as follow and be the source as well as the medium of enlightenment.

In offering the following suggestions for the classroom, I am aware of the odds against saying anything that might practically and often enough apply to every level of students. I have taught several age groups, young and old, and helped raise two sometime apprentices, a daughter and a son, but most of my instructional experience has been at the college graduate and undergraduate levels. Of my students who went on to teach, most are K-12 teachers. A few are art directors of school districts. From this experience and the reports of these former students, I think I can emphasize a few things that may be considered in most situations.

Though lectures are often appropriate, the majority of the time in art sessions is spent at work with various materials and evaluations of it. This fact alone explains the piecemeal, opportunistic, individual, reactional nature of most such instruction, however loose or tight the planning and however central or peripheral the teacher's style or presence. The rest of the time is divided between demonstrations and presentations of one kind or another. All of these are not only distinct options of equal potential but overlapping choices that may suddenly evolve from one another, depending on circumstances to which the teacher's purposes and sensitivities must be tuned.

Demonstration is critical. Apart from its obvious purpose to show how "this thing is possible," the demonstrator's competence is emphatically connected with a recognized pursuit that consumes time and thought beyond school age and has its own methods while being, like mathematics, widely applicable. The demonstration says, "This belongs not only to an already granted abstraction with its real center elsewhere, but is something actual and here as well, something that can be yours." Even the flaws, humorous difficulties, and odd occurences can serve, perhaps not as well as the successes, but as grounds for other insights, observations, and projects. In this sense, demonstration cannot irretrievably fail.

Here is an example of a basic painting demonstration meant more dramatically to convey, among other things, my point in trooping the famous intruders through Rembrandt's studio in chapter 2: a flexibility of medium so free and inexhaustible that any objective may benefit from any event without being prevented.

While discussing all sorts of technical matters, I begin a large painting. Gradually, after several configurations and many additions and subtractions to show different surfaces, relations, and so on, I turn the painting on its side. Together, we discuss its possibilities. Most see it as a developing landscape, let us say. Next, each student is given a chance to affect the work in any way (depending on their number I have limited them to a few moves or several minutes of work). As one might imagine, a good deal about the image and the students may be revealed. Sometimes a single configuration is cooperatively developed. More often, new directions rise up, or the whole "history" is suddenly lost in playfully total, energetic, even purposely destructive effects. Always there are beautiful, intriguing developments and a marvelous running commentary; always there are sighs of regret at what is lost and expressions of amazement at what has suddenly come about through casual effort. Eventually, I return to the painting and, perhaps deceptively discussing other matters, begin to work with whatever is there. If lucky, I can seem for quite a while simply to be bringing out what was "submerged" there—which is not entirely untrue. Soon, though, my contribution becomes strange, then a plainly purposeful overlay, even though I am also *relying* on the accumulated shapes and colors. As students begin to frown or bend sideways for a different orientation to the painting, I turn it back to its first position. The image is now obvious, and I add a few touches. Finally, I ask the first-arriving student to whom I had given a sealed envelope to tear it open and read aloud the contents. "In a room with a window open to a night sky," reads the student, "a woman wearing a large, dark hat holds a basket of bright flowers"—a preconceived description that fits the haphazardly gotten painting.

Yes, it is a shameful stunt, but for only moments does it seem magical or to have been about my performance. In spite of often stunning coincidences, that part of it burns away in the students' growing realization of how easy it was—of how forgiving and cooperative the medium can really be.

One may make many variations on this demonstration. In one, the "window . . . woman" (or some such) description is given as an assignment to one class. Meanwhile, a second class is taken through many "blind detours" (swapping canvases, turning them upside down, and so on) before being given the same assignment and only a minute or two to achieve it on the same surface. Each class is shown all of the work from both and, without explanations until later, preferences are discussed. Practically always, the works of the second class are preferred (discussing why they are or are not leads easily to other concerns). In any case, a highly suggestive difference is apparent, and it is the source of this difference *in their assumptions*, instead of the crazy mechanics of the second class, that becomes the real topic. Works from the first class tend to be anemic versions and show careful, uniform effort only toward what was mentioned; those of the second reveal a far wider, "undirected" range of qualities not specifically mentioned in the assignment but in rich extension and support of it.

The "presentations" I mentioned above mean anything from visiting teachers, students, and specialists to field trips and slide shows. However, I would like to comment on reproductions in general, because films, slides, and other electronic means offer many possibilities and are increasingly used.

What we know and feel about certain works, and about painting in general, comes from much varied experience and information, only a small part of which is study of the actual object. Most of us, I expect, wish it could be a larger part. For some, the shortcomings of reproductions are a small price to pay for an increased range of knowledge and familiarity. I cannot argue with them, but I would say unequivocally that it is a bargain of dangerous benefits for anyone, but particularly for the artist.

I value my books and collections of reproductions and turn to them often; however, they are also copies of works in their own right. Having necessarily loose relations to their sources, they are examples of another kind of discrimination as graphic art—a printed medley of designed intervals, shapes, sizes and continuity. There are the works of Kurt Schwitters, for example, and then there is the "meta-Schwitters" of the books, posters, and magazines. (He came to mind because so many of his collages were composed of pieces of posters, newspapers, and magazines.)

I am nevertheless aware of the realities of schools, where the need to provide valuable information and visual experience for large numbers of students is met in part with reproductions. Aside from a wide range of the highest quality available, there are ways to increase their value. Several quite different slides of the same work immediately remind the student of the relativities at play. Where feasible, some effort to make the projected image of slides the same dimensions as the actual work is revealing and worth the trouble. A very few actual, exemplary paintings will lend their substance to many reproductions.

However, nothing so increases the value of such aids as the frank teacher who discusses this topic and does not take reproductions or their uses for granted; whose use of them admits the many distortions of the actuality. In addition to the utter impairment of size's import, there is a critical difference between looking at a light bulb through a slide, or the ink of a bookplate, and looking at the tissues and materials of the real surface. The identifying "face" is there in the print, betrayed in some degree, but the "body" of the impelling and irreplaceable object is missing. Nevertheless, sensing what a reproduction may withhold in what it provides—seeing it as a "meta-work" of interest *and* a flawed substitute—further trains the imagination and the senses.

In addition to all that goes into good teaching in art, there is a general approach or attitude that is particularly favorable, and I would like to end with a rough characterization of it. It has to do with an active and delving (though of course not exclusive) interest in visual perception.

The activities of the mind are always related to the world received by the senses.[4] Therefore, one of art's firmest connections with the rest of the curriculum is its purposeful manifestations and study of appearance. (I mean, of course, any appearance, not only art—and any art, not only that which sets out to copy or represent appearances.) Whatever else art classes may be about, they benefit from a teacher's willingness at every opportunity to become involved with the data, habits, and characteristics of perception.

The involvement—or rather, consciousness of how fully one is already involved—does not come easily. Perception is taken for granted, and our routines help it to forget itself in being functional. We are willing to grant that there are physiological differences in vision or theoretical features due to unusual conditions and cultural or social causes, but we are reluctant to look further into the fundamental, equally circumstantial quality of our own "everyday" visual conditions. That is, although we rarely note it (and then as triviality), the relativity of vision is accepted in principle, but only up to a point. Beyond it, the profusion is "read" largely in constant, already received, and unexamined ways. In denying informal investigation of this as a gainful study in art, or even the connection between vision and art as marginal at best, some would unknowingly undercut the central experience of making and apprehending art and what it provides as preparation for other fields of study.

There will be moments when these opinions are persuasive, but they and other, perhaps material problems are effectively balanced in the moments of simply beginning. One gains confidence from the fact that visual relationships, oddities, artlike phenomena, unifying cues, and other possibilities for study and comment are literally always and everywhere present. One must acknowledge for oneself that what is seen or not seen can be important; that visual pleasure and acuteness can be increased; that avidly and studiously looking is a profound adjunct to thinking, or can be another form of it; that what one knows, feels, and does is based in some measure on what one sees and has seen, the importance given to it, and the interpretations one made of it.

Vision is conditional, paradoxical, and eclectic. Appearances expose and reveal, but they also conceal and are complicated. The role these effects play in making and seeing art has been a subject for many commentators, from da Vinci to E. H. Gombrich, Anton Ehrenzweig, Maurice Merleau-Ponty, and many others of our time. Eventual familiarity with such studies is important; more essential, however, is the teacher's own first, faltering but instructive beginnings, in which these effects are engaged ad hoc, with no specific reference or goal.

The beginning may be or become narrowly technical or general and philosophic. Color, where Cézanne said the brain meets the universe, will perhaps be a center of engagement or subconsciously near by. Pasting a square inch of each of ten colors against a larger but contrasting field of the same colors easily shows what is *always* taking place: their relations alone create more than the ten colors of the paper, paint, or whatever is used. Regardless of different medium, size, subject matter, or historical period, art can bridge over such differences in the way it *looks;* therefore, one way of providing students with a sense of the "common bases" mentioned at the end of chapter 2 is an examination of the similar form and appearance of otherwise very different art. Computers can now deal more quickly with data than can humans, but we are unparalleled in our ability to recognize, imagine, and manipulate patterns,[5] another possible entry point to perception. By "doctoring" slides, slyly cropping one side of some famous paintings, for example, I once set off a chain-reaction that continued in unpredictable but productive forms for a year. However, perpeption opens up to ever more speculative issues. When we see, we go out as well as take in, we collect *and* project—nature is inside us, said Cézanne; yet, it is obviously a major channel of learning. "Vision alone makes us learn that beings that are different, 'exterior,' foreign to one another, are yet absolutely *together,* are 'simultaneity,'" wrote Merleau-Ponty.[6] Perception both demonstrates and undermines the "tremendous power of factional belief over the freedom of the mind."[7]

What distinguishes classes in which the beginning is made, helping to insure their connection with many other interests, and these with art, is the multiplex nature of that engagement—the decriptions, explanations, comparisons, analyses, guesses, random observations, verbal inventions, admissions, hands-on trials and experiments, pondering, and vital staring that takes place when how and what we see (and the causes and effects in art and life) are subjects in an art room environment.

I belong to the first generation of artists forced to witness the unquestionable, dawning possibility in fact of Nietzsche's century-old prediction, "The artist will soon come to be regarded as a splendid relic."[8] I suppose he left us and himself some breathing room: being regarded as a relic is yet different from being one. Besides, we are harmed by too greatly disliking our own time, and I have tried to convert even my negative feeling for that dawning and its causes to positive sources of work. Although I take some satisfaction in what I have actually accomplished (downcast as I have also been at not having realized more), I greatly value the sense of awareness and capability from which it came. Like the ratio of many scattered shreds to fewer Presentable Works, the artist's capacity exceeds the work. The work, no matter how good or numerous, is also an indication of how much dies with us. It is the tip of the proverbial iceberg. A proper view of creativity will always include technique as but part of a much larger, life-size "excess." (Teachers, too, inhabit an "excess" that students are rarely encouraged or enabled to "use up"; however, the students and *their* work are in part its proof.)

Even so, I agree that the tale instead of the teller, the work, not the artist, must be looked to. Misfortune for an artist is when sense of self and theory outstrip performance. My separable work and self are brought together only by me and in the flow and backflow of creation. For me, the best work always requires fluent relation with that "excess," no part of which is, once and for all, superfluous. But the work is the objective. Only its realizations justify. Every other benefit may be gotten some other way.

Personal accounts of creating sooner or later bump, or are thought to bump, against pride. Whether or not I am guilty of it, I do not regard the tendency and its loftier symptoms as "romantic," the charge with which the current "un-arting" protects itself—which I find ironic because of the romanticism of *that* quest. I regard the tendency as another often mistaken aspect of our topic. It is mistaken, first, due to a confusion of "loftiness" with yearning for an unattainable happiness or integration; then, second, to seeing even measured happiness as naive blindness. Injustice, the grimness of daily prospects, and the gloomy estimates of our globe's health are surely plain. But whatever it may finally send out, I cannot see the *act* of creation as mournful. Making enacts a frame of mind so prone to the remedial and possible that it never fails to inch away from the sorrowful as well as the joyful in order to consider its effects, uses, and sources. Whether this is seen as inhuman detachment, a prideful rebuke of misery's company, or a harmless home-movie of denial, it is actually but another operation in that mindframe's refusal of all that might keep it from the Whole, whether squeamishness before the dirty facts or fear of heights.

Although it has no recipes, creation seems born of a compulsion that can support as well as be at odds with "the present." If one of its demands is a base in the present, we should consider how it also helps to qualify that present, to define what is in the present, and how it occupies the present. If there is no past or future in art, as Picasso said, or if, as William Faulkner wrote, "the past isn't dead, it's not even past," it must mean that, whatever else creation consists of, it is possessed by the idea Delacroix noted in his journal, that "what has been said has still not been said enough."⁹ To say it well and again requires a continuing belief in the transcendence of re-mulling and chewing existence in order to make the other existence that is art. It requires toughness of a particular kind: burning without being consumed, remaining vulnerable to heartbreak, staying open to any knowledge while closing it unremittingly in one's medium, and beholding bottomless time's losses while steadfastly anticipating how one will continue and succeed against all odds at making something that re-creates, validates, and celebrates the way we are.

NOTES

1. Edward C. Banfield, *The Democratic Muse: Visual Arts and the Public Interest* (New York: Basic Books, 1984), 125.

2. *The Notebooks of Samuel Butler* (New York: AMC Press, 1968), 293.

3. Henry Adams, *The Education of Henry Adams* (New York: Modern Library, 1931), 20.

4. Hannah Arendt, *The Life of the Mind: Willing* (New York: Harcourt Brace Jovanovich, 1978), 143.

5. James Fallows, "Wake Up America," *New York Review*, 1 March 1990, 15.

6. Maurice Merleau-Ponty, "Eye and Mind," *The Primacy of Perception and Other Essays*, ed. James M. Edie (Evanston: Northwestern University Press, 1964), 187.

7. Richard Mitchell, *The Leaning Tower of Babel and Other Affronts from the Underground Grammarian* (Boston: Little, Brown and Company, 1984), 275.

8. In *Human, All-Too-Human*, quoted in Bernard Yack, *The Longing for Total Revolution* (Princeton: Princeton University Press, 1986), 341.

9. Walter Pach, trans., *The Journal of Eugene Delacroix* (New York: Viking Press, 1972), 88–89.

PART 2

Education's Four Competing Traditions of Art Making

7

Bringing Art Making into the School

For as long as there have been artists, there have been others fascinated by them. Artists, at many times, have been vested with quasi-magical powers. Observers keep being intrigued by how artists get their ideas, how they follow their own paths, how they create their own audiences, and how they relate to the particular issues of their times. That fascination, particularly in the nineteenth century, led to a notion that the person who is an artist could be a model for the ideal learner. Some interpreted romantic writers, such as Rousseau and Wordsworth, as saying that artists could be the inspiration for ideas for teaching. In our century, others took one more step in that direction. They concluded that the person who is an artist, by that very fact, is ideally suited and ready to teach art, particularly to the young. I do not subscribe to this view. In the pages to come I propose an alternative interpretation of the studio artist's contribution to education, one that I see as both realistic and historically grounded.

My view is that we have a more than a hundred year old American heritage of educators being fascinated with particular attributes of artists' work. Generation after generation, they extract one small piece of the artist's process, they rename that piece and reset it, like a gem, into an entirely other context, the school. For a while that piece becomes the basis of art teaching. For example, since artists work in studios, in the 1960s open classroom educators thought that the new education should simulate studios. In the early twentieth century, educators who were proponents of the Sloyd method of woodworking, stressed students being taught to form their own objects from start to finish because artists themselves make objects that way. In the early years of the profession, "the gem" of the artist's process that was reset, was the forming of the perfect line. Since artists precisely controlled the lines they drew, children had to be taught to draw steady, even lines.

In our time, the Getty Center for Education in the Arts continues the educational fascination with the artist. In its advocacy for art education, it has directed attention to the artist's process, along with that of other art professionals. The center encourages teachers today to develop a methodology for teaching that coordinates aspects of the artist's studio process along with art history, art criticism, and aesthetics. It is the center's interest in art making that led to the writing of this volume. Maurice Brown and I share the responsibility of helping readers identify attributes of art making. In particular I explore art making in light of its past and potential contributions to establishing the purposes and operations of art teaching.

An Orientation to the Profession of Art Teaching

One premise of my essay is that the role of the teacher, the one responsible for bringing art making into young people's education, needs to be differentiated from the role of the artist, the one whose mind is full of ideas centering primarily on personal work. That does not mean that one individual may not do both. Many do, but those who are the best teachers differentiate their roles and their purposes in doing these two different types of work.

For almost two decades in the art college where I teach, I have talked with artists who are drawn to art teaching. Some who had little or no encouragement as children long to provide for others what they themselves missed. Because others had early stimulation that led them to think of themselves as artists very young, they tell me they want to give children the advantages and benefits they themselves received. Many of these aspirants express their ideal teaching as a sort of importation of their own studio lives to the school. They seem to say, "Install me into the school and surely art will bloom there. What could be better than to plant the studio, like a garden, right there in the school!" But, teaching is not like that. The art making of one's private studio cannot be lifted, whole-cloth, unchanged and placed in the school. The freedom to continually go in and out, to check in on one's work, finding it different at each turn, as Maurice Brown has described, is something quite different than the work of schools.

The studio transplant idea is not unique to inexperienced students. It inspired such recent widespread programs as "artists-in-residence" or "artists-in-the-schools" but by now it seems naive. Artists-in-residence who find themselves in school situations that invite them to set up their own work spaces there, soon recognize that being an artist in the school building is not enough. The school itself has powerful and attractive agendas that draw adults into relationships with children. For me and many who were artists-in-residence, our simply being in schools became our first lesson in how to listen to and think about children.

Professional transformation happens in many small steps. Those artists who decide they wish to become teachers learn to say goodbye to that "room of one's own" and the solitary work they do there, at least for the time they are in schools. For that part of each day, they forfeit control of their own time. No longer are they free to pace themselves, to come and go, to work and stop working. No longer are they engaged in the sustained work that demands, first and foremost, that they attend to what is on their own minds. No longer may they thrive in that complexity that evolves when they are alone and making intricate connections betwen their own thoughts. Unlike those artists described in Maurice Brown's essay, who are concerned with matters far from the reach of words, those who become teachers are expected to explain their ideas.

Maurice Brown and I agree that everyone's understanding of art is improved by real efforts to produce art. Studio involvement seems certain to enhance whatever art teaching one may do. But only those who have significant studio experience and who accept that the school is something quite new to them can begin to recognize the opportunity teaching may be for them. Once they are given space and time within the school, they will learn that the art making they will teach is hardly their own adult studio process; it is an enterprise in service of learners.

Schools as institutions could not be further from that studio process. In schools, many small people and fewer larger ones are all collected together. Schools are distracting social places. Schools do their job by organizing people so they can attend to and can communicate with one another in time chunks diametrically opposite from studio time. Schools chop time into bits. Whether or not there are different specialty teachers, time in the school day is subdivided because different content areas are allowed to have just so many minutes. So even if the studio model otherwise suited children's needs, it could hardly fit into the discontinuous, chopped up bits of school time. No matter how excellent the school, no matter how well-intentioned the teachers, the schools' priorities cannot be those of artists working in their own spaces.

What Are the Steps in Preparing to Teach?

First of all, ideally, those who would teach need time to observe children's inborn art making appetite. "Appetite" is the name I give to this eagerness, even hunger, built into the human system. It exists prior to any instruction. It is what draws children to a medium, to form something with their minds and hands. When Maurice Brown tells us that as a child he drew before he walked, he is documenting this appetite.

Those who want to teach can benefit from watching and listening to children as they discover language, make up games, and find ways of making relationships with others. These early forms of behavior all survive in later stages of artistic activity.

To prepare for teaching, people also need time to watch children in groups, because groups tend to be how children are organized in schools. They need to listen to the best kind of teacher talk, that is talk, that though presented to a group, stimulates each mind in its own quite private and richly personal way. They need to imagine forms of art talk and art making that can be social, in which children can benefit from the presence of others.

Each school is a community, so it is important to consider how art making fits in. In Maurice Brown's elementary schooling, the school copier was the disseminator of art. Some schools make much of contest winners and spread the news to local papers. Some schools equate art with the ornamentation of corridors, most conspicuously around holidays. Each school has some ideas of what art making is good for. An orientation to what is valued within a school helps new teachers decide what else might be valued.

The Profession's Continual Reinterpretation of Art Making

Each new teacher enters an everchanging profession. As I see it, over and over again, teachers of art keep having to invent ways that art making can fit into the larger agenda of schools. In the United States, wherever art making has been there in the school day, the art for which the school committee paid had to be conceived to provide specific benefits upon which the city or town had already agreed. Art making either fit in or gets dropped out. Studio processes are viable in schools only as long as they support and mesh with the current consensus of what schools should accomplish. In that respect, art must do what other subjects have done and still do. It must help children grow in directions the community values.

Even though the problem—figuring out and describing how studio work may fit in—is the same for each new wave of teachers, each generation's programs are always different. This should not surprise us. Teachers' ideas keep changing because school priorities themselves keep changing, and indeed so too does the art world. The many changes and adaptations of studio processes fill a large part of this essay.

Each generation answers anew the question, How can the art making process begin and grow in young lives? What it is that teachers do depends on how they answer this question. In our century, educators answered it by looking to the field of psychology. From what they read and heard, the expression of feelings, like breathing, was necessary. They valued art because it enabled children to be themselves and to unfold their feelings. The younger the children, the less encumbered their art was believed to be by the ideas of their elders. Adults believed art's role in education could be to provide an emotionally safe haven. Schools defended art, whether it was art with finger paints or crayons or clay, for its protection of expression.

Twentieth-century art educators have relied upon psychologists' now familiar and productive ways to inquire about artistic development. We looked at children's ages and suggested predictable stages of graphic development. We identified norms. Certain regularities, for example, the circle, the tadpole figure, the continuous contour, came to be accepted as spontaneous, natural occurrences in artistic development. Art educators enthusiastically adopted the view that art making was inherent in all children's growth. Drawing, painting, and sculpting came to be viewed as universal, even ordinary behaviors, with changes manifest at each new stage. Skill was presumed to unfold naturally, largely independent of social, artistic, or economic circumstances.

Art educators adopted psychologists' developmental model as a scaffold onto which to attach different age-related curricula. The model asserts that, as children grow, their emotional and cognitive capacities change. Teachers, trained according to these ideas, learned to respect these differences and to design lessons to make the most of them. Teachers taught with the aim of having children draw, sculpt, and paint in ways that helped children to flower at a particular stage of development.

Now, as we reach the end of the century, expression no longer seems so prized. The education pendulum has swung in the opposite direction. The innovations of this century now are seen as neglect, leaving children simply to develop according to their appropriate stage, with little intervention. School committees, if they devote their scarce dollars to an art program, want to see children advancing. Their progress should be measureable. Not surprisingly, this shift is compelling those who work with children to adjust their content, to shape an art curriculum that fits the new pressures. This climate is leading teachers to design more directed ways of thinking about artistic growth. Not so long ago what was considered adult intrusion, even contamination, now is prized education. Teachers are creating didactic, formal instruction about the art of adults, the art housed in museums, the art around which art history tends to be written. They combine art viewing with art making, some even are recommending that taboo of fifty years ago, copying art works. Other teachers make art making a corollary of writing.

Drawing, sculpting, and painting become partners to narrative writing. Visual observation of all the detail of the immediate world at one's doorstep now is welcome in schools. Explicit references to the children's ethnic, cultural, economic experiences are all part of this new realism.

Choices

Now on the verge of a new century, we need to see how much teachers determine what children do. Teachers, whatever they do, are powerful agents. They support certain kinds of activities and discourage others. Fifty years ago, when teachers allowed children to use only fat brushes thick with tempera paint, they controlled the images children could make. Perhaps those teachers, who thought they were so freeing, in fact were requiring certain types of children's art to be models for other children. In retrospect, expressivity itself looks as if it were a style with its own conventions.

So, how do we choose what we teach? Once people decide to teach, they face many choices. Each class is a new choice. In the coming chapters I show an array of possibilities, mostly, but not exclusively, related to drawing and painting (my own interests). These ideas have already been tried and tested by a century of art educators. That the choices make a difference will become apparent. Even the choices of particular methods teachers use in classrooms interpret the art making powers of the young. They reveal whether we expect a lot or a little.

At times people have viewed art teaching as if there were negligible consequences to what we do. That is hardly the case. In our time, when cultural diversity and economic inequity are among the most distinctive features of the overall American school population, when more languages are spoken by schoolchildren than even at the turn of the century, when children's physical safety even within schools is hardly ensured, the position of neutrality or benign neglect is no longer acceptable. What we do needs to make a difference. Children grow in a society that transmits values to them. As instruments of that society, teachers convey to children whatever they believe children are capable of at a given time. Those who would teach need to figure out for themselves what they feel is most empowering to children and to deliver that in their classrooms.

Never in any era was teaching the sole invention of a single expert, no matter how influential a certain leader may have been. The power of the ideas of art education's patriarchs, Walter Smith in the 1870s, or Arthur Wesley Dow at the turn of the century, or Viktor Lowenfeld at mid-century,[1] derived from the fact that other people, primarily teachers, responded to and saw opportunities in their ideas. These writers captured certain worries and aspirations to which teachers could relate.

It was teachers' use of their ideas that made these writers authorities. To a much greater extent than we might imagine, whether the ideas were ever acted upon depended on the actions of a multitude of individual teachers. The teacher decides what is important. And the teacher after all is the one who is with the children. Our past overreliance on the idea of authorities has masked how decisive teachers' actions are. To a far greater degree than history would suggest, the individual teacher's scope of influence—what happens in the classroom—is the result of the teacher's choice.

To be conscious choosers of their own direction, teachers need to see from what they are choosing. That has not been easy. My aim in this volume is to aid with this process. For more than a century, people have engaged children with art making, saying that, like Mom and apple pie, art was good for you. But in the midst of the enthusiasms, we hadn't noticed how frequently the actual justifications and methods for teaching art kept changing. One decade argued that art making was good for one reason. Then a decade later, people discounted that and upheld a new and better idea. Those who would teach art need to be alert to the inconsistencies in the different arguments. Contradictions exist between teaching for the spirit and teaching for the marketplace. Shaping a work force is quite another thing than cultivating a child's individual judgment. These various rationales have competed with one another for over a hundred years.

American art teaching unfortunately has tended to compete with itself. Ideas compete with one another or become mixed together. It has been hard to see what is going on. Hopefully, my contribution here will help teachers sort out differences so that they may identify their own best reasons for teaching art.

Why the Choice Matters

While the teacher is in the midst of thrashing through all these different ideas, there sit the children, patiently waiting for art. The choice the teacher makes matters. Whatever the teacher does with the children actually will shape the children's concept of art for life.

Here is a paradox that we would do well to keep in mind. The art making the young experience in schools can only be a tiny fragment of all that art making is. The piece children see is that which schools deem appropriate and manageable within a certain class size and within the school's small units of time. The children's concept of art comes from school art, the ways art is represented in the curriculum. For most children, those who don't have parents who are artists, who aren't taken on trips to art museums or offered Saturday morning art classes, the school's art class presents them with the art they will store in their memories. Whether art seems to them to be something trivial or central, whether art is bland or emotionally charged, whether art seems to belong to them or to some other class of people, all will be decided in these tiny bits of art in the school week. Our choices have lasting effects, for as children grow older, whatever they remember doing as art in school is what they will categorize as art.

NOTE

1. Walter Smith, *Art Education, Scholastic and Industrial* (Boston: James R. Osgood, 1872); Arthur Wesley Dow, *Composition: A Series of Exercises Selected from a New System of Art Education* (New York: Baker and Taylor, 1899); Viktor Lowenfeld, *Creative and Mental Growth* (New York: Macmillan, 1947).

8

Looking at Our Personal Histories and Educational Legacies

We each carry within us our own history in art. We carry within us memories of places where we went to school, of what some of the rooms looked like, and even of some pictures that hung on the walls. We may recall some teachers and even what they said. Our personal histories contain the perhaps too brief flowering of our very early art making and how people then supported us. We carry vestiges of our parents' and grandparents' educations too. We know their history through things they showed us and told us. We can extrapolate from these to earlier times even before our own grandparents were born. This history can be a storehouse of resources for us as teachers.

In the spring of 1924, when my father was a college student in upper Manhattan, he enrolled in a geology course in which the professor required the students to keep field notebooks. In his notebook my father drew complex patterns of parallel curves and tiny nets of x's. These indicated the relative depth and position of mica, quartz, and garnet in the rock beds at Fort George Hill only two hundred yards from a New York City subway station. Many years ago, when I was still a child, my father showed this book to me. He told me how he enjoyed picturing the layers in the ground under his feet. From his talking about inking in those lines and coloring those layers of rock, I first learned how much my father had liked to draw.

Meanwhile, also in the 1920s, my mother, who as yet was unacquainted with my father, was a student at the downtown end of Manhattan island. She attended Cooper Union, a school that provided a tuition-free professional art education. There she learned to use charcoal to render the shadows on figures that were plaster casts. Years later, she told me of the deadliness of doing these assignments. She would have preferred to be drawing from her mind, or at least from life. As a young person, I had no idea to what she was responding. Today, I know she was reacting to the still rumbling controversies aroused by the International Exhibition of Modern Art that everyone

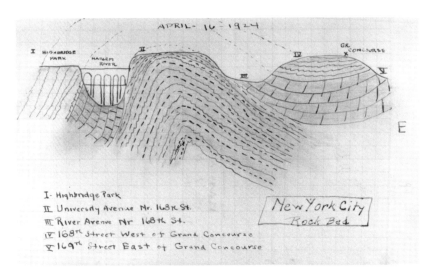

Figure 13. New York City Rock Bed, Harold Korzenik

called "The Armory Show," held in New York City in 1913. "Without doubt this most important single exhibition ever held in America . . . acted on the complacency of American art like a powerful shock. After the Armory show American art was never the same again."[1] By the twenties, the academicians who taught my mother were in a head-on collision with "contemporary artists." My mother's schooling was wedged between the conservatism of plaster cast assignments and "modernism" that was in the process of being born.

Both of my parents were prepared for their college educations by the New York City public schools. Their two families had settled in New York in the crushing crowds of late nineteenth-century immigration. The schools not only taught them lessons but served as their sanctuaries from the streets. Many children, including my father and mother, felt that school protected them from the daily physical attacks. My parents' elementary and secondary school years extended between the teens and the early twenties when art making was valued in schools as part of Americanization, a national preoccupation. Giant festivals and exhibitions, such as the "America's Making" of 1921 sponsored by the New York City public schools, presented performances and displays of the arts and traditions of immigrants' native countries along with the arts and skills of which they had become masters here.[2] Huge audiences attended, trying to make sense of the foreign-born strangers in American society. These well-funded enterprises were intended to persuade the children and their parents—my parents and my grandparents—that they were indeed welcome here. The public school became America's hope for a better future. In my parents' cases, that meant that they and their families might make a fresh albeit impoverished new start here, free from the persecution they had fled in their respective parts of Poland and Lithuania. These two young people, who were to become my parents, remained proud of their public high school and elementary school educations throughout their lives. When we were old enough to appreciate it, they talked to my sister and me about their schools, the teachers, the prizes they won, the interests they developed and the friends they made there.

This story of my parents' education is also an account of my own. My father's geology book and my mother's Cooper Union portfolio are now mine. They are bits of our family I carry into my adult life. These pieces of history help me assemble my own private history and that of my profession, art education. Their drawings, which I saw in my early years, turn out to have been the ideal stimuli and encouragement for the child I was.

For as long as I can remember, I have been absorbed by looking at and making pictures. Even before I went to school, I was hungry for ideas about art. Because drawing and painting already were important to me, I remembered my parents' art stories. When I was a child, I attended schools in that same school system, but my experience was different from theirs. Some teachers seemed less devoted and more distracted than the teachers my parents talked about. Postwar New York families relied on and trusted their children's teachers less. Schools were becoming unsettled places. Yet, after I graduated from college and came back to New York, I surprised myself by returning to that same system that had been so significant for our family, becoming an art teacher.

That was more than a quarter of a century ago. Those two objects, my father's geology book and my mother's Cooper Union portfolio, and more student art work that I have acquired over the years since I have become a college professor, now nourish my professional interest in the varieties of art educational experience. I am interested in schools and why they teach art. I want to know what schools ask students to draw, what examples they present to students as models from which to learn, and to what degree teachers control how students execute particular assignments. I am fascinated by the differences in what teachers have believed an art education can be for.

I now collect not only students' sketchbooks and portfolios from different eras, but also art stories. Hearing of my interest, people tend to pour forth their own still-vivid childhood art memories. The tales abound of a certain kind of teacher or uncle or neighbor who offered the person, then a child, a significant glimpse of art making. Sometimes, too, people report painful memories. All these stories, often passed over as trivial, are rich ore to mine. These memories offer us access to information that is central to art education. They tell us how people feel about how and what they were taught. They tell us what left an impression on people. They help us see the forgotten, neglected, or rejected directions art education might now be reconsidering. The varieties of artistic education are stunning, particularly because at any one point when we are absorbed in our contemporary way of doing things, we become deaf and blind to alternatives. Listening to and reading people's personal stories can be the beginnings of collecting alternatives.

Understanding art from the personal appeals to me. It is inherently democratic. I have my history. You have yours. In this spirit, Levi and Smith, in the introductory volume to this series, cite Jaques Barzun: "Art is inescapably pluralistic. It thrives on diversity."[3] Each of our histories determines our own bias. I have my bias as you have yours. The bias we each have, if conscious and examined, can be our strength. The task of this essay is to review the plurality of teachers' different reasons for using art making so that each of us may identify our own selves in relation to them, so we may teach using our own ideas and those of others akin to us.

It is a truism that teachers tend to teach as they were taught. If that is so, then our knowing our personal histories becomes particularly critical. We need to ask: What were our parents' attitudes toward art? What about art drew them or repelled them? What art was there in the house? If there were pictures, for example, what did people say about them? When and where did we attend school? How were we treated as children? Who was the authority figure? Who decided what we learned? Why did they decide that? Which, of the many possible views of art then current, did our teachers present to us? As we review our own histories, we see how the schools' representations of art to children become highly sensitive gauges of society's changing demands. In the process, we can learn about the political and social climate of our childhoods.

But teachers want to do more than just repeat how they were taught. Each of us carries our dreams and our ideas about how we want to make a difference. This essay provides a method for widening those options in personal and professional ways. To engage the reader with a democratic, pluralistic view of education, I describe many educators from art education's past. I selected them to offer us a way to recognize our pasts and the options we missed. These become a collection of examples to which we can relate.

This essay offers the reader an encounter with the array of studio-based teaching practices in our field. Though autobiographical work is important, it is not the central task of this essay. Over the years in my various roles—as a New York City art teacher, director of various Boston school projects, and some twenty years as a college professor preparing artists to be art teachers—I've had a sense of what supports the growth and longevity of the art teacher. Teachers who feel them-selves the authors of what they do, who can explain what they do, who believe in what they do, who don't feel isolated in what they do, seem to get pleasure out of their work and seem the most effective. It is for this reason that I place such importance on the matter of finding one's own rationale, one's biases, one's own place in the field.

Our Educational Legacies

Every culture sets aside resources for the education of its young. Schools have to decide what, if anything, they will do with the phe-nomenon of the child's appetite to make objects and images. Schools' interpretations of children's art making have been astonishingly dif-ferent. My purpose here is to identify the sometimes rival reasons for including art making in schooling, not to select any best way, but to preserve the variety itself. Among other things, this will help us under-stand something of our national disposition toward art.

Art making within a school never simply lifts and reproduces whole-cloth the studio processes of artists, whatever form they take at any given time. Art making within the precincts of a school always has to meet particular expectations. Schools have certain missions and objectives. Art making in schools always in one way or another is related to these. Those who pay for and plan for schools generate, or more often select, from a popular "menu," the reasons why art making may happen within them. Art making in schools is always there for one or another of these reasons. The diversity of those reasons and the programs spawned from them will be our concern from here on.

Hand-me-downs

Educational ideas, whether they are radical or conservative, intended to shock or intended to appease, are hand-me-downs. Whether we are conscious of it or not, whether we know a particular source or not, instruction tends to engage students with material that is the legacy of centuries. If our grandparents were children in this country, they were taught according to certain then-current ideas in American education. When our parents were children, their teachers probably repeated lessons they and our grandparents heard as children. And our parents and their peers, with some adjusting for new needs, pass along their ideas to us. As with many societal institutions, an undercurrent of tradition carries us forward.

What are the hand-me-downs? When as children we "play school," we intuitively rehearse some of them. But the facts of schoolroom life are elusive. Like dancing, teaching vanishes once it is over. Teaching involves people acting in time. Education history really can't capture it; reports after the fact are something else. To really know what happens we need to witness the lesson itself, the things that happen in time. As Richard Wollheim stated in his essay "The Art Lesson," in *Of Art and the Mind* (1973), a close examination of teaching practice "can allow us a special insight into the nature of that which it is a lesson in."[4]

Since in most cases we are not there in the classroom, the next best thing for understanding art teaching is paying attention to the many shreds of evidence that survive from the actual time and locale. Classroom textbooks, drawing manuals, teaching charts, exercise sheets, drawing slates, rewards of merit, teacher's guides, even local newspapers and commentaries, all may be sources for reconstructing a certain time in school.

The Three-Part Legacy

In my search for ephemera of art education, the bits of paper evidence of what people said and did, I came upon a thin yellow pamphlet dated 1877. It was titled *Some Reasons Why Drawing Should be Taught in Our Common Schools.* All I knew about it was printed on its cover: that it was a published lecture and the author-lecturer was Langdon S. Thompson. He was identified at length as superintendent of drawing in the public schools of Sandusky, Ohio, and a faculty member at Purdue University. The black letters on the golden-yellow cover explained that this was a speech for the National Education Association's membership at its 1877 annual meeting.

Since I have been looking at nineteenth-century papers on art teaching for a long time, I had good reason to pay attention to this pamphlet. I knew the year was critical in the history of American art education. The Philadelphia Exposition that marked the nation's centennial had just closed in the previous November. Thousands of Americans who had never before viewed art had traipsed from gallery to gallery through the exposition looking at the pride of nations from all over the world. They had become excited that we had hosted this extravaganza and that we had much to display in machinery as well as the arts. But the overriding sense was that we, as a country, had to struggle mightily to catch up aesthetically with other nations.

So by 1877 when Thompson lectured, I knew his audience would have been hungry for art information. In the decades following the exposition, tons of art publications sold: books on good taste, painting and drawing manuals, and magazines teaching children how to get their start in art. At the same time, passionate, forceful, and well-financed arguments were being made for the art education of children and adolescents. And one conspicuous need was for many art teachers. One supplier, that fledgling school, Massachusetts Normal Art School, founded in 1873, already had three years' worth of portfolios on display at the centennial. The art and the teaching method it represented attracted worldwide attention. The states that sought aesthetic improvement hired the women and men trained there.

So by 1877 the audience would have been primed to hear whatever Thompson had to say. His title conveyed exactly the content of his speech. He outlined three reasons why drawing should be taught in schools. One he called disciplinarian. Its purpose, he said, was the development of intelligence, exercising perception, judgment and imagination. The second he termed utilitarian. This argument judges drawing's worth as a school subject in terms of its practical utility in everyday life, particularly how it will help the child grow into an adult who can use art to earn a living. The third rationale, the aesthetic, is concerned with the development of taste, love of the beautiful, that which will "warm into activity the higher soul capacities and thereby assist in elevating man to the highest degree of culture known or imagined in this life."[5]

In the random find of this yellow pamphlet, I realized I had something particularly useful for understanding art in education. It struck me that Thompson's three rationales blazed trails that, by our time, had become roads. Three maps now could be drawn from Thompson's time to ours, tracing the three directions of teaching. We can look at any moment of teaching to ask, Which of these routes did this teacher take? Let's remember, Thompson was no major force. He didn't pave these three roads. They simply grew from paths to roads through repeated use.

Earlier I said that art making needed to fit into the schools' already established structures. Thompson recognized this. So his "reasons" conform to currently accepted educational objectives. A close look at how Thompson crafted each of his rationales is proof of the extent to which schools justified art making by making it mesh with an already accepted educational objective.

Let's take a closer look at how Thompson actually force-fitted art making into each of the schools' objectives. When Thompson characterizes the "disciplinarian purpose," he refers to the schools' concern with the development of intelligence. Thompson separates intelligence into parts that match testable facets of the school curriculum: reading, spelling, penmanship, geography, and arithmetic. He attempts to persuade his listeners that drawing may be an aid for learning them all.

Training in drawing assists in reading by helping the student recognize forms by sight. The more you draw, the more you notice subtle distinctions about lines and shapes of letters and whole words. Drawing also assists not only reading but spelling, since the development of spelling is helped by a trained memory of forms. As Thompson states, "Memory drawing educates and strengthens the power to recall forms."[6] Memory drawing, a trusted aspect of drawing instruction, was originally developed by a virtually forgotten French artist-teacher, LeCoq de Boisbaudran.[7] Drawing was understood to consist of many different routines, each of which might support the improvement of a particular school skill.

Reading and spelling were the prerequisites for that other skill, penmanship, the sign of the educated person of the nineteenth century. As early as 1847, John Gadsby Chapman promoted the alliance of drawing and writing when he stated that "Anyone who can learn to write can learn to draw."[8] Because educated people observed that drawing and writing both require quick eyes and a controlled hand, there was no controversy about urging young people to study drawing to improve their penmanship.

Geography, too, would be retained better, because when a student drew, he or she built skills used in making maps or reading maps. Drawing fixes in the mind complex relationships of space. Boundaries between states and nations, once drawn, would be remembered.

Another part of training the intelligence is the grasping of arithmetic concepts. Drawing, Thompson argued, also is ideally suited to arithmetic because it helps the student practice conceptualizing and symbolizing. "The power of abstraction is the chief mathematical faculty," he said, "and probably no school exercise has ever been invented, better calculated to lead the mind away from the concrete to the abstract, than inventive drawing, dictation drawing and designing."[9]

According to Thompson, the practice of drawing is useful not only for mastery of particular school subjects but because it prepares a "habit of mind" that can be applied to all objects of investigation. Drawing serves, as does language, as a mediator of thought and information. Thompson claims that the exercise of drawing demands making an abstraction, making something other than a replica of the directly sensed world. The person who makes a drawing uses his or her mind to abstract ideas that produce visible results, that is, the lines on a paper. Drawing trains the attention. It demands thinking about what you want to represent and then paying close and continued attention to the effect of the marks on the piece of paper and modifying them to get the effect you want. Drawing requires placement of marks, comparison of one mark to another and of different parts of the whole page in relation to one another. Thompson's rationale for teaching drawing is to promote intelligence.

Thompson's "utilitarian rationale" was shaped to conform to another mission of schools: preparing students for jobs. Thompson tells us that learning to draw will enhance a student's future employability: "It is estimated that nine-tenths of all the occupations into which labor is divided require a knowledge of drawing and that the remaining one-tenth receives the lowest wages. Everything that is well-made—from a toy house to a cathedral . . . is made from a drawing."[10]

In nineteenth-century America, excellence in any occupation was judged by the capacity to draw; that is, to think and communicate by drawing.[11] The waning of the apprenticeship model of learning, in Thompson's eyes, left society with a great loss. Education had to compensate for the learning that would have occurred naturally within an apprenticeship, and drawing was one way to do this. Thompson points out that for any occupation, drawing provides three different skills: drawing for yourself (accounting for the relationships of parts, calculating scale, and so forth), reading other people's drawings, and finally making drawings for others to be able to read and use. Instead of setting up separate shops or studios for each of the many possible occupations, teaching drawing could prepare everyone together. Thompson argued that it was cost-efficient simply to teach everyone at once the use of the pencil, the compass and the ruler, enabling them to apply their skills as they would in future years. Perhaps because most people around him already agreed, Thompson's simplest and most persuasive argument was for teaching drawing in preparation for the trades and occupations: "To sum up the utilitarian phase . . . we live in a universe of matter. We are surrounded by it on all sides. . . . All matter has extension, the result of which is form. . . . In the battle for material existence we are struggling to change the form or shape of the various kinds of matter around us. . . . The people of the world are engaged in the preparation, production, and distribution, of different forms of matter. . . . He who has the best knowledge of forms that surround him and the greatest power to change those forms at will, is the best able to cope."[12]

That "material existence," the "preparation, production, and distribution of different forms of matter" was becoming equally the concern of women and men. Impressed by the Centennial Exposition's displays of the work of women of London, from book illustration and book binding to ceramics, Doulton Ware and Lambeth Faience, many looked at women as workers. Women making artistic crafts and objects, so sought in the marketplace, could do wonders by joining the American labor force and contributing to the economy. Thompson explicitly emphasizes the advantages that the utilitarian rationale offered women. He prophecies, "When drawing and designing have been well taught in our schools for some time, we shall find women becoming engravers on wood and stone, designers of ornament for calico . . . for carpets, oilcloths, wall-papers, and decorators of pottery and table ware."[13] In fact, by 1877, some women already were so employed. Women were hired to do art labor, as it was called, that is, the production of objects of ceramics, glass, metals, and cloth. By the turn of the century, 90 percent of the students at Massachusetts Normal Art School were women.[14]

Though each worker, female and male, would receive better pay were she or he able to draw, the individual family economy hardly justified the investment in utilitarian drawing training. At issue was the national economy. Like many of his contemporaries, Thompson prized drawing instruction for its potential impact on our nation's industries. Drawing would improve our ability to compete internationally. The conflict was between nations. The battles were within industry. Drawing instruction became comparable to and as important as military training. Massachusetts Normal Art School students were even referred to as the "art army."

Most agreed that European countries already had a head start in supremacy for the markets of the world. The French and English were seen as leaders, along with the Germans, Austrians, Belgians, and Russians. They had foreseen international economic contests and protected their advantage by establishing drawing schools and "by arming every child with a lead pencil, ruler and compass, and teaching him how to use them."[15] Thompson reported that an American journalist for the *New York Independent*, like many of his compatriots, regretted that "We are now paying a good many millions of dollars yearly to France for *mere style* in cotton goods. . . . It is the elegance, the superior taste, the artistic designs of the French calicoes . . . which our own calicoes do not possess. . . . It should be the aim of our manufacturers to compete with them."[16]

Thompson's language becomes stilted when he shifts to defending art making on aesthetic grounds. He equates *aesthetic* advancement with the progress of civilization. The aesthetic purpose of the study of drawing, he claimed, was to permit a person to "converse with a picture and find an agreeable companion in a statue." The aesthetic neither matched conventional school subjects, arithmetic, geography, and so on, nor directly promised an expanded economy. The aesthetic rationale did promise to cultivate students' taste to make them into consumers: "It [the aesthetic training] gives him [the student] a kind of property in everything he sees . . . discovers in it a multitude of charms that conceal themselves from the generality of mankind."[17] Art, according to many periodicals of the time, met a need in the growing affluent class. The acquisition of art was a way of displaying, if not flaunting, new wealth.

But the public schools were not bastions of the affluent. The aesthetic rationale presented more of a problem when considering those who weren't well-off. The argument blurs here. Thompson, still arguing for drawing, describes the student's relationship to objects. Looking at art gave one a kind of property. It was the next best thing to owning the objects. The suggestion here is that, through the exercise of the aesthetic in drawing, a person gains something that raises him or her above the rest of humankind. Whereas in the utilitarian argument, the value of drawing served 90 percent of the people, and only the lowest paid 10 percent weren't served, in the case of the aesthetic, the proportions seem to be reversed. Thompson implies that learning to draw raises one class of people above another portion of the population, who are forever doomed to an inferior state. Though the love of beauty is claimed to be a universal desire and though democracy and the civilized state are expected to make such beauty available to all, few of the many cultivate this sensibility.

As I see it, as the field of art education took form the three rationales that Thompson charted became fixed. In time these three conceptions and goals of art teaching became unwitting rivals. In each subsequent era, teachers, art magazines, professors, and textbook authors have had to choose. They sometimes shifted from one rationale to another. Each view would gain authority for a time, only to be ridiculed and replaced by another.

The Two-Part Legacy

There is another, older legacy that we carry on in teaching. Unlike the legacy we have just reviewed, which enhanced and advanced art education, this one has tended to undermine it.

A long time ago education was split in two. One part included domains that purportedly trained the mind. The other, deemed inferior, involved training the mind along with the hands. The latter was relegated to the lower classes. Though we are virtually unconscious of it, this hand-me-down that we carry within us ranks and determines the prestige and priority of certain school subjects. Art as a school subject has been contaminated by this disdain for work with the hands. The prejudice against art derives from an association of handwork, working with materials, with the lower, less-educated classes.

This prejudice is damaging. Our society today is reaping the ignorance and incompetence in handling materials that were created by it. Children and adults who are good with their hands are maligned and presumed to be intellectually less able. In most schools, children, praised for being "good with their hands," know that they are receiving rather backhanded complements. This is hardly new. Anyone whose work required skills with the hands and brain, anyone who fabricated, repaired, or conserved objects, anyone who created objects or taught others to create them, through the centuries, was subject to this view, as Rudolf Arnheim documented in *Visual Thinking* (1969). Maurice Brown shows how current this prejudice still is when he describes how intense critical intellectuality today, sometimes playfully, sometimes combatively, seeks superiority and control over the artist.

Those educators seated listening to Langdon Thompson at the National Education Association convention back in 1877 didn't have to be told about this hierarchy. They knew it. The learning that involved no stuff, no physical thing, they knew as the liberal arts. The liberal arts included studies far removed from utility. The liberal arts studies included the contemplative efforts of the mind: language, literature, music, philosophy, science, and mathematics. The manual arts made one's hands dirty. Minds and hands were needed in drafting, model making, shipbuilding, toolmaking, printing, and carpentry.

In an upwardly mobile nation like the United States in 1877, the division between studies transferred to attitudes toward work itself. The work you did defined who you were. With the growth of industrialization in cities, clean work, office work, divided some people from those who worked with their hands. The prejudice persists. Art making requires the use of the hands. The very thing so satisfying to the child and adult alike, the pleasure of actual manipulation of materials, remains an embarrassment. Art making still carries a stigma.

We, as educators, have to cope with these legacies. As long as art making holds some place in the school day, the purposes for art's being a school subject at all keep being calibrated against these legacies. We keep trying to elevate art making to make it more acceptable within the context of education's different ideological prejudices and rivalries.

Some people imagine they may protect art as a school subject by dropping the studio component entirely. If art were only lectures and tests, they suggest, art would seem more like science and history. Without art making neither messy classrooms nor dirty hands would stir up the old prejudices. The content of art in schools continues to jockey uncomfortably back and forth from one sort of teaching to another, while the eager children of each generation inherit whichever rationale is in favor at their particular time.

NOTES

1. Milton W. Brown, *American Painting from the Armory Show to the Depression* (Princeton: Princeton University Press, 1955).

2. Allen H. Eaton, *Immigrant Gifts to American Life* (New York: Russell Sage Foundation, 1932).

3. Albert William Levi and Ralph A. Smith, *Art Education: A Critical Necessity* (Urbana: University of Illinois Press, 1991).

4. Richard Wollheim, *Of Art and the Mind* (London: Allen Lane, 1973), 144

5. Langdon S. Thompson, "Some Reasons Why Drawing Should be Taught in Our Common Schools" [lecture] (Louisville: National Education Association, 1877), 13.

6. Ibid., 14.

7. Lecoq de Boisbaudran, *The Training of the Memory in Art and the Education of the Artist* (London: Macmillan and Co., Ltd., 1911).

8. John Gadsby Chapman, *Chapman's American Drawing-Book* (New York: J. S. Redfield, 1848), 1..

9. Thompson, "Some Reasons," 14.

10. Ibid., 17.

11. See Diana Korzenik, *Drawn to Art: A Nineteenth-Century American Dream* (Hanover, N.H.: University Press of New England, 1985).

12. Thompson, "Some Reasons," 18.

13. Ibid., 19.

14. Diana Korzenik, "The Art Education of Working Women, 1873-1903," in *Pilgrims and Pioneers: New England Women in the Arts*, ed. Alicia Faxon and Sylvia Moore (New York: Midmarch Arts Press, 1987).

15. Thompson, "Some Reasons," 20.

16. Ibid., 22.

17. Ibid., 23.

9

Transition to the Traditions: Art Making as Study Skills

Describing art education in the twentieth century, Arthur Efland wrote about, the "School Art Style." "School art" is not the same thing as child art. School art is an institutional style in its own right.[1] Efland describes the complex role the art teacher plays. The teacher's actions within the school must conform to stated and hidden expectations, potentially undermining the very best contributions art making otherwise might make to children's lives. Efland concludes his analysis of the constraints of teaching art in schools, writing, "What I suspect is that the school art style tells us a lot more about schools and less about students and what is on their minds."[2] I concur.

Once art enters schools, inevitably it is transformed. From the start of this essay I take this as a given. I see the profession of teaching young people in schools as having opened only particular paths to us. These paths are the "reasons," the objectives, for our teaching.

In the profession's formative years, Thompson's "three reasons" were starting points. The field of art teaching now has grown and taken on predictable forms. In the more than a hundred years since Thompson, because the teaching profession continued to use his "reasons," I now regard them as "traditions." One can see it when one looks at the shards of evidence from the last hundred years of art teaching: students' drawing books, school committee reports, art teaching magazines, textbooks, and teachers' own notes from their college preparation. The profession's formalization has been as much the product of the marketing of magazines, art supplies, and textbooks as of teacher preparation programs.

By the start of this century, a substantial number of art teachers became an audience for one another. They paid attention to each other. They went to conferences, even overseas. They read each others' articles. They tended to organize their teaching much along the lines of schools' priorities. They were proud of their contribution to children's lives.

From our view at the end of the century, a now vastly larger profession still teaches according to the rationales of our predecessors. Whether or not we are aware of it, we emulate what previous art teachers have done. I believe we do this to identify ourselves as participants in our profession, first, because the traditions give teachers a sense of belonging. They keep us connected with the successes of our predecessors. Second, they remind us of how art may stay in line with the schools' goals.

In the sections to come, I provide a sampling of teaching done across this country by a vast number of people. Though they followed in one of the "traditions," these people should be deemed neither as conservatives nor traditionals. Some were even rebels. Each tradition engaged imaginative and innovative minds, looking for ways art making could become more significant within schools.

Tradition 1: Art Making as Study Skills

Annie, a seven-year-old, is discovering the pleasures of sitting still and letting her mind be active. She engages herself making dramas happen on a paper in front of her on the kitchen table. With pencil on paper, she is thinking about and picturing the members of her family, none of whom is there with her. She talks to herself, describing each person, as she guides her hand. She plans who should be bigger than whom, who should wear what. She starts drawing two people. They are large and high up on the page. The one she makes be the father wears a shirt she constructs out of a grid of straight lines. With the same care she will later exercise in drawing maps for geography, she forms precise lines on the clothes for the figure she calls "Mother." Then Annie draws herself and her brother. Both are smaller and lower down on the page near its bottom edge. Annie counts to make sure the people have all their fingers. With control similar to that required in spacing words in a penmanship lesson, she draws the ground line connecting the four people.

If they were in that kitchen, Annie's parents would notice how attentive she is when she is drawing. They could see her thinking about what she is doing. They could hear her talking about how one mark takes up a certain amount of space, how it can be made to fit next to another. They could hear her figuring aloud how one shape can hide another. They could hear her talking about how her marks form branches that sprout leaves, how the tree trunks she is drawing connect to root forms hidden under the earth. Drawing helps children organize what they have seen. It also helps them listen to and remember what

Figure 14. Anatomy of a Cow

they've heard, for example, about trees and about their families. Whatever at the time children think is important about trees or people or whatever, they can draw. The drawings are their own ideas.

This has everything to do with education. When adults watch children draw and eavesdrop on children talking as they draw, they appreciate how drawing focuses children's attention. Wise teachers who have noticed this, tap children's art making capacities for teaching the sciences, social studies, mathematics, geography, and even reading and writing.

Teachers working in this vein are participants in what I term the "Study Skills Tradition." Such teachers value art making as a tool for children's learning other school subjects. Such teaching may involve not only art making, but art viewing and writing about art, but whatever the process, the goal, the reason for the teaching, is the child's better grasp of subjects such as, geography, spelling, history, or mathematics.

A History

While it is obvious today that children may learn school studies by drawing, it hasn't always seemed so apparent. Periodically, one or another teacher discovers the power of drawing in the main school subjects, and if the educational climate is right, everyone says, "Of course." However, although drawing seems to be as old as human nature, drawing's place in schooling certainly is not.

How is it that Thompson back in 1877 was able to realize that art making was the means by which students may learn to read, to write, to do math and geography? The answer has many parts. One part concerns changes in the technology of producing books. For art making to become a possible part of the school curriculum, the mid-nineteenth-century burgeoning of illustrated printing had to have been already underway. As pictured texts became cheaper to produce, American readers could appreciate for themselves how much they could learn from pictures. Pictures taught everything about structure and function, whether it be for the propagation of flowers or the fabrication of fire engines.

But another part of the answer comes from another set of innovations that took place within education itself. Were it not for that revolution, schools still would group students of all ages together doing identical tasks to learn to read, write, and cipher. Each would take turns repeating words and numbers orally by rote and then sit silently at desks writing sentences the teacher directed them to copy onto their lined copybooks.

This revolution was introduced not by Thompson toward the end of the nineteenth century, but by Jean Jacques Rousseau a century before him. Rousseau, and the inventive educators who subsequently applied and extended his ideas, proved what is now obvious: that art making is a tool for school studies.

In his book, *Émile*, his proposal for a new education for boys, Rousseau gives us his concepts of education, particularly how the senses, the natural instincts and desires are the route to learning. According to Rousseau, the boy should learn only to make his own direct observations. He should be encouraged to question and be active in nature. Whatever he learns for himself is far more useful than whatever he might learn through the filtered experience of a book's author. Rousseau shows us how the boy drawing from nature is in the right relationship to the physical world. Drawing is the child's opportunity to look, notice, ask questions, and record what he sees with marks he can master, however wobbly. "Children, being great imitators, all try to draw; and my pupil will study this art, not precisely for its own sake, but to give him a good eye and a supple hand. . . . I wish him to have no other master than Nature, no other model than the objects themselves. . . . I know that this method will, for a long time, lead to unrecognizable daubs. . . . By way of recompense, he certainly will acquire a more accurate eye and a steadier hand; he will learn to know the true relations of size and shape between animals, plants and other natural objects."[3]

The "unrecognizable daubs" didn't trouble Rousseau. His concept was based upon the notion that immature behaviors are appropriate to early stages of development. Rousseau conceived of each stage of childhood benefiting from a teaching method designed to suit it. The physical, the basis for the learning in the earliest stage, provided the foundation for the rest. Children's physical, sensory experiences should precede and have priority over language. Rousseau recommended that adults inhibit their tendency to supply children with names for everything: "It is a great disadvantage for him [the student] to have more words than ideas, and to know how to say more things than he can think."[4]

Rousseau characterized his approach as the education of interest. The boy learns best who follows his natural inclinations. The education of interest exercises the capacities of childhood and liberates the child's appetites and interests. Unfortunately the education of the girl lacked these advantages. But were it not for Rousseau's theories of the boy's development and his application of his theories to education, boys' and girls' so evident art making appetite probably would never have been harnessed for the education that was to come.

Though Rousseau lacked a specific program of education, his ideas remain necessary but not sufficient to account for art making's history in general education. Those who followed Rousseau took from him the idea that children learn differently at different ages and made classroom methods out of it. One was Heinrich Pestalozzi (1746–1827). Through developing his own schools in Switzerland's Neuhof and Yverdon, Pestalozzi studied the needs of children and the best methods for teaching them. Shaping his methods out of Rousseau's ideas of stage-related learning, Pestalozzi worked to adjust subject matter to the child's capacity. His methods involved sensory experiences and simplifications appropriate to the child's level. Teachers took an already familiar single object and used "object lessons" to teach the child simplified concepts of number and language and what Pestalozzi called "the ABC's of spatial form." Teachers helped the children name the straight, curved, and angular edges that they saw in objects. Then they practiced these as elements in drawing. Though today few see drawing as the massing together of disparate bits or elements, Pestalozzi's system made drawing a necessary school skill.

The methods that Frederick Froebel (1782–1852) developed for the kindergarten, which Elizabeth Peabody referred to as the "Art Academy for Children," gave children's art work an even more significant role in the curriculum. Froebel, one of Pestalozzi's students at his institute at Yverdon, admired his teacher's methods. He also wanted to improve upon what he saw as their limitations: their mechanical and disjointed instructional procedures. Froebel developed a vast theory and specific methods to implement it, picking up where "object lessons" had left off. His innovations became the first kindergarten, established in Blankenburg, Germany, in 1837. Whereas in a Pestalozzian classroom the choice of the object in "the object lesson" may have been casual, in the kindergarten the choice of particular objects was precisely determined. Froebel developed guidelines for the fabrication of what he called "the gifts": woolen crocheted balls, wooden cylinders and cubes, and other educational equipment. These objects were intended to be art media, vehicles enabling children to bring their inner thoughts into the outside world.

Through manipulating the differently sliced wooden cubes, the third, fourth, fifth, and sixth of Froebel's "gifts," children grasped in their hands and their minds entities that could be thought of as numbers. Children's route to arriving at an understanding of number was to be a sculptural process. Froebel called children's solid creations of mathematical ideas "forms of knowledge." But other purposes too were served by these same small, wooden, variously proportioned rectangles. They were for children's building their understanding of such familiar domestic objects as tables and chairs, called "forms of life." Finally, these same blocks served yet a third purpose. With them the child could explore "forms of beauty," which Froebel understood as whatever simple, symmetrical, formal arrangements the child found pleasing. The kindergarten expanded the menu of media with which children learn. Block play, like drawing, clay work, painting, singing, dancing, and dramatic play, became part of school.

This tradition, the legacy of nineteenth-century romanticism, had its patriarchs; Rousseau begat Pestalozzi, who begat Froebel. They represent and did create the educational revolution that gave art making its place in schools. Though it seems obvious, it is important to say that these men necessarily were removed from the multitude of school houses in the towns and villages that adopted their ideas. In America as well as Europe, many attentive teachers no doubt experimented with and arrived at methods we now associate with the patriarchs. Here Alcott, Parker, and others, most of whose names we will never know, developed their own "object lessons," their ways to help children to observe nature and to describe familiar objects. To whomever one attributes the radical changes in education, they forever changed the dominance of words and numbers as the sum and substance of schooling. This revolution placed art making at the heart of the general curriculum.

By 1876, parents in the United States were becoming aware of the new movements. Those who could attend the Centennial Exposition studied the fair's education displays. There many parents, including Frank Lloyd Wright's mother, bought Froebel's "gifts" to take home to their children. By this time an American company was already manufacturing and distributing these items. That same year Thomas Eakins, the American painter so sensitive to the changing educational opportunities, commented both on art making and on education by painting *Baby at Play*. Here in paint is his appreciation of the child's concentration exercised in the building of block structures.

Even earlier, educators in America applied elements of the new theories in their teaching. In the 1830s, Bronson Alcott and the art teacher he hired, Francis Graeter, followed the advice Rousseau offered for Émile with Boston's Temple School children. With their drawing books in hand, the students went outdoors to draw from observation. Facing the Temple School facade or a tree, the children drew what they saw. When they were done they returned inside to record their day in their journals. Journal keeping included redrawing in their notebooks the artworks they had just drawn outside. The second drawing became an occasion for self-reflection. It taught children that drawing can be a way of thinking and that the thinking involved in drawing could help

Figure 15. *Baby at Play*, Thomas Eakins

them reflect on all their studies. Interspersed throughout the journal were writings and drawings covering all school subjects. Bronson Alcott, perhaps best known through his daughter Louisa's account of their family life, *Little Women*, made children's individual, personal experience the basis of his teaching. Children were to be the sources of their own ideas. The school's obligation was to give children opportunities to express their ideas and experiences, whether in writing, conversations, or drawing. Children were encouraged to use all the forms of expression. In the journal of one of Alcott students, surviving in the collection of Fruitlands Museums in Harvard, Massachusetts, we can see the various studies that incorporated drawing.

Dr. Alcott, as he liked to be called, and Mr. Graeter were hardly alone with these ideas. Elizabeth Peabody, who wrote *Record of a School* (1835), documenting Alcott's Temple School teaching, was also a proponent of these new ideas. As the founder of New England's first kindergarten, along with Mrs. Carl Schurz, William Torrey Harris, and Susan Blow, she was part of the movement that established kindergartens in this country. Peabody also promoted new educational ideas at her Boston bookshop, which became a gathering place for writers, teachers, and other intellectuals, including her brother-in-law, Horace Mann, the husband of her sister, Mary. Mann, who served as Massachusetts's first secretary of education, and his wife, who shared the passion for education, traveled through Europe looking for educational innovations. Then "E. P. Peabody," the publisher with an imprint in her own name, spread the ideas they found in this country. One such publication was *The Common School Drawing Master* of 1846.

Another educator deeply influenced by the European innovators was Francis Wayland Parker. With an interruption in his teaching career caused by his service in the Civil War, he returned home as "Col. Parker" to assume an eighth-grade teaching position at North Grammar School in Manchester, New Hampshire. Newspapers there reported that, even though his students were well beyond kindergarten age, Parker was experimenting with Froebel's ideas. In the years to follow, Parker developed his own system incorporating Froebel's theories. He condensed his system into a single graphic chart, so teachers could visually grasp its essence. The chart pictured children's relationships to the knowledge they will attain from education. The chart is a circle with the child at its center. The child draws to him or her all ideas, attending to and taking in stimulation from the outside world. As an assimilator of ideas, the child also extends outward, expressing and interpreting whatever passes through the filter of personal experience. According to Parker, learning required both processes: attention and expression. The teachers' job was to plan for and to provide for both. Attention meant providing time and stimuli for the child's taking in ideas: looking, listening, and reading. Expression meant providing time for the child's giving form to the thoughts triggered by these inputs. Expression has nine modes: writing, singing, dancing, speaking, building, sculpting , drawing, gesturing, and making. According to Parker, through these modes a child may acquire all knowledge for which schooling is responsible. Parker trained teachers, across all the school subjects, to use art making to help children take in and express their ideas.

Educational ideas of the nineteenth century were like pebbles tossed into a vast American lake. The effects of those pebbles were rings with ever enlarging circles around them. Parker's ideas influenced John Dewey, who in turn developed ideas in his laboratory school that have been so pervasive in the twentieth century that no one alive today has been untouched by them. Dewey, acknowledging his inheritance, wrote of Parker that he "more nearly than any other person . . . [was] . . . the father of the progressive education movement."[5]

Using Parker's concepts of expression and attention, Dewey carried forward the idea that the art instinct should animate the general curriculum in schools of the twentieth century. He wanted schools to be transformed into places where children make things. Dewey decribed his frustration, ferreting through school supply stores, looking for desks that would permit the sort of education he valued. He recalled a salesperson telling him, "I am afraid we do not have what you want. You want something at which the children may work; these [desks] are all for listening."[6]

Drawing, for Dewey, taps the social instinct and is a vehicle for expressing, reflecting upon, and developing dialogue with others on any subject: "The egoistic and limited interest of little children is in this manner capable of infinite expansion." The instinct of investigation seems to grow out of the combination of the constructive impulse and the conversational. Of drawing, Dewey says: "Let the child first express his impulse, and then through criticism, question, and suggestion bring him to consciousness of what he has done, and what he needs to do. . . . There is no distinction between experimental science for little children and the work done in the carpenter's shop . . . and so the expressive impulse of children, the art instinct, grows out of the communicating and constructive instincts."[7]

In Dewey's words we hear his predecessors. We hear the now long tradition of using art making to help children acquire school skills. In Dewey's words we can hear Rousseau guiding Émile. We can recognize Froebel urging kindergarten teachers to provide children with materials for externalizing their thinking. We can see parallels to Alcott's advising his students to redraw their own drawings in their journals. And we know we see applications of Parker's system of attention and expression, because Dewey himself has written of his admiration for Parker.

And the tradition is carried on. Drawing as an approach to acquiring school skills continuously threads through twentieth-century education. One publication that established art making as a route to children's geographical thinking was Lucy Sprague Mitchell's *Young Geographers: How They Explore the World and How They Map the World*, first published in 1934. Mitchell charted the stages of children's geographic thinking, aligning the stages of development with categories essential to learning at each stage. Mitchell shows how early geographical thinking begins. Children explore the space relationships between things and express that understanding through play even before they walk. As children's interests in space broaden, their spatial representations become more complex. By age five, children are making block maps, clay maps, and what they think of as airplane views of space. Mitchell tells us: "Thinking forever consists of seeing relationships: art, which from this point of view is matured play, forever consists of the expression of relations through images. . . . [The school] has become a . . . laboratory-studio equipped with tools for study and media for expression. . . . The art element does not vitiate but may even enhance the scientific. . . . All maps must be expressed through some symbol. For geographic thinking, I believe image symbols should precede abstract symbols."[8]

Teachers today who would work in this tradition could introduce children to art that explicitly incorporates imagery used in teaching writing, mathematics, science, and geography. One might develop an age/stage appropriate curriculum around the presence of letter forms in students' lives. Students could invent images in which written letters actually appear. To support this, teachers might show students nineteenth-century trompe l'oeil paintings by Americans like Harnett and Peto. The same might be done for numbers, maps, scientific studies of bones and flowers. Such artwork in school might join together the two types of education traditionally split assunder, the manual arts and the liberal arts. The study skills approach challenges that assumption that learning done in the making of things associated with manual arts is separate from learning acquired only by reading and writing, associated with the liberal arts.

From the Artists' View

At first glance, one might say that study skills teaching is not art, that it is a dilution and a distortion of art. Yet from artists' recollections we can see the pleasure and stimulation that such studies can yeild. Glimpsing a teaching method from the eyes of an artist, such as Lee Krasner, helps us recognize how seeds of the artist's process may be captured in certain school activities. Krasner remembers elementary social studies and the making of maps that was part of that curriculum: "One activity useful to the making of good citizens was making maps, making the American terrain concrete and seeable. . . . Every time I see a Jasper Johns map, I remember how crazy I was for doing that thing."[9] I have similar vivid memories.

The Art for Study Skills tradition benefits more students than those who are artists-to-be. It give students access to art making processes without having to ever answer the question of whether they wished to be artists. For example, in the fifth grade, if the teacher is assigning the drawing of maps, everyone does one. As a result, some young people discover art making who otherwise might never have touched it. How many nineteenth-century women, in their learning how to paint flowers while studying botany, discovered their love of color and drawing? We know as a result of that instruction that some continued to paint as amateurs when a career in art was not a possibility. How many amateur artists in our century were like my father, who accounted for his enthusiasm for drawing and painting rocks, by pointing to his school notebook full of geology drawings?

NOTES

1. Arthur D. Efland,"The School Art Style," *Studies in Art Education,* vol. 17, no 2 (1976): 37-38.

2. Ibid., 43.

3. Jean Jacques Rousseau, *Jean Jacques Rousseau: His Educational Theories Selected from Émile, Julie, and His Other Writings,* ed. R. L. Archer (Woodbury, N.Y.: Barrons Educational Series, 1964), 133.

4. Paul Monroe, *A Textbook of the History of Education* (New York: Macmillan, 1920), 561.

5. John Dewey, "How Much Freedom in New Schools?" *New Republic,* 9 July 1930; reprinted in Josepth Ratner, ed., *Education Today* (New York: G. P. Putnam's Sons, 1940), 217.

6. John Dewey, *The School and Society* (1900); reprinted in *The Child and the Curriculum, the School and Society* (Chicago: University of Chicago Press, 1956), 31.

7. Ibid., 43, 40, 44.

8. Lucy Sprague Mitchell, *Young Geographers: How They Explore the World and How They Map the World* (New York: Bank Street College of Education, 1934), 39, 48, 71.

9. Krasner is quoted in Eleanor Munro, *Originals: American Women Artists* (New York: Simon & Schuster, 1979), 105.

10

Art Making for Jobs

To orient ourselves to the next tradition, the jobs tradition, in which we think of art making in terms of what it may contribute to the young person's future employment, we will acquaint ourselves with one child. At age two, Charles began his self-appointed task. He would sit at the table daily, even before breakfast, drawing very rapidly. In that first year his yield was over three hundred drawings. His annual output declined slightly in each subsequent year until he turned age seven. Then his productivity peaked. Of the 903 drawings he produced in his seventh year, the majority (389) were trains. The rest were related to trains: timetables, road maps, men, women, subway systems, inventions, radio circuits, planes, house wiring, landscapes, elevators, and trolleys.[1]

The psychologist Gertrude Hildreth documented Charles's childhood. Charles's mother, who fortunately had saved the over four thousand drawings her son made between ages two and eleven, told Hildreth,

> From the beginning, Charles considered his drawing as work, and concentrated seriously on it. . . . There were two railroad lines not far from our house. When Charles was six months old his favorite ride in his carriage was along "Railroad Avenue.". . . At seven months of age he rode in the front seat with his father to and from the commuting train, watching everything with intense interest. . . . As he grew older and could use his kiddie car, he made trips to the tracks alone. He seemed to know the exact times the trains were due. . . . He mapped out routes on the sidewalk and rode his "expresses" and "locals" making regular stops at his stations. At ten his tracks were in the road and his bicycle was his train. . . . At age twelve and after, he continued work with his miniature electric railroad. . . . Charles' interest in science and mechanics reflects special capacities. . . . He has never cared much for reading.[2]

Throughout his childhood, Charles used drawing to understand trains. His childhood occupation seems to have prepared him to do the work he ultimately chose for his career. I met Charles when he was forty-two years old and had become a computer expert at a federal branch office of the Department of Transportation. His job dealt with designing systems that regulate the speed, arrival, and departure of trains at busy, complex intersections. His work involved solving problems remarkably similar to those that had riveted his attention as a child.

On their own, children work at drawing. They direct themselves. They practice conceptual and mechanical skills as they draw. Early pictures, like those Charles drew, may signal later lifetime interests. Though children may busy themselves with work on their own and may, like Charles, never consciously see the connection between their early art interest and their later careers, teachers at times have directed them to use this capacity.

For more than a century, art teachers have organized art teaching around skills that may be applied specifically to jobs students may have as adults. In large part, art education's proliferation in American public schools in the nineteenth century was due to this enthusiasm. Of all the rationales that Americans have developed to promote the study of art making, perhaps this type is most easily described.

History

Education that specifically prepares students for work grew out of a curious paradox. At schools in the nineteenth century, children were removed from the community in which, up to then, they had watched, listened to, and mixed with working adults. The schoolchild was deprived of contact with people who were at work. As a result the child's understanding of work was severely limited. The school thus may be seen as creating the problem of children's ignorance of work, of tools, and of skills of the hands, eyes, and brain. By the beginning of the twentieth century people agreed: "Everyday lost by the apprentice system was gained by the school, until imperceptibly under steady pressure, the school came to stand alone as the only means of training, and the child came to be almost wholly separated from the ordinary activities of life."[2] The school had become the instrument that was to solve the very problem it had, in part, created.

Back when Thompson addressed the National Education Association in 1877, one problem had become apparent to all. Nations were in a "battle for material existence,"[3] competing with one another to produce the finest, most desirable marketable products. Our country feared it couldn't hold its own. The schools were enlisted to help. Separate shops replicating now-lost apprenticeships could not be the answer.

Figure 16. Fashion design class at the museum

They would have been too costly. Besides, schools had other priorities. They were not supposed to be workplaces. Creating a school subject called "drawing" was proposed as a solution. Many believed that if students studied drawing at school, they would be far more employable, bringing useful skills to whatever trades they entered as adults.

The idea of using schools to prepare students for work was a dramatic contrast with the schooling that started in this country two hundred and fifty years ago. American formal education was begun in 1635 with the establishment of the Boston Latin School. The boys who attended it and those schools that later emulated it came from homes where parents had no need for their sons to contribute to the family economy. Modeled on British grammar schools, whatever the boys learned there came through their reading of the scriptures and the classics. The Latin school offered them a certain preparation and polish required for entry to the university and the professions.

A serious gap exists in our knowlege of analogous female education contemporaneous with that of the Latin school. Many long-lasting and sometimes well-equipped schools for young women seem to have existed.[4] We know teachers taught schoolgirls to produce embroideries, which keep surfacing in today's auctions. Though some researchers can identify certain teachers by name and recognize their students' styles in needlework pictures on silk, known as "schoolgirl art," we don't yet know all the teachers' reasons for offering this instruction.

But though schools for the privileged may have carried on their mission well into the nineteenth century, publicly supported schools were pressed to change and broaden their mission. With the growth of industry, society needed to reorganize itself. Publicly supported schools in each city and town participated in the changes, serving their more diverse populations of young people. The schools were adjusting to prepare children to become workers. Schools needed to invent a curriculum to educate all those who intended not to go to the university. Art making as preparation for adult work evolved along two paths: (1) Work that would meet the challenge of industry. Art skills would help students take their roles in production; (2) Work to counteract the effects of industry. Art for nonindustrial work offering a criticism and corrective for the damages wrought by industrialization.

In promoting art making for jobs, American teachers pursued both of these directions. As we read of the various movements and arguments, we need to remember that the person who cast the argument in most cases was not the person teaching in the classroom. The person who conceived of a campaign on behalf of one or another idea had to inculcate that approach into the minds of teachers. For ideas to become current, they had to get exposure. Lectures, teacher institutes, newspapers, the growing list of books on how to teach art, and the periodicals developing for the professions all helped. But whether ideas did or did not take form in a particular classroom depended on the teachers and their access to information.

From Industry to "Laborphobia"

It wasn't enough that the sons of the wealthy could attend Latin or other schools of that ilk. A growing work force needed to be developed. To understand how ill-prepared for this task the schools were, one has only to read Horace Mann's despair over his state's public schools in the 1840s. Students who did undertake some years of locally provided schooling sat through their lessons in dilapidated school buildings; lessons were taught according to no plan and by teachers who were untrained and lacked exposure to new educational ideas. Even before 1852, when his state passed its compulsory education law, growing numbers of students were making demands on the system of free common schools. Schools had custodial and educational responsibility for the often rowdy young, many of whom were unsure of why they had to go to these places called schools. And little help could be expected from parents, both of whom were sometimes at work for as many as twelve hours a day.

In order to preserve and perpetuate the ideal of democracy, the common school had to create the possibility of the American ideal: equality. Local school reports and newspapers fostered the notion that, in a society that was growing ever more conspicuously unequal with a growing affluent class, improved common schools could promise upward mobility for diligent girls and boys.

Mann, as Massachusetts's secretary of education, undertook the mission of making people care for the education of those too poor to pay for private schooling. His treatments for these problems were no local matter; they were spread through *The Common School Journal* that he edited. It offered methods and inspiration to the nation. As part of this program, Horace and Mary Mann ferreted through schools in Europe, looking for curriculum methods. Elizabeth Peabody, Mary's sister-in-law, contributed to their efforts by publishing and selling books related to the good ideas they found.

In 1846, perhaps to justify Mann's extravagance in commissioning and printing the steel-engraved plates illustrating Schmid's lessons in *The Common School Journal*, Peabody herself republished this work under the title *The Common School Drawing Master*, "so that every student could have the book to himself."[5] *The Common School Drawing*

Master described the methods of a drawing teacher, Peter Schmid of Berlin, who Peabody tells us was recognized as extraordinarily gifted early in life. To redeem himself from the warping of wrong art teachings advocated by a German prince who meant to help him, Schmid devoted himself to "a series of experiments analyzing his own process of mind." His self-reflective research led to a reform in the methods of teaching in the schools of his native country, where he generated the exercises Peabody reissued here for Americans. Peabody assured her readers that Schmid "answers all purposes of mechanical drawing. The most complicated machinery, furniture, &c, can, by its aid, be drawn in perspective."[6]

Schmid's system consisted of twenty-four lessons based on nineteen rectilinear solid blocks. Instruction sheets directed the student to draw the blocks in various prescribed configurations. On the instructions, each corner of the block was labeled by a different letter of the alphabet. The student's task was to connect the dots, as it were, between the letters at each block's corner. Proportions were to be rigidly observed with hard, thin, even and equal in weight, precise pencil lines.

Schmid's method, first published here in 1845 in *Common School Journal*, promised to be a solution to the rowdy students who needed some productive direction: "How are young students to spend the residue of a session three hours long? They are not to whisper, they are not to manufacture and to fillip spitballs. They are not to try the law of projectiles by quill or an elastic bit of wood. . . . What then is to be done? We answer, 'Find them an occupation; direct this activity instead of suppressing it.'. . . For all these purposes, there is no single resource so valuable as drawing."[7]

Unlike the study skills approach, which tapped the spontaneous art making capacities of children, art making for jobs concerned itself more with the shaping of the adults the children were to become. The spontaneous behavior of children seemed to threaten Mann. He feared that once drawing entered the school curriculum, the rigorous practice of Schmid's methods might deteriorate and give way to what he termed "mere play and picture making."[8] Mann was convinced that the children so in need of activity and discipline for their future lives would have the benefits of both through Peter Schmid's drawing lessons. The "occupation" of drawing promised to anticipate working-class students' future needs, as the study of Latin and Greek did for the children of wealth.

The importation of the Schmid ideas was significant because it was no isolated phenomenon. In 1848, an American, way ahead of his time as it turned out, Wiliam Minifie of Baltimore, wrote a *Textbook for*

Mechanical Drawing and an Essay on the Theory of Color. Minifie urged the public to support the inclusion of drawing as a common school subject: "We should call upon our manufacturers as the persons most directly interested, to be foremost in the good work. Let them start such schools for both sexes with liberality and then call upon our statesmen and capitalists for aid."[9]

Four years later, in 1852, Great Britain's Government Art School at South Kensington adopted this American's book as one of its texts. There a young student, Walter Smith, who was to become a leading figure in American art education, may have read Minifie as he prepared himself to improve art in Britain.

In the next eighteen years, the United States prepared itself to join the industrial art education movement well underway in England. One landmark of our country's commitment to art education for jobs was the signing of the Massachusetts Drawing Act of 1870, a fulfillment thirty years later of Minifie's vision. Merchants lobbied the legislature for the act, which made drawing a requirement in the schools and made evening drawing classes accessible to all adults in cities and towns with populations of over ten thousand. As the Senate Reports of 1885, *Art and Industry, Education in the Industrial and Fine Arts in the United States,* compiled by Isaac Edwards Clarke, indicated, this law reverberated across the states. Art instruction specifically oriented to work inspired other states to follow the lead. Maine in 1871 and New York in 1875 passed similar acts. Connecticut, Iowa, Wisconsin, and Ohio finally rejected such legislation after devoting much debate to the matter.

A British man, Walter Smith, whose first contact with the United States possibly was reading Minifie in his London school days, was the one who planted utilitarian art education in America. After he graduated from South Kensington (now the Royal College of Art) and had served as director of several art colleges in England, Smith was recommended by Sir Henry Cole, Director of the South Kensington School, as the best person to interpret the British system of industrial art here. Smith was hired jointly by the city of Boston and the state of Massachusetts and was commissioned by his new employers first to tour the country to acquire art instruction methods and art examples to show to Americans.

He arrived in 1871, ready to go. Once here, Smith devised a systematic curriculum. His sequentially ordered lessons counteracted the planlessness of which Horace Mann had despaired. Smith's curriculum extended from elementary through high school. In 1873 he topped it off, shaping and then directing Massachusetts Normal Art School, with a curriculum for adults whom he would prepare to be designers and drawing teachers who themselves would perpetuate art education for students' future jobs. The graduating artists, "the art army," as they liked to call themselves, spread Smith's ideas across the states.

In Smith's curriculum, children were provided with drawing cards and printed booklets of geometrical flat figures in progressions so that the learner could first master simple straight lines, then progress to curves and complex combinations of these. The program resembled Pestalozzi's ABC's of spatial form, though here the objective was to master pattern and ornament that would be applied in all the materials being fabricated in the burgeoning art industries.

Industrial art education became firmly rooted in public education. Whether the student started drawing from flat copies or geometrical solids, as later teachers preferred, the purpose was the perfection of drawing for its service to the innumerable art industries' technical fabrications processes: cast metal, wrought metal, carved objects, printed fabrics, pottery and porcelain, cut and engraved glass, and graphic reproductions.[10] Here was proof of Thompson's later contention that drawing in the schools promoted the growing art industries.

Art making in schools became a virtual crusade. Philadelphia, where the viewers at the Centennial Exposition had admired the first fruits of the Massachusetts Drawing Act, became the center of a new activity: the minor arts, which Charles Godfrey Leland introduced into the public schools as "manual training." Its threefold virtues were preparation of children for labor, curbing idleness, and promoting morality. No longer exclusively concerned with drawing, the minor arts included many media. In 1879 Leland produced his comprehensive guide, *The Minor Arts*, explaining woodworking, stencilling, repoussé, and other crafts based upon his own studies.

Born in Philadelphia in 1824, from old New England stock, Leland attended Princeton, studied in Germany, and lived as an expatriate man of letters in London, where he witnessed the revival of the decorative arts. Leland chose to take classes at South Kensington, the same school where Walter Smith prepared. In addition, Leland consulted directly with William Morris, the leader of the Arts and Crafts Movement, on the "lost" medieval technique of waxed leather. In 1880, a year after Walter Smith had addressed the Pennsylvania legislature on behalf of the virtues of an industrial art education, Leland returned to Philadelphia. His state's leaders were ready now to accept some new form of industrial art or manual training that could serve the growing populations of public schools, orphanages, and asylums. The decorative arts were Leland's solution.

At this time, educators and psychologists were fascinated by childhood and the uniqueness of the child's mind. In 1883 G. Stanley Hall published his study *On the Content of Children's Minds,* looking at the concepts that children entering their first year of school brought with them. The art equivalent to Hall's question was expressed in Leland's curiousity about children's minds. He concluded that children were developmentally fit to pursue studies of ornament because of "the universal truth that man develops the ornamental during the infancy of every race before the useful."[11] Leland's developmental defense for teaching decorative arts suited his time perfectly.

Leland wrestled with the same problem that had occupied his predecessors. How could young people be prepared for specific trades in schools without training them in those specific trades? Leland's solution was the "manual arts." Leland shared with his Massachusetts compatriots an unbridled optimism for the economic advantages of art education. A generalized decorative art training for any child between the ages of twelve and fifteen would teach the child enough "decorative outline" later to design carpet for a factory, to work at a metal foundry, or to become a salesperson or a buyer of dry goods. Leland saw only good coming from his ideas. Students could sell or use the works they made. They would develop a taste for more beautiful objects that they then would buy. The flourishing of the minor arts, he argued, might even lead to advancing the fine arts.

In 1880 the Philadelphia Board of Education provided Leland with the Hollingsworth School to set up as his model. In that year he addressed the Philadelphia Social Science Association on the subject of "Industrial and Decorative Art in the Public Schools." He argued that the two pressing problems of the time were providing work for everyone and devising means for education that would provide both mental discipline and practical skill. Leland lamented people's loss of interest in making decorative objects. He blamed machinery for the degradation of handwork. He saw in the revival of handwork skills the provision for work for the masses because such work is slower and employs more workers than fabrication dependent upon machines. He promised a national artistic renewal and condescendingly dreamed that art and art industry can be brought back again and down to the humble multitude.[12]

Leland faulted both models, England's South Kensington and Boston's Massachusetts Normal Art School, for being elitist. Leland worried about the impoverished students unable to go to an urban center and pay room and board for training in a specialized institute of higher education. He directed his attention to the slow student who showed little interest in artistic ability. Neither the students' originality nor their initiative was his concern. In fact he thought these were of such little consequence that he recommended that the government patent office might provide students with printed patterns for their elementary decorative work. His attention was devoted to the local school and the earlier years of schooling. The manual arts movement in the schools became one more effort to cope with the vanishing opportunities for apprenticeships and the too limited vocational preparation in schools.

The ever-widening class distinctions that haunted the United States became evident in conceptions of art teaching. In the nineteenth century the new discovery within the field of art, industrial art education, was deemed inferior and was relegated to the working class while fine art remained a privileged preserve. When Charles Leland developed his innovations he created another split: this time within industrial art education. The industrial drawing movement was a privileged bastion of urban sophistication in comparison with the manual arts. Manual arts was a movement enabling the lowest classes to flower. Two student groups, up to then given little particular attention, were targeted for this new movement. One group was the poorer, rural, less able students. The other population was inferior not by ability or economics, but by chronological age: students of intermediate schools. It is a curious pattern that each jobs-orientated educational innovation has seized upon art making as a way of rescuing one neglected segment of the population. The newly identified group is separated off from other people, who are presumed superior, more able, and slightly more privileged.

The utilitarian orientation in art teaching took various names: industrial arts, decorative arts, minor arts, or manual arts. Sometimes it was called "constructive work." Stirred by the 1876 centennial and the influx of artistic objects and ideas about the making of such objects, Americans continued to retrieve educational ideas from abroad. One viewer, Dr. Runkle, president of Massachusetts Institute of Technology, was impressed particularly by what he saw at the Centennial Exposition of the work of the Moscow Technical School. Under this influence, he formulated "type exercises"[13] explicitly designed to familiarize technical students with different tools and processes. Type exercises filtered down into secondary education, where manual training programs developed along the lines of the Moscow Technical School. The movement rapidly spread across the states, even into the elementary schools.

In contrast to the Moscow training system, which involved procedures solely for the purpose of exercising and perfecting certain technical skills, Sloyd, a Swedish elementary-level method of manual training, had students acquiring skills while they actually fabricated whole usable objects. The incentives for learning were making and having some thing of one's own, something made from idea to finish and perceived as useful. Gustaf Larson, the proponent of Sloyd, prized children's finding use and satisfaction in their work.

That Sloyd methods looked innovative reveals how much work had changed in American society. Craftspeople customarily had formed objects from idea to finish. But as production was broken into bits in the mills, workers learned only their one part of any fabrication process. When Sloyd came along and advised students to make a thing whole, that idea seemed an innovation. Sloyd, a revolution that required schools to equip rooms with expensive worktables and tools, embodied a romance and nostalgia about work from a now lost past. Sloyd's popularity was a criticism of the industrial art education that we see growing at the turn of the century.

The notion of using art making to prepare for future work had many subdivisions and alternatives. With each innovation the field split again. Some refined the industrial applications, while others, like Charles Leland, advocated slowing down labor and emphasizing handwork as preparation for commericial production. The manual arts movement at times split from the art education movement. At other times they joined forces. In the early twentieth century, manual arts teachers were as numerous as art teachers, and two periodicals supported the joint professions. One was *The Manual Training Magazine,* a bimonthly begun in 1899 and edited by Charles Bennett. The second periodical was a monthly, *The Applied Arts Book,* begun in 1901 and edited by Frederick H. Daniels. In 1902, when Henry Turner Bailey became its editor, he renamed it *The School Arts Book.* For the next fifteen years Bailey, as editor, continued the debate about the relationship of art making to work. What is art's best contribution to the child's future employment?

The new century called for a fresh start. Schools were blamed for a lazy and incompetent new generation. In 1906 Bailey, addressing the American Institute of Education on "The Arts and Crafts in the Public School" pleaded that conditions of our time demanded a new school subject. Assessing the past fifty years' failures, he said: "For a whole generation the feeling that the schools have offered a one-sided curriculum has been deepening like a rising tide. The farmer and the businessman and the educator all agree that the new generation of boys and girls have an aversion to honest hard work and simple pleasures."[14] Bailey called the aversion to work "laborphobia." He attributed it, in part, to the decay of the apprenticeship system and recommended that "the school [that] came to stand alone as the only means of training" shift its orientation. It should cease preparing students for the performance of job-related skills and instead should concentrate on cultivating students' incentive to work.

Meanwhile the nature of work itself was changing. Bailey noted that not only changes in the workplace, but changes in the home were depriving the child of an understanding of work. Laborsaving devices, cooking with gas and electricity, milk delivered to the home, mail arriving by postal carriers, all were mystifications, removing too many stages of human work from children's sight. "If the public school is ever to give children anything like the discipline they used to receive in the home and the workshop," he wrote, "all this [curriculum] must be modified in the direction of the concrete, the genuine." The teacher was left responsible to make sense of these changes. Bailey said the old methods knock the vitality out of the child. The school separates the child from life. "As soon as nature has brought the child to the point where he has gained complete control of his powers of locomotion, we teachers caught him and make him sit still six hours a day. . . . As soon as he could use his fingers and thumbs in a hundred skillful ways we took from him everything he tried to use in school except a pencil."[15]

The progressive education movement took up the challenge. In *The School and Society* (1900), John Dewey addressed objections of materialism and the tendency toward menial training for occupations being taught in the school. He recast the argument. The change had to be in the awareness, the mind, of the person who is a worker. The change is "in the consciousness of the one who does the work that his activity shall have meaning to himself. . . . The world in which most of us live is a world in which everyone has a calling and an occupation, something to do . . . the great thing for the one as for the other is that each shall have had the education which enables him to see within his daily work all there is in it of large and human significance."[16] Dewey's ideas were yet another form of education for work that avoided the explicit training for trades. His larger, more social view of work promoted schools as places where children work and learn about other people's work.

Art Making as an Alternative Form of Work

That other direction in education, which sought not to adapt art making to industrial society but to be a criticism of it and a resistance to it, nonetheless remained concerned with work. Here the artist became a model of an alternative kind of worker. The artist corrects for the damages wrought by industrialization. Art makers criticize industrial processes by not conforming to them.[17]

John Ruskin (1819–1900), the "aesthetic czar of the Anglo-American world,"[18] devoted his life to this problem. Ruskin believed that the careful observation of a rock, the drawing of a landscape, morally improved the person who did it. His concern was the contribution of art to labor. He believed art had the power to improve society, so he judged art by moral and social criteria. Ruskin's attitudes matched those flourishing in the United States, particularly after the Civil War.[19] Ruskin became influential on art education here because he thought about the mind and feelings of the worker. Ruskin wondered how the worker felt while forming an object: Was the work done for enjoyment? Was the carver happy while working? Ruskin's admiration for the Gothic style in architecture was due to his belief that the Gothic style alone encouraged even the lowliest worker to express the soul and the mind in the work.[20] The personal touch became the mark of art, evidence that the worker was in touch, literally, with the work. Pleasure, in-touchness with work, was the measure of its goodness. Ruskin opposed teaching art making for industries. Ruskin "did not want to teach accurate command of mathematical forms which were deemed useful in their applications to industry. . . . Try first to manufacture a Raphael, then let Raphael direct your manufacture."[21]

As Ruskin saw it, the way industry divided the work shattered the worker. Assigning different workers piecemeal tasks, consecutive stages of completion of the work on one product, deprived the worker of identification with the entire cycle of forming something. This was the very problem the Sloyd method sought to solve. Art making, touching and forming something whole, could heal not only the individual but the society. The cure for the alienated workers, unruly street crowds, and the badly behaved schoolchildren was work in which people could find pleasure. Though Ruskin did not favor democracy in politics, nor feminism, nor the workers' control of production, he did think society should take charge paternalistically and organize life so that children would grow into adults having learned to use their hands and their heads.

William Morris, the renowned founder of his company, Morris, Marshall and Faulkner and Co. in London in 1861, differed from Ruskin on the matter of the machine. Morris's objections were not directed toward the machine. Machines, Morris believed, could free workers from some drudgery and he built into the work process as much room for expressive individuality as possible. Morris made himself a student of unfamiliar and discarded work processes and made a virtue of learning to dye, weave, embroider, and print, looking always to make the best use of materials. Within one decade Morris's company proved that a person could still find pleasure in work that yielded highly marketable products. But in time this proved an illusion. Morris eventually accepted that the workforce had to be divided into managers and planners on one hand and interchangeable unskilled laborers on the other.[22] The only processes exempt from this that kept the human touch throughout were painting, sculpting, and architecture.

Ruskin and Morris served as models for Americans who sought alternatives. They were attracted to the ideals of both these men who refused to be led by industry. They liked the idea that art elevated labor, that the aesthetic, the in-touchness of the fine arts could improve work conditions, and that beauty was available to everyone.

This ideal permeated our schools in the form of the Arts and Crafts ideals. Unlike the South Kensington and its offspring schools that for generations influenced England, here industrial drawing had had a very much shorter life. There was less to overthrow and the Arts and Crafts Movement that replaced it perpetuated Ruskin's and Morris's social attitudes. The craftsperson became an ideal, an independent soul who joined aesthetics, skill, freedom, and responsibility. In an economic system apparently stacked against quality, where profits were more important than the time it took to do things well, the craftsperson's priorities, using fine materials and devoting whatever time the work required, were heard as implicit challenges to industry.

But money was a problem. Turning their backs on industry, craftspeople neeeded to look elsewhere for income. They faced a choice. Either they could sell their products to manufacturers, who controlled the working conditions and the profits, or they could seek a financial livelihood by becoming teachers and pursue their art work, expecting little or no money for it. Teaching, deemed more morally acceptable than compromising one's craft, took on a central position in the Arts and Crafts Movement. Education within the movement came to be about work that involved "the winning of character not information, the teaching of the idea of service rather than that of acquisition; the education that tends to brotherhood and cooperation. Art came to mean anything that was well done."[23]

Arts and crafts education took two forms in the first decade of this century; education via independent arts and crafts societies and via the public schools. Thousands of handicrafts groups sprang up, carrying on the traditions of the voluntary societies of the nineteenth century. Public schools also encouraged the formation of groups. These societies offered classes, lectures, and exhibitions much as had the voluntary societies and local art associations before them. When the Boston Society of Arts and Crafts, founded in 1897, developed a salesroom and jury system to develop a market and standards many groups across the country copied them. Beginning in 1901, the society also published a magazine, *Handicraft*, a forum for education. Everyone read it. It announced exhibitions, reviewed books, and listed services and printed lectures. Like the lyceum audiences half a century before them, the craft groups across the country wanted to book the *Handicraft* lecturers for such subjects as Ruskin, Morris, Oriental and native American crafts, architecture, and processes required for specific crafts. Looking back, the Boston Society of Arts and Crafts, with all its moralizing, failed as education. Neither the promised change in class segregation nor the improved distribution of art ever came to pass. It became a purely commercial operation.

But the public schools did grow as a substantial conduit for ideas on the Arts and Crafts Movement. Schools introduced social ideals and new notions about work. Schools taught work with paper, clay, wood, and metals. As Eileen Boris notes, "They strove to elevate and refine the work of the artisan and at the same time to make the work of the artisan practical and essential. . . . School room crafts taught ethics as well as skills."[24] But the question remained, What was the relationship of art making to work?

Art making in this tradition of education shifted in its interpretation of the student. From being the originator and source of an object, the student became a maker of objects in order to become a better consumer. Consuming became work. Homemaking came to be viewed as a job. Teachers turned into tastemakers. In 1903, for example, children made small houses, decorating each detail down to the wallpaper and floor coverings. In 1906, the *Schools Arts Book* recommended a course in home decoration. As Boris notes, "The school curriculum reinforced social prejudices by presenting propertied class spatial arrangements as ideal, if not the norm. In his house, one small boy said he did not care to trouble over windows in the second story of his house, since the servant girl could sleep there."[25] But no curriculum was out there for children whose family's homes had no sitting rooms.

Nonindustrial work became the subject for other voices and other publications. Gustav Stickley and his magazine, *The Craftsman*, aimed to dignify manual labor. Through manual training in public schools, Stickley foresaw saving children from slums, providing skills for the middle class, and removing children of the wealthy from their parasitic leisure. Manual training became the education too for immigrants judged in need of jobs. The newly arriving Mexicans, Jews, Slavs, and Poles had access to manual training classes, as indeed my parents did, through both public schools and vacation schools. The model perhaps was the Gary, Indiana, public school system, which from 1907 through 1938, was superintended by William Wirt, whose vision of education was that schools were responsible for compensating for all urban blight. Vocational classes were oriented toward specific trades and skills, while other parts of the curriculum included drawing, arts and crafts, nature study, laboratories, music and dancing. All were parts of a larger vision in which the school was the place not only for these, but for health care, recreation, and neighborhood life. Art making in the Gary schools primed one for trades within a caring, healthful community. Learning a trade here provided quite a contrast to the dire threats to health and safety posed by the mills.

Modern Reconciliation of Industry and Art

The variations of the interpretation of art and work are endless. But the story here cannot close without a discussion of the impact of the Bauhaus. Across Europe, the Arts and Crafts Movement had revived many variations of medieval guilds, creating a handmade style in wallpapers, silverware, jewelry, textiles, and furniture. Germans, attracted to what they saw and read, in 1907 organized themselves into their own association of German design workers. But these manufacturers, architects, and craftspeople were "intent on an improvement of production through the collaboration of art, industry and the crafts."[26] From this association grew the Bauhaus, an educational experiment, which unlike the Arts and Crafts Movement accepted industry as a viable, equal partner.

In 1919, as Walter Gropius took over leadership of the crafts school of the Weimar Academy of Fine Arts, he dreamed of creating a new profession for what he saw as a new society. The controversy of his time was between standardization, construed as the result of industry, and spontaneity, construed as pertaining to art. Through Gropius's ingenious recognition of the capacity of industry, he resolved the conflict by preserving both: "It is possible to have an infinite number of variations of every plan type by differing combinations of standard elements." In no way did industrial mass production have to squelch invention; in no way did the products of industry have to be deadly. Artists would be able to see the capacities of industry and "breathe life into the dead product of the machine."[27]

The very acceptance of the changing culture and the place of industry within it must have been energizing to all who were engaged with these questions. After artists' bemoaning of the development of industry, the Bauhaus attitude must have been an exhilarating, welcome change. Gropius's curriculum plan for the Bauhaus demanded that artists offer their talents and learn to work directly with experts in mass production. People at all levels of work experience were trained to work together in teams. Like the products they created, the Bauhaus curriculum was thought of as standardized modules. Modules consisted of both practical and formal learning, coordinated toward different ends. Learning about materials and processes was the practical end while the formal end involved art history and theory. The modules were to be taught by artists, who weren't to be called faculty but rather "masters." Lyonel Feininger, Johannes Itten, and Gerhardt Marks were among them. In addition to masters, there were the "apprentices" and "journeymen," people from ages seventeen to forty, who anywhere else might have been called students. The school was organized to enable these diverse people to work together on all projects.

In 1923 in the United States, Charles Alpheus Bennet, familiar with experiments in Germany and known for his advocacy of the manual arts, proposed a National School of Industrial Art. He said that "Such a school should cover not one industry. . . . but several groups of industries in which design in form and color is an important factor. It should be to all the art industries what post-graduate courses in the universities are to the professions. It would be a place of research. . . . It would give artists a higher type of special training than can be obtained at the present time."[28] Bennet's scheme was intended to impact young people's opportunities as well: "Such a school is much needed to elevate the standard of teaching in technical high schools, industrial schools, and vocational schools. If such a school were available . . . as a training center for the higher branches of the manual arts, such a school would supply a need."[29]

Americans were intrigued by the German innovations in relating art to industry. By 1933, five years after Gropius gave up leadership of the Bauhaus and Hans Meyer, a left-wing, politically active, community-oriented Swiss had taken over, the Nazis forced the closing of the school. Students and staff were denied access to the premises as the Nazis searched it for evidence of Communist activity. Thus began the artists' exodus to points around the globe. Their Bauhaus experience came with them wherever they settled. Klee went to Switzerland. Kandinsky went to Paris. But most "masters" headed toward the United States. Gropius came to head Harvard's School of Architecture (now Design), later to be joined by Marcel Breuer. Mies Van Der Rohe went to the Illinois Institute of Technology (then the Armour Institute). Chicago inherited Moholy-Nagy, who founded a New Bauhaus, later called Institute of Design, and Joseph Albers went to North Carolina's legendary Black Mountain College.

The rise of Hitler and the horrors that were the cause of the closing of the Bauhaus were to remain with the world too long. In that despairing climate there still were those who remained hopeful and carried on the Bauhaus's mission and convictions. American design and education benefited from the accomplishments and values of these people. They designed the objects we hold and sit on and use every day. With an unexpected twist, through the machine and standardization, the Bauhaus artists realized some aspects of the Arts and Crafts ideal. The artists became active within industry, impressing their skills and visions onto the processes of industry. Here was a larger vision in which artists altered industry and which resulted in the aesthetic pervading everyday life.

The Bauhaus also altered how people thought about art making for children and adolescents. Herbert Read, whose work was popular here, thrashed out the issues in his 1935 commentary on the Bauhaus, *Art and Industry.* He supported the idea that artists might build upon what was healthy and artistically usable in industry *and* in art. Machines in no way necessitated loss of spirit or form. Read, in short, identified the real problem as how to think out new aesthetic standards for new methods of production. Four years earlier, Read had written his *Meaning in Art* and confirmed that aesthetic sensibility exists in each person.

Read regrets that education separates the fine and applied arts and that the art of the machine age is relegated to the technical school. Read saw that the art education around him was too much oriented to fine art and to making the child an artist, divorcing the learner from what Read saw as "the significant art of his age. . . . What we do at present is to teach, not only potential artists, but the potential citizens who are to live in a modern age, the practise and technique of an individualistic art which not one boy in a million will ever practise with profit and distinction."[30]

Read's is a utilitarian complaint. His bottom line is jobs, and no employment seemed foreseeable from the archaic fine arts. "We might as well teach potential motor mechanics to drive horses," he said. "Let all other forms of art instruction be assimilated into the *Fachschule* (specialized industry schools), or where those do not exist, to the factories themselves. The only alternative is to convert the schools into factories—which is exactly what the Bauhaus was in Germany: a school with the complete productive capacities of a factory, an industrial system in miniature."[31]

From the Artist's View

This tradition of teaching brought artists, who would never have imagined themselves as fine artists because their social class neither exposed them to art nor permitted the luxury of imagining a future without earning a living. Were it not for their schools' offering Commercial Art and other courses under more modern rubrics, they might never have learned the use of certain tools, the design of letter forms, patterning for wallpapers and textiles that gave them both a livelihood and imagery for more personal work.

Artists trained in this tradition faced what Maurice Brown has called the Muse of Realization. Things that are made must work. Packaging must hold. A building must stand. From the jobs tradition, artists learn to test their tools and to control their materials.

At the same time, artists trained with a jobs orientation indirectly have been orientated, through the vocational mindset, to considering the needs of the viewer, the hypothetical consumer who will pay the bill. Some would argue that this experience is invaluable to all artists.

But above all, artists trained in this tradition face a question that never goes away, "How can art making be work for which one is paid?"

NOTES

1. Gertrude Hildreth, *The Child Mind in Evolution: A Study of Developmental Sequences in Drawing* (New York: King's Crown Press, 1941), 24, 18, 11–13.

2. Henry Turner Bailey, "The Arts and Crafts in the Public Schools" [lecture] (Worchester, Mass.: Davis Press, 1907), 5.

3. Langdon S. Thompson, "Some Reasons Why Drawing Should be Taught in Our Common Schools" [lecture] (Louisville: National Education Association, 1877), 18.

4. Betty Ring, *American Needlework Treasures* (New York: E. P. Dutton, 1987), 3.

5. Peter Schmid, *The Common School Drawing-Master, Containing Schmid's Practical Perspective* (Boston: E. P. Peabody, 1846), iii.

6. Ibid., iv.

7. Frederick M. Logan, *Growth of Art in American Schools* (New York: Harper & Brothers, 1955), 22.

8. Ibid., 21.

9. William Minifie, *Popular Lectures on Drawing and Design Delivered at the Public Meetings of the School of Design at the Mayland Institute* (Baltimore, 1854), 57.

10. *The Antefix Papers: Papers on Art Educational Subjects,* ed. Charles Callahan Perkins (Boston: Massachusetts Art Teachers' Association, 1875).

11. Eileen Boris, *Art and Labor: Ruskin, Morris and the Craftsman Ideal in America* (Philadelphia: Temple University Press, 1986), 84.

12. Charles Godfrey Leland, *The Minor Arts, Porcelain Painting, Wood-Carving, Stencilling, Modelling, Mosaic Work, &c.* (London: Macmillan and Co., 1880), 5.

13. James Parton Haney, *Art Education in the Public Schools of the United States* (New York: American Art Annual, 1908), 56.

14. Bailey, "Arts and Crafts," 3.

15. Ibid., 13, 10.

16. John Dewey, *The School and Society* (1900); reprinted in *The Child and the Curriculum, the School and Society* (Chicago: University of Chicago Press, 1956), 23–24.

17. This section was suggested by Phyllis Ewen, "Art-Making: An Alternative to Work," *The Journal* (Massachusetts College of Art), Spring 1976.

18. Boris, *Art and Labor*, 4.

19. Roger Stein, *John Ruskin and Aesthetic Thought in America, 1840–1900* (Cambridge: Harvard University Press, 1967).

20. Boris, *Art and Labor*, 4.

21. John Ruskin, *The Elements of Drawing in Three Letters to Beginners* (New York: John Wiley, 1863), xi.

22. Boris, *Art and Labor*, 10.

23. Ibid., 30.

24. Ibid., 86.

25. Ibid., 87.

26. Gillian Naylor, *The Bauhaus* (New York: E. P. Dutton and Co., 1968), 20.

27. Ibid., 30, 34.

28. Charles Alpheus Bennet, *Art Training for Life and for Industry* (Peoria, Ill.: Manual Arts Press, 1923), 51.

29. Ibid., 52.

30. Herbert Read, *Art and Industry* (1953; reprint, Bloomington: Indiana University Press, 1961), 128.

31. Ibid., 129, 313.

11

Art Making for the Spirit

The third tradition requires an entirely different attitude. Instead of thinking of the future the child will have, this form of teaching centers on the feelings and the imaginative life of the child in the present moment. We will start as before, focusing on a single child.

> Then I saw one little girl working by herself in a corner of the room almost with her back to the rest. . . . She was laying out on her desk, by touch, a string of "sausages" of clay, which she rolled and placed with great devotion, feeling their position in relation to one another. When I saw her at work she had completed one oval of such sausages and was making another inside it. She seemed to be working to some intense inner dictation so, not wanting to disturb her, I waited until . . . the others were clearing up. . . . Inside the inner oval she had placed three upright pillars, of which the middle one was the larger, more squat and hung with fruitlike appendages. . . . she looked at her work for a few moments, then ran to the front of the room where I provided a bag of powdered flint to dry up the clay. . . . She came back with a handful of this and, laughing, scattered it over the pillars. . . . "It's a rosegarden" she said . . . "it's a rosegarden and this is the wall around it. You come in here," indicating an opening in the outer wall with her finger. "But you cannot get into the garden. You have to come round that way [between the outer and the inner wall] and then you come into the garden this way." The opening of the inner oval was at the *opposite* side to the outer one and now, with her forefinger, she traced the path into the inner garden. "And here," she said, "there are fountains," and again she lifted a little of the white powdered flint and scattered it. . . . "There are fountains and there are flowers and rose-trees and lovely smells."[1]

The writer of this observation is the teacher Seonaid Robertson, who encouraged the twelve-year-old to sculpt this piece blindfolded. She did so because she believed that blindfolding helped children turn their minds inward toward their inner feelings. Her book *Rosegarden and Labyrinth* (1963) prizes making art because it permits people to encounter the feelings and wishes they quietly carry within. Teaching in this tradition, the teacher is oriented most to the student's inner life. Lessons are predicated on the importance of recognizing and activating the student's inner emotional and spiritual experience.

History

American education has a history of approach and avoidance of such inward, aesthetic, spiritual activity. People both craved and were repelled by it. Such art was not for us, at least not yet. An old debate is still ongoing. It concerns who can make art, when, and for what purposes. Back in the late eighteenth century, while many men and women here already were engaged in making and learning how to make objects we now view as art, many others agreed with John Adams that art study was something for which he, and by extension other Americans, should wait: "I must study politics and war so that my sons may have liberty—liberty to study mathematics and philosophy, geography, natural history, naval architecture, navigation, commerce and agriculture, in order to give their children a right to study painting, poetry, music and architecture."[2]

In that letter of Adams, the "painting" that his sons' children would have a right to study was hardly related to an urgent universal human need that we today recognize in all people across the world, even the poorest. Adams's art becomes something optional, which one comes to deserve and earn by having undertaken and having mastered more important and necessary matters. Adams's view still lives in the too-familiar public school schedule that relegates art to late Friday afternoons after all the other school work is done.

Americans were taught to believe that art was not in us. Art was what other people made, in other places that had other priorities. Perhaps the distrust grew from an ambivalence toward artistic Europe. People who had just left and turned their backs on Europe perhaps felt they could hardly now turn around and try to imitate her. Uneasiness with the aesthetic may also have grown here from art's association with religion, particularly with the Catholic church. Whatever the reasons, Americans doubted their entitlement to trust themselves to be the source of art.

Any emotional and spiritual content in art tended to be masked. In the minds of many, the best hope for getting anything that resembled art near children was to infiltrate schools by construing art making as being for something other than personal expression. If any art making might thrive, it would be because it promoted school study skills. Rembrandt Peale's *Graphics* of 1838 needed the protection of its subtitle: *A*

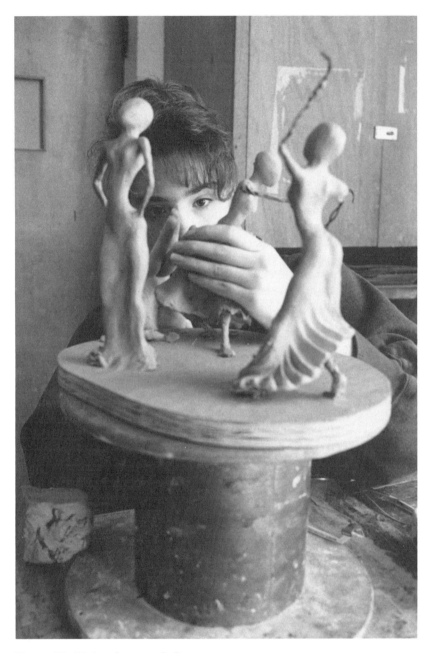

Figure 17. Giving form to feelings

Manual of Drawing and Writing. In fact, two traditions colluded, art making for study skills and for jobs. Both diminished or denied art's emotional and spiritual nourishment.

But on those occasions when educators defended the aesthetic, perhaps because they encountered resistance, they had trouble defining what they meant. We have only to refer back to Thompson's weak defense of the aesthetic advantages of drawing. The best he could say in his 1877 lecture was that drawing's purpose was to permit a person to "converse with a picture and find an agreeable companion in a statue."[3]

When educators defended the spiritual experience, art making differed dramatically from the prior two traditions. Individuals were viewed as full of feelings and ideas. Like the twelve-year-old girl described by Robertson, people are seen as creating from "some intense inner dictation." The benefit of such work was seen to be moral. Giving form to their ideas seemed both to be good for children and to make them be good. Writers benefited from a certain ambiguity in the word "goodness." Sometimes goodness was associated with the children's using their God-given natures: playing, being inventive. Sometimes goodness was associated with refinement, acquiring finer feelings, good behavior, and good taste. In the twentieth century, art making aided the child's psychological well-being. Goodness came to be linked with mental health. Creativity became a sign of it.

In the spiritual tradition, children are seen as full of ideas. Bronson Alcott's Temple School's teaching, as early as the 1830s, became a laboratory for culturing children's ideas. Alcott's method involved reflection and dialogue. Since he believed children had ideas and that they were worthwhile, he engaged them in conversations to hear what they thought. Like talk, drawing became a means for children to give form to what they saw. A drawing teacher, Francis Graeter, worked along with Alcott, encouraging the children to draw the Temple School classroom, inside and out, as well as the views they saw on walks around the school. Reflection on their ideas was incorporated even in drawing. First children were reflective in seeing and drawing what they saw. Then they reflected once again, redrawing in their journals their drawings from the art class of that day.

Books for teachers and parents also were guides. The words here signal the differences that are introduced by this tradition. As early as the mid-nineteenth century, we find concern with children's fancy, invention, imagination, beauty, self-reliance, and creativity. In the 1849 "Chambers' Educational Course," *Elements of Drawing and Perspective,* a reprint of a British manual, the author John Clark describes the child as distinguished by an appetite for making images. Since children are fond of drawing, they should do it. Good teaching should support that tendency in children: "They are delighted to scribble as their fancy suggests, or to copy toy-pictures which are presented for their amusement. . . . Followed up . . . these infant aspirations may lead to the development of a much valuable talent, that might otherwise have been left dormant and useless. . . . The exercises in the first place afford much pleasure and recreation of a harmless kind; if pursued with increasing interest, they will gradually inculcate a perception and a love of the beautiful, both in nature and in art."[4] Clark sees the child's mind as capable of inventing and expressing forms in which the child finds interest.

Drawing for Young Children (1848) is another teacher and parent guide reprinted from a British original. The author, anonymous perhaps because she was a woman, seems intimately familiar with children. This book describes children's pleasure in art making and hopes to extend that by helping children to teach themselves. The writer pleads on behalf of children's need for a few interesting occupations. Children will feel miserable, we are told, if they lack resources, like drawing, with which they can engage themselves. Drawing would "if generally disseminated, be a powerful means of increasing the innocent enjoyments, good feelings, and good taste of a community. . . . A very little assistance, encouragement, and sympathy, will enable the child to convert his rude power of imitation into a source of gratification, always increasing as he advances, and will unite it to the power of invention."[5] This 1848 guide describes children admiringly: "Besides . . . the numerous experiments on objects which they take delight in, they are constantly exerting their invention and imagination in curious imitations and recombinations of actions, gestures, and vocal sounds, &c., and feeding the mind with various wonders of animals, savages, giants, fairies, and all kinds of superior and inferior and extraordinary creations; and they are always fond of fun, which is a new and striking combination of old materials. We have only to train a faculty which is already, more or less, at work in every young child. There is a passiveness of mind . . . liable to become permanent if it is not corrected by these more self-relying and creative qualities."[6] "Self-relying and creative qualities" are not words we tend to associate with the mid-nineteenth century, but in fact not a few writers of that time made similar recommendations.

About thirty years later, all over the states children were reading a popular magazine, *Wide Awake*. One issue described a private Saturday art school in New York City, where, since 1878, children were encouraged to be children, where they pursued those "self-relying and creative qualities." After first appearing in *Wide Awake,* the news of the school was published again and again. It appeared in *Wide Awake's* story book *Some Curious Schools* (1880) and then again in many elegant gilded and chromolithographed gift editions under the title *Art for Young Folks* (1885). Miss F. E. Fryatt, the author, describes this new school called "The Children's Hour," launched by Mary Cook, one of the first pupils at the National Academy of Design. She and seven other women, all devoted to children's art training, had earlier formed a New York-based society, the "Ladies Art Association," which taught and then sent art teachers to all parts of the country. Cook chose the teacher for this special new school, Alice Donlevy, "one of the finest designers of illumination in the United States," who had been a protégée of an art education crusader, a fellow National Academy of Design alumnus, Henry Herrick.

Ms. F. E. Fryatt's text allows us to glimpse how art classes actually were taught at "The Children's Hour." One lesson in watercolor painting began with each child being encouraged to compose her or his own subject. Some chose from objects in the room, such as an adult might select for a still life, a vase or drapery. But most children selected objects frequently associated with their own age group. A boy brought in his ball. Another carried in a toy ship that he set to sail in a wash bowl. One boy brought his own bag of marbles and composed them on a blue paper and told the class, "Papa took me to a factory and I saw them blowing glass, and I know all about how the color gets in the glass."[7]

A collection of children's drawings and paintings were a feature of this novel school. The teacher encouraged children to look at these and to use other children's paintings for ideas and inspiration. The collection of drawings and paintings, solicited as they were from readers of *Wide Awake,* depicted people and places in many different parts of the country. This well-publicized school drew many curious visitors. Fryatt tells us that when the public asked Ms. Donlevy about the purpose of this enterprise and wondered if she imagined or intended that these children all would become artists, she answered: "In every case, No. . . . But I will tell you what my little people will be, if not artists in the future, at least refined, intelligent, useful citizens."[8]

While Alice Donlevy worked with her private children's classes of never more than ten, the public schools across the states inched toward a view of art making that left more room for the individual spirit than had either art for study skills or industrial drawing. Louis Prang, the lithographic entrepreneur so identified with Walter Smith and his utilitarian arguments for the public school, began to publish his own different art ideas in the late 1880s. The various editions of *Prang's Complete Course for Form Study and Drawing* by John S. Clark, Walter S. Perry, and Prang's wife, Mary Dana Hicks, showed small changes. Though the students still were required to complete identical drawing tasks, the images they were told to represent had more personal relevance. "A Toy House" was one assignment. Another, a flower pot, allowed children to draw what they saw growing in the particular flower pot before their eyes. The flower pot was significant. This object, albeit preselected, now could be drawn not by copying prepared line drawings but from the object itself seen from the child's own individual view. In just one more step, children would be making their own whole pictures showing whatever they found pleasing.

Within the next decade the three Prang authors, still cranking out drawing books used in schools across the states, took that next step. By 1898 *The Prang Elementary Course in Art Instruction* included glossy plates reproducing charcoal figure drawings by William Morris Hunt and John LaFarge, artists who exulted in expressivity. The assignments in that book, such as "Representation—Figure Studies," also provided space for the children to draw. Now they were allowed to draw whatever figure they liked in any position with any prop they wished. On the printed page titled "Representation—Figure Studies," each child completed the assignment by penciling what came to mind. Because his drawing book still survives, we can see one boy's interpretation of the task. He drew a boy standing beside a recent invention, the bicycle. For that assignment, each child would have imagined and drawn a different figure in a different posture. The Prang courses after the late 1880s devised a way that public school art included both art by the "masters" and art that reflected the individual child's ideas. New words in the "advice to teachers" section signal the changes: "increasing power of both appreciation and creation in the individual pupil . . . developing original power and facility in drawing as a means of art expression."[9] The "masters" appearing in this new Prang series were strange bedfellows. The variety of their styles was intended to encourage freedom and originality in the pupil's own work. Da Vinci, Raphael, and Rembrandt were listed as companions to contemporary, living American painters, such as Elihu Vedder, John Singer Sargent, Winslow Homer, Charles Woodbury, and Arthur Wesley Dow. Also in the list were three now forgotten women artists: Edith Clark, Lucy Fitch Perkins, and Anna Klumpke, and a curious and highly significant other source, named only as "Japanese artists."

Arthur Wesley Dow (1857–1922), one of those artists whose work was reproduced by Prang to benefit children's freedom and originality, himself became a major writer and teacher deeply influenced by the Japanese. Following the two decades of the Prang publications' virtual monopoly, Dow's methods became the most popular. His book *Composition,* copyrighted in 1899 and reappearing in many editions, became the basis for public school teaching well into this century. Dow's system offered optimism and opportunity to a new century. He refers less to painting and drawing and more to a "space art" for which his exercises are processes of assembling lines and masses. Music became Dow's analogy: "space art" was a "visual music."

Dow's experiments were an implicit criticism of academic art teaching, that is, any teaching that begins with objects, casts, or the figure. Dow regretted that for teachers academic work lacked the one vital element for which he believed art existed and that had as yet been given slight attention: beauty. He wanted to develop a method better than what he called "nature-copying," the approach by which he had been taught in Paris. Dow valued "self-expression," which he felt is usually deferred until the student has learned to draw through a course of cast drawing, perspective, history, and anatomy. Also, in regard to viewing works of art, Dow wished the pupil to respond to the object more than to facts about subject matter, history, derivation, and so on. Dow prized individual differences: if one's drawing was just like someone else's it would have no artistic value. Dow writes about the boundless possibilities of Mind and sees art as the expression of the personality of its creator.[10] Here was the spiritual tradition formed for the public school.

Dow's revolution would come about through his comparative study of the arts of many nations. Once back in Boston, with his interest in Japanese art and his acquaintance with the Japanese art expert Ernest Fenellosa, Dow formulated his new art education program, spending years in his Boston studio working out new ideas with the only recently available Japanese art materials.

Dow's *Composition* was a success. It caught on in schools because his methods were flexible. They were capable of being adapted to students of different ages. He wasn't discouraged by the child's lack of proficiency. Dow admired the young pupils whose work attempts to embody beauty in lines on paper, which he expected would lead to a desire to know more fully the character and shape of things. The success of his new methods was also due to their capacity to fit into various time schedules. Dow's exercises can vary and expand according to the age of the pupils and the limits of time. Appealing, too, must have been Dow's attempt to universalize art. His was a "world art." Dow's overarching concept of art included more than just Europe.

Americans could be less nervous learning from Sesshu and Kano Tanyo alongside Giotto and Leonardo. Also welcome was Dow's appreciation of art viewing as a basis of art making. His era's burgeoning of cheaper art reproduction made Dow's approach seem modern, taking advantage of what was newly available. Dow believed that nature will not teach the student composition. The student must learn as other artists like Giotto, Francesca, Kanawoka, and Turner learned, by the study of art itself and by their own continual creative effort.

Teachers crossed over the threshold into the new century with a new art teaching method, the novel content of which was epitomized by new words such as "notan" (the interaction of darks and lights) and new concepts such as "space art" and "visual music." This was the time when everyone was talking about being "modern." Being based in New York City, Dow no doubt had special influence on that city's teachers. His art ideas, though formed in the last years of the nineteenth century, meshed well with the art ideas also generated in New York at the Armory Show. Dow's would have been the words art teachers spoke to children such as my parents, who were in school in the teens and twenties. That is why "self expression" and "expressing one's personality" became such significant words in my mother's later criticism of her education.

The modern ideas were there, ready for others to pick up. Charles Woodbury and Elizabeth Perkins, who taught as a pair, had a following of adults, many of whom studied with them, not only to become better teachers, but because of their own art making ambitions. Many of those who were teachers got ideas from Woodbury and Perkins that they could bring to their classrooms. In the 1930s Woodbury and Perkins ran *The Art of Seeing* summer schools in Maine and Massachusetts. Their course, named after their 1925 book, reflected the book's popularity. The summer school brochure read: "Prove through Line and Color What You See, Why You See, What is Worth Seeing." Inside the folder was another slogan: "Mental Training through Drawing, Strict Integrity of Personal Expression." Some phrases in it are reminiscent of Dow. Others suggest that his influence was weakening. These new teachers promoted "sight training," a reform in the attitude toward vision. "The process of seeing is not the simple one of directing the eyes at a special spot and getting a correct and literal visual image as a result. . . . We do not take the trouble to look unless we have special interest in doing so."[11] Their teaching grows out of recognizing and validating what children watch and pay attention to. Woodbury and Perkins's tour de force was to develop a system of teaching that detached drawing from art. Drawing simply was one of the child's natural modes of expression.

In the 1920s Woodbury and Perkins had already charted the development of drawing in the child. According to their sequence, seeing leads to wanting to touch; touch is the reason for gesture; then reaching and gesture lead to drawing. Drawing is the method whereby individuals personally express themselves. According to these two teachers, all learning comes from experience reacted to by our spontaneous personal choices.

The objective throughout the spiritual tradition is "to leave open avenues for original observation."[12] Perhaps the seed of the Woodbury and Perkins approach, thirty years before, was the Prang drawing book of 1898 with its tentative, slightly shifting position in which the authors encouraged children to draw "the figure" in whatever ways interested them. The emphasis in this tradition is on how drawing affects the mind. The accomplishment of the final product was not the issue. The motives, ideas, and feelings of the child were what mattered.

As we noted earlier, even in the early nineteenth-century drawing manuals this tradition is distinguished by its respect for children's having their own mental resources. The child is viewed as full of ideas. The spiritual tradition encourages the expression of whatever is inherent in human development and allows it to unfold. Adult information and direction are seen as deterrents to the child's arriving at a private sense of what is important and what is beautiful.

Though these ideas gained currency and were associated with many individuals, their popularity in American twentieth-century public schools is mainly due to Viktor Lowenfeld, through his teaching, lecturing, and most important, his writing of *Creative and Mental Growth.* Though, as we have seen, "creativity," "self-expression" and "expressing personality" were in currency well before 1947, the date of his first edition, Lowenfeld made these into household words. Lowenfeld's methods fit in this tradition because of the seriousness he gave to children's feelings about their experiences. He writes of the "inner spirit" that comes from using one's own resources at whatever is one's stage of development. According to Lowenfeld, "If the child expresses himself according to his own level, he becomes encouraged by his own independent thinking by expressing his own thoughts and ideas by his own means. The independent, thinking child . . . will tackle any problem, emotional or mental, that he encounters in his life. Thus his expression also is an emotional outlet."[13] Art making, once thought to be a route to goodness through morality and finer feelings through the perception of beauty, now has taken on the mid-twentieth-century form of goodness, mental health.

Lowenfeld's concern was to preserve children's creative confidence. He blamed modern education for inhibiting children's natural powers and believed the way out of our problems was by training teachers who would alter and improve conditions by becoming appreciators of child development. Preservation of the aesthetic spirit depended more on knowing about children than on knowing about art. It is no accident that these ideas gained currency in the United States exactly when abstract expressionism was in the ascendancy in the New York art scene. In the eyes of abstract expressionist artists and critics, no aesthetic canon was available or desirable. What mattered was a process of authentic expression, being intimate with the medium and finding out what you and it could do. Abstract expressionists claimed they were concerned with process. Their growth required that their art change continually. An appealing final product was a trap one had to work to avoid. No product should take precedence over process. In *Creative and Mental Growth*, Lowenfeld warns us that though the best-intentioned teachers have heard that "the working process is of greater importance than the final outcome,"[14] they still lay stress on the final product. Teachers unwittingly may fall into the same trap the artists tried to avoid: seeking and prizing a certain look in their final product.

During the years when he was a student at the Art Students' League in New York, Mark Rothko had heard a lot about "expression."[15] For Rothko, making art became the expression of his personality. Therefore it isn't surprising that even with his acknowledged history at the Art Students' League studying with Max Weber, himself a student of Dow's, Rothko was fond of saying he was self-taught. The ideal of the time was to be uninfluenced. Rothko was one—though hardly the only—artist engaged with current ideals about art and children.

From 1929 through 1952 Rothko taught art to children in New York's Center Academy. Teaching enabled him to have an income and "to test his theory and reinforce his growing belief in art as man's expression of his total experience in the world."[16] In the mid-1930s, Rothko drafted a speech celebrating ten years of the art program at the Center Academy. He told his audience at the school that children's art taught viewers "the difference between sheer skill and skill that is linked in spirit, expressiveness and personality." In Rothko's approach to teaching, "the result is a constant creative activity in which the child creates an entire child-like cosmology which expressed the infinitely varied and exciting world of a child's fancies and experiences."[17] Rothko studied the literature on art education and children's artistic development. His sketchbooks include quotations from Franz Cizek, the Viennese teacher and advocate of child art, who taught through the first twenty years of this century by "the simple method of not teaching at all in the accepted sense, but letting the children teach themselves."[18] Cizek's words and student work were published and circulated around the world. They inspired Rothko for more than twelve years to take careful notes on what he learned from the children he taught. As Dore Ashton comments, "Rothko's notes on child education are invariably fervent."[19]

The aesthetic spirit of the twentieth century brought the artist and the teacher together. Many times they were one and the same person. Some American artists sought in children a way to make peace with a society that questioned the right of the artist to exist. Spiritual education became a way artists made themselves at home here. Perhaps they felt what Peter Marzio has said of the nineteenth-century art crusaders: "The true artist in a democratic society has to be a teacher."[20] A strong relationship exists between the mid-twentieth-century artists' need for tools for introspection and then-current ideas about the spirit and experience in children's art education. In this century, teaching children an approach to art making for the spirit became an opportunity not only for helping children but for aiding adult artists' appreciation of their own work process.

From the Artist's View

From my view as a painter, the art class—in this tradition—was the one time in my early schooling where I found it truly made a difference what I liked. The work required calling up images of feelings, interests, loves, and enthusiasms. This is what artists do. Because the only answer comes from the self, this approach is full of unknowns. Here is the beginning of the artist's process Maurice Brown has described, that tacking and trimming of a sailing ship at sea.

Artists work with their own experience. Perhaps through the invitation, say, to compare van Gogh's bedroom to their own and then to draw their own, the young person first encounters something they will never forget, about how private experience may be the source of their own creative work. To learn that each work and each artist is unique, that only each of us can supply our own answers, that the concentrated effort must be to search within, is to learn what every artist knows. This experience may fuel work for a lifetime.

NOTES

1. Seonaid M. Robertson, *Rosegarden and Labyrinth* (London: Routledge & Kegan Paul, 1963), 6–7.

2. John Adams, *Letters of John Adams, Addressed to His Wife*, edited by his grandson, Charles Francis Adams, letter no. 178, 1780 (Boston: Charles C. Little and James Brown, 1841), 2:68.

3. Langdon S. Thompson, "Some Reasons Why Drawing Should be Taught in Our Common Schools" [lecture] (Louisville: National Education Association, 1877), 23.

4. John Clark, *Elements of Drawing and Perspective Embracing Exercises for the Slate and the Blackboard Chambers' Educational Course* (New York: A. S. Barnes & Co.), iv.

5. Anonymous, *Drawing for Young Children* (New York: Charles S. Francis, 1848), 3.

6. Ibid., 7.

7. F. E. Fryatt, "The Children's Hour: A Novel Art School," in *Some Curious Schools* (Boston: D. Lothrop and Company, 1880), n.p.

8. Ibid.

9. John S. Clark, Walter S. Perry, and Mary D. Hicks, *Prang's Elementary Course in Art Instruction* (Boston: L. Prang Co., 1898).

10. See Arthur Wesley Dow, *Composition: A Series of Exercises Selected from a New System of Art Education* (New York: Baker and Taylor, 1899).

11. Charles Herbert Woodbury and Elizabeth Ward Perkins, *The Art of Seeing* (New York: Charles Scribner's Sons, n.d.), 3, 4.

12. Ibid., 32.

13. Viktor Lowenfeld, *Creative and Mental Growth* (New York: Macmillan, 1947), 4, 7.

14. Ibid., iv.

15. Dore Ashton, *About Rothko* (New York: Oxford University Press, 1983), 23.

16. Ibid., 19.

17. Ibid., 20.

18. Francesca Wilson, *A Lecture by Franz Cizek* (Children's Art Exhibition Fund, 1921), 1.

19. Ashton, *About Rothko*, 20.

20. Peter C. Marzio, *The Art Crusade: An Analysis of American Drawing Manuals, 1820–1860* (Washington, D.C.: Smithsonian Institution Press, 1976), 18.

12

Art Making for Understanding Ourselves and Others

Developing the concept of our field's traditions has engaged me for many years. For the volume edited by Stephen M. Dobbs, *Arts Education and Back to Basics* (1979), I first wrote about the three traditions I have just traced. At that time, though the three embraced a good portion of art making in schools, some approaches fit nowhere. Graduate students pointed out to me that a line of thinking yet to be represented needed to include the many variants of teaching organized around issues of community, group socialization, multiculturalism, or as it was once called, intergroup relations.

Their criticism prompted me to search to see what the roots of such work might be. As a result, I have now identified a fourth tradition, one of which Langdon Thompson never would have dreamed. First I shall describe how such teaching might look in a classroom today. Then, I will trace the way back to its origins.

Because Jorge and Edward need more space, their teacher suggests that they unroll their five feet of brown wrapping paper on the corridor floor just outside their second grade room. After some discussion, the children settle on painting a city park. Their paper, longer than they are tall, offers them plenty of room to paint all the things they imagine; the kids' homes just outside the park's edges, the spaces where kids play on see-saws and slides while grown-ups watch, paths where kids bike, trees for kids to climb, and perhaps even a pond for ducks.

They decide to paint the big areas first. Jorge starts the grass at one end. Ed starts it at the other. Jorge adds the trees. Then, in scale with his trees, he inserts his little figures biking and walking. Meanwhile Ed is painting people too. His are much larger than Jorge's. They eye each others' work. Ed brings the yellow paint to the middle of the mural, sits down on the floor. Swirling his brush in giant circles on the top half of the mural he forms his sun, making it larger, filling in much of the sky. Jorge yells, "You wrecked it."

Figure 18. Widening the spectrum of the art we show

Children such as Jorge and Ed not only differ in terms of their developmental stages and sophistication in art skills, they also differ in temperament. Jorge darts from one corner to the other five feet away, quickly placing his little people. Ed is slower. He works sensuously, circling his sun over and over again. Many differences appear between any pair of students. Had the teacher paired a girl and a boy, a whole new set of issues would have entered the picture. So, too, if the teacher had introduced an older child. What difference might it have made if one of the pair had been born in another country, had known different kinds of parks, say, in Sweden or Japan? What if one girl, who had spent her first five years in Haiti, decided to paint all the houses around the park bright pinks and orange and blue the way the wooden houses are in Port-au-Prince? Her partner, who knew nothing of such houses, might well have objected, saying, "No. All houses are brick!"

In this section we look at art making in the fourth teaching tradition, the one in which teachers use art making to help children understand themselves and others. The teacher emphasizes interpersonal awareness. Students learn that art making can be both a reflection of the self and an occasion for relating oneself to others. Children are helped to see both likenesses and differences between individuals in pairs, in small groups, and across cultures. Children learn that art objects always mean something to the people who make them, and sometimes people's intentions require a special effort to understand.

The teacher who planned the mural making lesson for Jorge and Ed expected conflicts. She believes mural painting by pairs or groups of children is worthwhile because students express their ideas and each child learns to consider how the other person thinks. The teacher's goals with such a lesson are to have the students see the differences among them and to coordinate their ideas in some mutually agreeable ways. Art making becomes the way a group of students consider who the other person is, asking, Who am I? Who are you? How are we similar? How do we differ? Art making is an activity in which individuals' different styles of performance are quite obvious, as are the unique objects each person produces.

But in this tradition the teacher's goal is not exclusively social or psychological. This tradition also teaches about art. Students learn that painting is another form of telling. We do different things with paint than we do with words. On the brown wrapping paper, in colors, shapes, and sizes, children can show things they saw either as they look or how they wished they might be. They can also picture things they have never seen. Art making is so wide open that it can be an arena for negotiating their differences, as Jorge and Ed find out in finishing their mural. In the past, art's style changes may even be seen as a kind of negotiation. It is usual for one person to influence another person.

Another aspect of art that children learn is how much the artwork can matter. They learn how much feeling they can pour into their work. Children learn that they can see bits of themselves in what they make. Art is making one's own ideas be real. They come to be there for everyone to see. Students can come to understand that even art objects in museums are products of particular people who had temperaments, strong feelings, and ideas.

Students also learn that art grows from each person's uniqueness. Everyone who has taken a studio art class knows this. From one single assignment, even drawing from the same still life, varieties of interpretations emerge. Teachers working in the fourth tradition explicitly explore these differences. Unlike other school subjects where one right answer may be what the teacher seeks, in this tradition of teaching, differences are what matter most. Many responses are better than one.

People familiar with visual art might ask, What is new about this approach? Everyone who teaches any studio process makes reference to other people's work. Doesn't teaching each art making process, whether with clay or fibers or pencil or wood, bring to the well-trained teacher's mind different examples made by many people, even of different cultures? Since teachers show these objects to students, don't they thereby teach them about differences?

Yes and no. It is safe to say that all three of the teaching traditions we've just studied may do that. The study skills approach to art teaching may deal with people's differences as a way of reinforcing concepts in geography or social studies. In the jobs tradition, other cultures become source books for marketable form and pattern ideas for packaging, fashion, or graphic design. In the spiritual tradition, art of other people stimulates feelings and emotions that may be directed toward the student's own reflection. But the teaching that belongs in the fourth tradition is different from these three. Its objective is to help students ask, Who am I? Who are you? Empathy is what matters. Only when the objective of art making is the development of an awareness of self and others would the teaching approach be classified within this tradition.

History

The fourth tradition is younger than the other three. Teaching shifted its emphasis to the explicit encouragement of children's questions— Who am I? Who are you?—only when this country's big cities faced new problems. Several changes in education prepared the way for this new goal for art teaching. The first change is already familiar to us. It is the recognition that even a child could make art, inspired by Rousseau, who valued most not the art of museums but the awkward drawings that children created as they faced nature. This first change involved a growing appreciation of the normality of art making. Art could be made not only by the great genius or even the privileged person but also by ordinary people, even children.

The second change had to do with the classification of objects: What counts as art? Though most people are not aware of it, the concept of the art object is always changing. This is a tricky matter. For centuries, many objects we now consider art were not so classified. Only since the Renaissance have artists and patrons striven to elevate frescoes, oil paintings, and sculpture above the level of manual labor.[1] Through much of Western European history nothing made by children was considered art. But romanticism in the late eighteenth and early nineteenth century radically widened not only the public's notion of who could make art but the categories of objects to be called art. As children's forms came to be called "art," other forms, folk and traditional arts, formerly outside the pale of high art, also were included as "art."[2]

But two additional societal changes were necessary before schools created a place for the interpersonal goal for art making. One was our nation's growing heterogeneity. The other was a public response to it: a willingness, even eagerness, to look at and respect our differences. The two didn't occur simultaneously.

Let's look first at the facts of our heterogeneity. In the past hundred and fifty years, the United States has become more and more pluralistic. In the decade just before World War I, immigration averaged nearly a million a year. Thousands of strangers were struggling to find their way here. In recent years, more than a million people annually have become legal permanent residents. Their children sit in today's classrooms, eager to learn English and looking for help in their own languages: French, Chinese, Spanish, Portuguese, Japanese, Vietnamese, Khmer, Russian, and more.

For a long time this country has seen itself as one dominant culture. New groups had to conform. Education followed that spirit. Fortunately, we as a people kept redefining ourselves. Teachers realized they needed to address the students' needs. Americanization became the buzzword, but people debated how that word should be intepreted. Now our laws demand that neither language, nor culture, nor physical, nor intellectual, nor gender differences may be a basis for exclusion from school. As the laws change, schools change. Art making in schools also changes.

In summary, four changes in attitude led to the pluralism necessary for teaching in this tradition. They were: (1) that the ordinary person, and indeed child, may be an artist; (2) that objects other than traditional "high art" objects were art; (3) that our population's heterogeneity was growing; (4) that people were increasingly willing to confront diversity. Given these four preconditions, how did the more interpersonal view of art teaching develop? I see it as, not surprisingly, splitting off from another tradition: the art teaching that prepared students for jobs. The industrial drawing movement imported here by Walter Smith relied upon art examples from Europe. A British repository of graphic forms called *The Grammar of Ornament* (1868) was the primary source that fed art students pattern ideas from around the world. Students imitated and practiced these ornamental designs, as if they were applying them to the products fabricated by local industries: wall coverings, textiles, lace tablecloths, and ironwork.

This most important work, preparing the way for the new tradition, was written by Owen Jones, an Englishman. Jones explained his work as an effort to organize the testimony of travelers who confirmed that "there is scarcely a people, in however early a stage of civilization, with whom the desire for ornament is not a strong instinct."[3] His lavishly chromolithographed volume acquired by public school libraries here in the United States introduced students to the world's many cultures. He labeled the images "Egyptian, Assyrian, Persian, Greek, Pompeian, Roman, Byzantine, Arabian, Turkish, Moresque, Indian, Hindoo, Chinese, Celtic" and "Ornament of Savage Tribes" (referring to the forms on objects from Fiji, the Sandwich Islands, New Hebrides, Tahiti, and New Zealand).

Though it was nowhere stated as its aim, I believe Jones's work helped people acknowledge the varieties of art histories that people of different cultures brought with them when they settled in industrialized centers. The generations of students who saw this book in America were the same people facing growing numbers of puzzling foreigners in their midst. In cities like New York and Chicago they saw people from some of the cultures represented in this book.

The Grammar of Ornament, and the industrial drawing movement that grew along with it, not only embodied a cultural pluralism, but it also established new ideas about what was art. Textiles, pottery, weapons, basket weaving, tiles, forms outside the fine arts wre grouped together as expressions of people's aesthetic. Readers of the book learned to admire folk and traditional objects and patterns applied to them. Even tattooing counted as art: "Man's earliest ambition is to create.

To this feeling must be ascribed the tattooing of the human face and body, resorted to by the savage to increase the expression by which he seeks to strike terror on his enemies or rivals, or to create what appears to him a new beauty."[4]

Owen Jones was a cultural romantic. To him peasants in all their poverty seemed rich in art. People in distant nations, devoid of industrialization, preserved an artistic integrity that we in urban industrialized societies unfortunately had lost. Manufacturing was a poison, and the antidote for it was artistic decoration, or, better yet, the creation of the whole object, handmade.

Jones drew a parallel between the beauty of the forms remote peoples create and the art of children. The diverse world of art that he cataloged in his book was proof to him of the same appetite to make art that we see everyday in children around us. As he put it, "The efforts of a people in an early stage of civilization are like those of children, though presenting a want of power, they possess a grace and naivete rarely found in middle age, and never in manhood's decline."[5]

When Jones observed that "the works of a people in an early stage of civilization are like those of children," he was saying that children had their own personal expression and artistic integrity. But Jones revealed his cultural chauvinism and condescension by classifying children's art making with that of peasants or "primitive" people. Nevertheless, his was a new viewpoint in a more modern cosmopolitan city, and schools could be the institutions that protected and nurtured these capacities.

The nineteenth century was engaged in a vast, worldwide search for beautiful objects. Travelers often became collectors who brought back treasures, many of which fortunately were given to newly established museums. Thus two notions of pluralism spread. One was an appreciation of the fact that the people of the world were rich with cultures of their own. The second was an acceptance that whatever these people made, however naive, decorative, or expressive the forms, was art. Because of changing attitudes, the schools, coping with the hordes of immigrants, may have had a bit more curiosity and respect for the various unfamiliar cultures in their midst. But it was the settlement house movement, not the schools, that first applied these new attitudes to the teaching of art. Its leaders, who broke ground on so many social issues at the turn of the century, did so also in terms of art teaching. The approach they developed fits this fourth tradition only partially. They did not yet ask, Who am I ? Who are you? They concerned themselves mostly with the second question, Who are you?

The Vision of Hull-House

The interpersonal use of art making was part of a social experiment: Chicago's Hull-House, created to provide a center for civic and social life for the poor, needy immigrants who were arriving in Chicago in the late nineteenth century. Hull-House had many agendas. Some were direct services. Educational programs included a kindergarten, day nursery, drama groups, clubs, concerts, multilingual lending library, and classes and art galleries. Other direct services were a relief fund, a public kitchen, and even the prototype for meals-on-wheels, an outgoing food service for invalids. Of all the services, it is reported that the Butler Art Gallery was in even more demand than the public kitchen!

Hull-House also instituted and maintained public educational and philanthropic enterprises to raise public awareness of the conditions of the poor. Hull-House served too as an agency for research and advocacy for political action to improve conditions. As a result of Hull-House's activism, Chicago passed child labor laws, anti-sweat shop laws, sanitation and building codes, and established juvenile courts and a system of playgrounds.

This ambitious social project had art as its center in three particular schemes; the Butler Art Gallery, the ongoing studio art classes, and the Labor Museum. These three served as probes, sending out feelers as to how art making could serve the needs of people who were at the diametrically opposite end of society from those most nineteenth-century Americans associated with art.

We know that Hull-House's founder, Jane Addams (1860–1939), went to England, as many Americans did, to get ideas. She was seeking models for institutions that didn't exist here. Two centers similar to her then indistinct vision of Hull-House already existed in London. One was Toynbee Hall and the other was Walter Besant's People's Palace. Seeing these gave her a mind full of ideas with which she returned to Chicago, where she rented an old mansion that was to become Hull-House.

When Jane Addams, with her former Rockford Female Academy classmate Ellen Gates Starr (1859–1940), developed art ideas for Hull-House, where did their ideas come from? As Stankiewicz[6] outlined, Addams and Starr started off with different sorts of art exposure. Addams had studied watercolor painting, while Starr had grown up watching her paternal grandmother weaving and spinning. As they traveled and studied in Europe, what drew their attention? Might they have seen actual objects such as those on which Jones's illustrations were based and that London's Victoria and Albert Museum was then collecting by the wagon load? Might they have been influenced by Owen Jones's characterization of the world's cultures?

Whether or not Addams read Jones, she shared his romanticism. She wrote of her own struggle with art in that "Dresden winter" of her European tour when she was "given over to much reading of 'The History of Art' and to much visiting of its art gallery. I would invariably suffer a moral revulsion against this feverish search after culture."[7] Jane Addams preferred the crafts. She was moved by seeing people practice them. Seeing a woman "spinning a thread by the simple stick spindle so reminiscent of all southern Europe gave me the clew [*sic*] that was needed." Years later Addams wrote of her "overmastering desire to reveal the humbler immigrant parents to their own children" through their craft skills. She worried that women expert in their crafts had "lost their hold on their Americanized children."[8] Generations who were becoming alienated from each other, and people with so little language in common they could barely talk, each might have some craft skill that Addams wanted to perpetuate.

It was a commonplace to see fine art as a bastion of the wealthy. It was a radical idea to conceive of the poor as having an interest in art. But that was the idea Addams and Starr shared. Addams observed that "older immigrants do not expect the solace of art in this country. . . . One Italian man expressed great surprise when he found that Americans liked pictures."[9] She realized that the people who loved art in their native lands didn't even know a public art gallery existed in their own city. This was one symptom of a pattern she saw of "extreme isolation," of people ghettoized and trapped in their impoverished neighborhoods. So art was brought to Hull-House by establishing the Butler Art Gallery, the first building erected for Hull-House, opening in June 1891. The Art Institute of Chicago, which Ellen Gates Starr's aunt Eliza Starr had helped found, agreed to prepare loan exhibits for the gallery. It continued to do so until the Art Institite itself opened for free on Sunday afternoons. Addams proudly described the Butler Art Gallery as "the first permanent art gallery in an industrial district, [which] proved even more popular than the public kitchen."[10]

In fact, Hull-House had three different ideas of how art could be meaningful in the lives of the industrial neighborhood. Viewing art loaned from the Art Institute of Chicago was one. Another was to offer the people opportunities to actually paint, draw, and make prints. The third was the Labor Museum.

From 1893 until her death in 1942, Enella Benedict created art studios at Hull-House and she taught classes that were held in them: classes in painting, etching and lithography, and nature sketching.[11] They were filled by young and older people who, as Jane Addams wrote, were "escaping from dreariness."[12]

Sharing an idea growing at that time, Addams and Starr saw art interests an inevitable consequence of skill in handwork. They saw those skilled at their culture's handiwork as ripe for more opportunity to share what they knew. That led to their creation of the third Hull-House art program: the Labor Museum. The European peasants in Hull-House's midst, however poor, seemed to Addams and Starr makers of a pure, unspoiled, and dying art. The people too seemed vestiges of a passing world. The Labor Museum created at Hull-House displayed these vanishing art forms and the idealized people who created them. Each Saturday night Hull-House neighbors were invited to come and demonstrate their traditional skills.[13] At the Labor Museum they not only demonstrated rug hooking, spinning, and basket making but also sold the products of their labors. Loans from Chicago's Field Museum to the Labor Museum enriched the display, so that people could view objects made by the immigrants' own ancestors. Sicilian, Greek, Dutch, Irish, Syrian, and Russian treasures offered people the opportunity to reminisce and perpetuate their folk arts. It also gave them a sense of continuity and value, helping them to bridge their European and American experience. The goal here was to offer neighborhood people a way to show who they were. Their crafts became the means of appreciating other people.

Of the three Hull-House art endeavors, the Butler Art Gallery, the studio classes, and the Labor Museum, the one most explicitly devoted to interpersonal relationships was the Labor Museum. It was a model for art programming devoted to helping people understand one another, even across barriers of culture and language.

The Schools

Had Hull-House not been good at establishing formal connections between institutions, perhaps its innovations would have been limited. But Hull-House wanted to export art ideas to the city at large, and its mission grew to include the extension of its activities to greater Chicago. So, though the initial concept was to bring art to Hull-House through cooperation with the Art Institute of Chicago and then with the Field Museum, the influence went in both directions. As much as objects came into Hull-House, the more populist view of art spread out into Chicago itself. The Art Institute, for example, became sensitive to people who couldn't afford to pay, and it established free days.

Another target, particularly of Ellen Gates Starr, was Chicago's schools. But the development of art making programs sensitive to differences, that could help people understand others, was no continuous story of progress. There were ups and downs. The program Ellen Gates Starr brought to the Chicago public schools lacked the vision of her work at Hull-House. In 1893 Starr had founded and served as the first president of the Chicago Public School Art Society, feeding "the hungry individual soul . . . [that] . . . without art will have passed unsolaced and unfed."[14] Like others in her time, Starr felt that people's aesthetic was being contaminated by industrialization. If they imitated American taste, the children of rural peasants now in Chicago were at risk of losing their artistic sensibility. These after all were the same children Addams worried about, who were becoming alienated from their own parents, the makers of the pure forms on view at the Labor Museum and the descendants of the makers of the objects from the Field Museum. Starr believed the schools could stem the tide.

However, in the schools the arts were seen neither as bridges to students' homeland cultures nor as sources of pride and self-esteem. Instead, they promised moral improvement. Integrity and honesty of construction were attributes believed to permeate not only art objects, but also the lives of those touched by art. Handmade things were signs of the good life. Weaving, it was said, improved women's moral fiber! Perhaps there was more talking about the virtues of handwork than the doing of it. When Hull-House started, Addams regrets, schools offered little in actual handwork.[15]

The art that Starr brought to the Chicago public schools didn't involve making objects at all. Her emphasis switched from art making to viewing. The Chicago Public School Art Society, which she initiated and then directed, was an offshoot of her idea of a Hull-House art collection. She saw to it that a set of framed study-photographs, largely of paintings, was made available for use in Hull-House's art classes and was also available on loan to individual students who requested them. The Chicago Public School Art Society expanded the loan collection and extended an invitation to the public schools to use it. The aim of the society was to cultivate the physical appearance of schools. Since the children were from poor families whose homelife was seen as deprived, the society decided that schools should become surrogate homes. Rather than appreciating the distinct and rich cultures these people had, the society sought to impose taste. Instead of showcasing the talents and skills of the immigrants, instead of giving them opportunities to make things of significance to them, the society emphasized what the people lacked. The society collection became known not only for photographs of paintings but also for its original prints and plaster casts that families and schools could borrow, as they could borrow books from a public library, to improve the aesthetics of their surroundings.

The Chicago Public School Art Society surveyed most schools, checking their aesthetic conditions. They didn't trust that teachers had their own taste. The society's activists appropriated the schools, decorating them as if they were their own. By 1914 the society had made an impact on the curriculum. Schoolchildren were organized in groups to view art in museums. According to the mission of the society, the art museum trip supported the art spirit that was everywhere else threatened by modern life.

How did someone who had appreciated the importance of making art in the settlement house context forget that to which she had been so sensitive? Once engaged with the schools, the settlement house movement's leader changed. She became a "moral environmentalist."[16] Contrary to the Labor Museum ideals, all art forms were not treated as equals. What had been respect became condescension. What started as an appreciation of people's differences subtly shifted to aesthetic conversion. Starr's contribution to the Chicago public schools lacked a social vision. Children tended to be kept in their social place so that, for example, the manual arts of the jobs tradition was the preferred art for children in working-class districts.

From our position at the end of the century, we may wonder about that romantic belief about the purity of "peasant crafts." Why did Starr not transplant her beliefs into schools? Were the leaders at Hull-House and its counterparts in New York, Richmond Hull-House and the Greenwich House, and in Boston, Denison House and the South End House, caught up in an upper-class reconstruction of an imagined "traditional culture"? Was this "traditional culture" too far removed from the reality of children's needs to be useful in teaching them?

Immigration presented American education with a tricky legacy. As different people arrived in the cities, Americans tried to decide what to make of them. With a slight adjustment, any one-room schoolhouse, some imagined, might offer the same promise that the Labor Museum had offered. Some still thought schools could conserve these otherwise disappearing arts. Teachers could take on the role of surrogate parents. Teachers, who so often are asked to fill in the gaps left elsewhere in society, were told that they could preserve the old traditional arts. Even if they had no handcraft in their own heritage, they could learn some token skills that would apply to crafts of different cultures. With some practice they could then teach children to make traditional furniture, embroideries, weavings, toy wagons, and holiday ornaments. *The*

School Arts Book, a magazine born at the start of the century, was dotted with ideas for all children to learn to make traditional folk arts of different cultures, for example, Norwegian and Swedish embroidery and dolls in traditional dress. As part of its multiculturalism, in the year 1911 the magazine featured one culture each month on its front cover. Each issue had a large graphic form representing a particular culture: September was the Egyptian papyrus; October, the Greek anthemion; November, the Assyrian palmette; and December, the Roman acanthus, proof that art was about the world's diversity.

By the 1920s the idea of traditional crafts in schools was not entirely lost but it was less rooted in the ethnic traditions. The motive for teaching crafts had changed. Crafts were less about passing on different art traditions and instilling ethnic pride and more intended to engage children in pleasurable occupations. Jane Addams noted that the crafts that survived in the newer education under the influence of John Dewey, then in Chicago, involved adapting handcraft "for the delight of children."[17]

Underneath the romanticism of traditional crafts a question remained. It gnawed at people. Were these new people to be a burden and a drain on American society? Or could they be expected to be clever and resourceful enough to rise out of the slums? Jacob Riis saw the perpetual movement out of the slums as proof of people's drives to improve their lives. The system of slums itself tested their mettle. Each departure from the slums was proof of these people's talents.[18]

People's differences can be seen as either good or bad. One may emphasize skills a group of people are lacking or one may see each group as having their own gifts, "hoping their roots might strike deeply into the new soil to which they were being transplanted."[19] Seeing the new people as bringing their own gifts was Allen Eaton's view in his *Immigrant Gifts to American Life* (1932). As field secretary for the American Federation of the Arts, Eaton advised those planning public art exhibitions to Americanize people by "utilizing a common interest in aesthetics to promote a better understanding of social and civic values."[20]

All over the country, statewide "Homeland Exhibitions" expressed appreciation of the immigrants' contributions. In New York City in the fall of 1921, a year's preparation culminated in that giant public festival, "America's Making Exposition," which, as I noted earlier, involved many children, probably including my own parents. The children and their families who participated in the "America's Making Exposition" saw not only immigrant traditions but also displays of contemporary widespread contributions to American life of the various cultures, including American blacks and thirty-two recent immigrant groups. The thousands who attended heard acknowledgment for the first time that immigrants were assets, bringing gifts to those already settled. Speeches, amplified by motion pictures, pageants, exhibitions, and other forms of entertainment all reinforced the spirit of appreciation and gratitude. Instead of nostalgia, the emphasis was on people's current contributions to American life. This new approach was the brainchild of the New York State Department of Education, which, through the Department of Immigrant Education, had helped sponsor previous "homeland events" in Buffalo, Albany, and Rochester. For the whole year of 1921, the "America's Making Exposition" became central to the public schools' curriculum. Children and their teachers created 2,265 pageants, which more than a million and a half New Yorkers attended.[21]

The "America's Making Exposition" signaled a shift. It is difficult to appreciate today how much learning about art and artists here in this country in the first half of this century was about forging connections between unfamiliar people. No longer were immigrants celebrated for their Old World skills. The arts were among the things for which the new foreign-born citizens were appreciated. The arts were what some of them produced here. People from foreign lands who had learned to make sculpture continued to make their sculpture here. In the eyes of many, sculpture remained a foreigners' thing. People tended to associate sculpture with men from Ireland, England, France, and Germany who happened by then to be living here.[22] For example, the now renowned sculptor Augustus St. Gaudens, whom we think of as our great American sculptor, back then was like his parents, who were identified as newly settled Irish and symbolized many families' struggles to get a foothold here. In the 1930s, when Americans were "consciously trying to cultivate the love of beauty, [it was noted that] . . . we find ourselves in possession of a wealth of resources. . . . we discover rich sources of inspiration in the contributions of men and women who have come to us from other lands."[23]

The appreciation of people's cultures had been further stirred by a national attempt to regulate immigration back in 1921 with the first "Quota Law." That law was followed in 1924 with the Johnson-Reed Act, which reduced total immigration from Europe and Asia and maintained what was called "the national origins idea," restricting people by nationality and favoring only those from northwestern Europe.[24] With the sudden reversal in immigration patterns, handmade work, and the human values associated with it, became especially prized. A certain nostalgia surrounded unusual handmade objects. With "easy transportation, factory-made products and the cinema," art, crafts, and the "festivals where workers danced their hearts out" threatened to disappear.[25] The arts needed to be protected and preserved, and museums promised some hope. They at least conserved objects. John Cotton Dana, director of the Free Library and Museum of Newark, New Jersey, particularly stimulated the care of folk art objects and wrote about their implications for education.

But the fourth tradition's ideal, understanding oneself and others, concerned not only foreigners entering the country. It had to include Americans themselves. This larger vision was to transform us all. The question was not only Who are you? but also Who am I? The whole society could become art makers; as Allen Eaton said, "Sensitive people who knew not the rules of composition and color but who felt strongly the impulse to create beautiful objects and responded to that impulse, will not only help us to appreciate more fully the folk culture of many homelands from which America is made up, but they will give us a vision of what we may reasonably hope to see in a renaissance of all the arts in this country."[26]

In some sense the art programs of the Works Progress Administration's Federal Art Project (WPA/FAP) were an effort to fulfill that vision. In the economically depressed states across the country, where governmentally initiated work projects were conceived to revitalize every part of American life, artists bloomed everywhere. Artists were employed as teachers of children, as managers of public art programs, as easel painters, as poster designers, as visual documenters of early American crafts, as muralists in public places, post offices, prisons, and airports. They trained many people who never before would have conceived of themselves making art. "The renaissance of all the arts in this country" was one hope that accompanied the WPA's working artists. As Holger Cahill, the national director of the WPA Federal Art Project for the years 1935 through 1943, said: "One of the things which the history of art indicates is that great art arises in situations where there is a great deal of artistic activity."[27] The WPA/FAP vision survives even in the project's effort to document itself: "This democratic procedure [of having the story come from the lips of the Project workers] . . . reaped a rich harvest far beyond our wildest expectations. We found that artists, contrary to prevailing opinion, have something vital to say about themselves, about their crafts, about the world they live in."[28] The WPA/FAP was the twentieth-century expression of the mid-nineteenth-century ideal of Owen Jones: every person is seen as carrying her or his own sense of beauty and capable of giving form to it.

The profession of art education in the 1941 *Yearbook* of the National Society for the Study of Education misses the richness suggested by the scope of the WPA/FAP. Art tends to be described as something that is good for you. Teaching seems to be imposing taste. Even Thomas Munro, curator of education at the Cleveland Art Museum, who argues for the wider view of what will count as art, as editor of the 1941 yearbook barely includes the notion that children have their own preferences, their own aesthetics, their own cultures. The cultural diversity that characterized the United States of the mid-twentieth century gets only brief mention in a section on the determinants of artistic ability. There Munro suggests the aesthetic influence of language and special traditions. He asks such cultural and economic questions as: "In what ways does the American environment in general predispose a child to different tendencies from those of France or Germany? That of New York City as compared with a small rural town? . . . What difference does it make whether a child grows up on a level of luxury, of modest comfort, and of bare subsistence?"[29] But the yearbook considers these questions only as abstract matters. Nowhere is there discussion of the ramifications of these for teaching.

By contrast, two years later in England, Herbert Read's *Education through Art* pushed these questions much further, right into the arena of the classroom. His book, which was popular here, had as its thesis that art should be the basis of education because it exercises people's differences. The classroom should be a microcosm for the practice of democracy. As Read put it, "The essence of democracy lies in individualism, variety and organic differentiation."[30] Read's ideal is a community of people who help each other, who allow differences. He wants to discourage society's striving to conform to one ideal.

Herbert Read believed that people perceive the world differently. These differences can be classified by types. To each type there corresponds a distinctly different form of artistic expression. The art studio is where children practice democracy. The single most important feature Read observed in classrooms was atmosphere; he noted the importance of a democratic, accepting climate that induces children to pursue their own work. According to Read, "The first aim of the art teacher should be to bring about the highest degree of correlation between the child's temperament and its modes of expression." But this is not construed for one child alone: "The purpose of education is integration—the preparation of the individual child for his place in society, not only vocationally but spiritually and mentally."[31]

What encourages individuals within a group to be themselves artistically? People continue to ask that question. In recent years the federal government has supported high school Magnet Art programs. Such programs draw diverse students away from their local schools to a school that integrates students by dint of their common interest in art. These school art programs intend to encourage individual aesthetic differences. In a sense, they revive the spirit of the "America's Making Exposition." In some schools this has led to debates about ethnicity and aesthetics. Why, only once a year in Black History Month, for example, do we see art that we should see all the rest of the year? Much is missing from art textbooks and our own teaching, and indeed from museums and galleries, that represents the diversity of the world's aesthetics.

J. Eugene Grigsby, Jr., in *Art and Ethnics*,[32] raises a related problem: in the effort to recognize diversity and to celebrate differences between people, art programs can fix people in slots. Groups are labeled, described, and celebrated. Stereotypes are perpetuated, perhaps even generated. Preservation of traditions may take precedence over individual growth. The romanticizing of ethnicities has its own inertia. Students feel pressured to conform to the available group prototypes. Grigsby points out that group identification may have its built-in protective shield against assimilation, but people shouldn't and can't be forced to keep working in the vein of their forebears. Grigsby rightly points out that today people don't even have that choice because of the too-narrow sample of visual art available. Students don't even have the opportunity to acquaint themselves with the varieties of visual heritages there are. Not only do books in the United States lack examples of art by blacks, Mexicans, Cubans, and Puerto Ricans, but they continue to perpetuate the notion that art history is the story of certain white men. By widening the spectrum of the art we show children, as Owen Jones did back in the mid-nineteenth century, we may again present to students a sense of the world's and their own imagination.

Today, school interracial, interethnic, and even intergenerational art programs continue to explore art making for its power to help us to consider how we think, how the other person thinks, and how we differ from one another. The human potential movement and the increasing use of psychology as content in education has brought group process into the classroom. *Art for Intergroup Relations Education*, a curriculum on which I worked in the 1970s, is one example. It explores the child's sense of self and the ways others accept, reject, or reward him or her. The topics of community-making are the very themes for art. *Groups*, *Prejudice*, *Feelings*, *People Change*, and *Conflict*, each a teacher's guide title, are the subjects toward which the children's art making is directed. Children's ideas and experiences determine how they express these themes. Their expressing their ideas in art becomes the route to mutual respect.

Since we don't teach the traditional crafts in the art curriculum as teachers did in 1910, since many of us no longer have our immigrant forebears who can flesh out for us the now-diluted traditions we carry within us, what can help us answer the question, Who are we? We know there are still differences, but it is hardly clear how to express them. Art making in the tradition of helping students understand themselves and others can be one way.

In this chapter I have outlined a tradition in art teaching that involves knowing more about oneself, recognizing the differences between individuals in terms of temperament, attitudes, and culture, and learning how the art making process can lead to stronger interpersonal relationships. I have traced the inputs in this tradition from Rousseau's approval of the child as artist, to the acceptance of a wider definition of art including all cultural artifacts, to seeing how these ideas served Americans in coping with the problems of America as a supposed "melting pot." The needs addressed by this tradition are by no means past. Statistics tell us that those we call minorities today are to be the majority in the not too distant future.

From the Artist's View

Artists recognize in this tradition the richness of influence. This tradition emphasizes what Maurice Brown and I both believe, that no creative prowess of the mind can be free of outside impressions. In this tradition we are all influences for one another and we are steeped in all we bring. Images and objects become reflections of self and glimpses into others. Art is no mere academic exercise. Art here is the glue, the stuff that has bound communities together for centuries.

Artists will recognize in this tradition an explosion of possibilities. Art is not just European art, but includes all the forms of cultures around the world. If my own education had been of this sort, American art, which was barely taught in the United States in the fifties and sixties, would have been available to me early. Jewish art, too. And I might have met Islamic Art, and art of the many cultures of Africa. Instead I had to find on my own the multitude of forms that inspire so many of us in folk art, domestic arts (quilting, needlework, furniture, and so on), and popular arts.

The artist gains the strongest, most real grasp of history because, as Brown writes, "it is the artist who encounters the whole of human history in his or her lifetime" (see chapter 6). Artists continually look. We look at what people make. We look for what fascinates and what resonates within us. The widening of sources for imagery can be a stimulus to new work. The cherishing, not only of the differences of objects made but of the people who make them, is the legacy artists may recognize in this sort of teaching.

NOTES

1. Rudolf Wittkower and Margot Wittkower, *Born under Saturn* (New York: Random House, 1963).

2. Diana Korzenik, "The Artist as Model Learner," in *The Educational Legacy of Romanticism*, ed. John Willinsky (Calgary, Alberta: Wilfred Laurier University Press, 1990).

3. Owen Jones, *The Grammar of Ornament* (London: Bernard Quaritch, 1868), 13.

4. Ibid.

5. Ibid., 15.

6. Mary Ann Stankiewicz, "Art at Hull-House: 1889–1901, Jane Addams and Ellen Gates Starr," *Women's Art Journal*, vol. 10, no.1 (Spring/Summer 1989).

7. Jane Addams, *Twenty Years at Hull-House* (New York: Macmillan, 1930; reprint, Urbana: University of Illinois Press, 1990), 75.

8. Ibid., 235–36, 234, 235.

9. Ibid., 372.

10. Ibid.

11. Stankiewicz, "Art at Hull-House," 36–37.

12. Addams, *Twenty Years at Hull-House*, 374.

13. Stankiewicz, "Art at Hull-House," 37.

14. Addams, *Twenty Years at Hull-House*, 372.

15. Ibid., 106.

16. Eileen Boris, *Art and Labor: Ruskin, Morris and the Craftsman Ideal in America* (Philadelphia: Temple University Press, 1986), 96.

17. Addams, *Twenty Years at Hull-House*, 106.

18. Jacob Riis, *The Children of the Poor* (New York: Charles Scribner's Sons, 1892), 2.

19. Allen H. Eaton, *Immigrant Gifts to American Life* (New York: Russell Sage Foundation, 1932), 10.

20. Ibid.

21. Ibid., 90.

22. Ibid., 117.

23. Ibid., 12.

24. *Scribner's Dictionary of American History*, 8 vols. (New York: Scribners and Sons, 1978), 8:342.

25. Eaton, *Immigrant Gifts*, 155.

26. Ibid., 158.

27. Francis V. O'Connor, *Art for the Millions* (New York: New York Graphic Society, 1973), 35.

28. Ibid., 13.

29. Guy M. Whipple, ed., "Art in American Life and Education," *Fortieth Yearbook of the National Society for the Study of Education* (Bloomington, Ill.: Public School Publishing Company, 1941), 272.

30. Herbert Read, *Education through Art* (London: Faber & Faber, 1943), 4.

31. Ibid., 104, 231.

32. J. Eugene Grigsby, Jr., *Art and Ethnics* (Dubuque, Iowa: William C. Brown, 1977).

13

Conclusion: Who Chooses?

In these chapters my priority has been to identify a range of ideas that motivate the teaching of art making. Ideas make a difference. Among other things, they suggest different ways we may envision our students. In a Martin Buber anecdote, cited by Marilyn Zurmuehlen, a teacher realizes that, though he did not choose his students, "he can choose how he thinks about them. He chooses to think beyond what they appear at the moment to what they can become."[1] Sometimes subtle differences in ideas lead to distinctly different views of students and their needs. The following examples illustrate this point.

Four Lessons

In four different eighth grade classrooms in four schools, teachers have arranged objects on a high table. Each arrangement includes a cow's skull. Around each high table a group of thirteen-year-old girls and boys are seated at individual desks. They all face the skull. Superficially these four lessons might look alike. But in each case the teacher's ideas and the rationale or objective for teaching the lesson are entirely different.

In one of the classes the students drawing the skull are participating in a science lesson. The teacher intends for them to compare the form of the cow skull with that of another animal's head they studied the day before. In the second school the eighth grade is studying the skull to develop a simplified pattern design that could be transferred to a textile to be printed on huge bolts of cloth, then cut and sewn and sold as shirts. That teacher's objective concerns having the students consider issues related to careers in one of the design fields. In the third classroom the teacher oversees students drawing the skull, helping them find their own best form for expressing their feelings about life and death. After years of teaching, this person knows how riveting a subject this is for adolescents who relish reflection and the expression of feelings. Finally, in the fourth school the teacher's objective is to have the students draw the skull in order to prompt talk about their feelings. The teacher's objective is to have students compare how people across cultures have similar feelings.

Were we looking at these four classes through walls of one-way glass that block out all sound, the student groups might all appear to be doing the same thing. Without hearing the teacher and students talking, we could not guess why the teacher was having the students do this work. But in an actual classroom situation where we do hear the teacher and students the expectations become unmistakably different.

In the eighth grade where the students are drawing the skull for a science objective, the motivation might have begun with a study of one or two slides of animal anatomy. The teacher might ask the students, "What can we learn by observing bones? Why are artists the people who documented skeletal structures? What do artists know? Why are medical illustrators still preferred for drawing scientific studies?" Students may compare the relative advantages of drawing and photography for analyzing structure.

In the second school the eighth grade is studying the skull to create a simplified pattern to be printed on huge bolts of cloth, to be cut and sewn as shirts. The teacher might distribute small samples of differently textured cloth and then ask about how the cow skull could be an inspiration for designing for each: "What features of the cow skull form might be used?" Discussion proceeds to how textile design sometimes uses recognizable references, say to skulls, and is sometimes admired for its abstraction, for the remoteness of its form from any reference. The students then might work on the problem of abstracting from the skull features that suit the specified fabric the teacher just gave them.

In the third classroom the teacher is helping students relate to their feelings about life and death, encouraging the students to generate the many personal reasons a painter might choose to work from a skull. The teacher confirms their ideas by noting that "Centuries of painters have incorporated skulls into their art for just those reasons." The teacher, standing beside a Picasso cow skull painting in actual size reproduction, asks the students to describe what they see in order to launch students into making their own skull ideas in thumbnail sketches.

Finally, in the fourth school the teacher's objective is to have the students draw the skull to prompt talk about their culture and traditions. The teacher stops everyone's drawing at a certain point to show them the popular skull-headed clay figures Mexican sculptors have made for "Dia de las Muertos" (Day of the Dead). The teacher sees the students' growing curiosity and respect for a culture new to most of them. The Day of the Dead leads to discussion of why each of us makes objects. The teacher turns the students' attention to their own values by asking, "What do each of you believe the objects we make are good for?"

The Complexity within Creating

All four lessons may be successful or deadly. As Zurmuehlen writes, the hazard in all this complexity of media and ideas is that students may be busy with materials and yet not tap into their own ideas. Such busyness substitutes "a superficial appearance of intentional symbolization for the real condition" of making art from one's own motives.[2] All depends upon whether the teacher takes the students and art making seriously enough so students become engaged with their own intentions. In each case the components of the artist's process are there. But the lesson can come alive only in the students' immersion in the making process. Teachers need to provide time and quiet so that students' minds may concentrate their hands and the paint or charcoal on whatever is happening before their eyes.

That this exciting engagement happens is due, in good measure, to the teacher's own personal convictions. Teaching starts in teachers' minds. Each skull lesson was each teacher's creative product. Before the students are presented with anything, teachers already have ideas. A teacher may recall his or her own fascination, at age thirteen, with dark, moody art. That same teacher may be fascinated by science, may be an enthusiast of the nineteenth-century naturalist Louis Agassiz, who required that all his science students learn to draw in minute detail each creature they studied. Another teacher may have just seen an exhibition of Dutch seventeenth-century paintings that include skulls and connected that with the fact a Mexican-American parent could come in as a guest artist, and demonstrate the making of those popular skull-headed Day of the Dead figures. The teachers who have designed their own skull lessons did so because of whatever their minds already hold. Teaching comes out of a context, part of which comes from the schools, part of which comes from what teachers already know about their students. Another part of the teacher's sources, of course, comes from whatever teachers themselves love. Ideally, we each take all this and adjust it to our students' stage of development.

Proponents of discipline-based art education have identified four adult roles as the sources for art teaching: the aesthetician, the critic, the art historian, and the studio artist. These roles inform one another and are interdependent. For example, the critic has studied art history and brings several theoretical models of art history to the writing of criticism. The art historian, say one who is particularly expert in the history of printmaking, ideally has actually made prints using etching, aquatint, lithography, and wood engraving and knows intimately the difference each procedure makes. Each of these roles alone involves a universe of adult concerns specific to that field. An adult in any of these four roles has taken years of courses, has read innumerable books, has viewed years and years of exhibitions and, in the case of the artist, has generated perhaps decades of images. These four expert roles may suggest an array of teaching possibilities.

But let us remember that within the role of the studio artist alone there is complexity enough to yield a bounty of ideas for teaching. The subject of this volume has been exactly that, how the artist's work may be and has been a source of ideas for teaching. Anticipating our efforts, Edmund Feldman in his 1982 book, *The Artist,* showed how the functions of the many artists active in society vary: the naive artist, the revolutionary artist, the illustrator, the folk artist, the industrial designer, the hero of the fine arts, and "the gallery idol."[3]

As if these many categories of artists (which in themselves are great simplifications) were not complex enough, Howard Becker argued in his book, *Art Worlds,*[4] also published in 1982, that the artist never can be considered as a figure alone. Artists belong to many systems. They are part of business. Artists' work may not be cordoned off from the work of other people who depend economically and socially upon their production. Though this is not the place to explore the many roles of artists, it is necessary to say that there is no one model for the artist; that there is a vast amount to know about artists' work; and that the work is subtle and complex and far beyond the grasp of children.

So how can teachers tap artists as sources in their teaching? Many things that artists know can be learned by children. Since the early nineteenth century there has been a fascination with how artists can be like young people, and vice versa.[5] Teachers have to extract from the complex world of adult artists' experiences that which is appropriate to children and congruent with their recognized needs. Because the needs of children are already coded into the general missions of schools, art making in schools tends to conform again and again to one of the four traditions. The traditions, let us remember, promoted: (1) understanding of school subjects; (2) preparation for jobs; (3) expression of feelings; and (4) making relationships between individuals in a group.

Amazingly, even when conforming to school situations, art making may retain features of the mature adult process. It is noteworthy too that adult art can remind us of what we did as children. As I said at the very start, I believe school-based art making captures different facets of the adult art making processes:

1. *The study skills tradition* teaches students that art may be *about* anything. Artists use a medium to reflect on situations they have in mind. No subject is outside of art. Just as words may help us think, so do the colors of paint and lumps of clay. For example, a painter may find interest in the different shapes of the continents, the relationships of oceans to land. As a child, Lee Krasner, and the many other children like her who drew maps in school, later had a personal, internalized way to respond to Jasper Johns's map paintings. In art teaching in the study skills tradition, children learn that in making forms artists think about anything they have in mind.

2. *The jobs tradition* teaches that artists' work is part of the economy. In any era, all products must be designed and fabricated, and everyone engaged with art at one or another stage of its production is paid. In the jobs tradition the artists' process requires professional techniques, the current type, layout and pattern making devices used in contemporary production. As new technology enters production in the world of business, so that technology enters curriculum. Today's study of computer graphics is one example.

3. *The art making for the spirit tradition* teaches students that artists seek opportunities for taking time to reflect on feelings. Centuries of artists have used painting and sculpture to reflect upon their homes, their own appearances, their feelings about aging, their love for friends and members of their family, the spiritual life, whatever is important to them.

4. *The art for understanding oneself and others tradition* teaches students that artists reflect not only on themselves. Art also celebrates likenesses and differences between individuals and across cultures. Such teaching suggests how artists of different groups use their work to express ideas of the group. Hopefully, students come away from such teaching appreciating how art making grows in the context of a community.

How Teaching Is Like Art Making

Out of all the complexity that is art making, the teacher shapes a lesson, something derived from the teacher's own personal educational history, knowledge of the needs of children, constraints of schools, and knowledge of the field of art. But from this vast array, how does one choose what to teach and who really decides?

Education is rarely talked of on the scale on which it is actually lived. Schooling is many tiny acts children and teachers do together. Most of the undertakings within schools are like lives in homes. Decisions are made on a personal and intimate scale. Even within the vast public school systems the actual classroom activity remains on a personal scale. This is one of the appeals of teaching. Yet the facts of this personal scale have eluded description. They tend to be disregarded. Education is also work done by people not in classrooms. They are at different layers in the education hierarchy. They are viewed as being higher up, and they have different responsibilities.

To understand how decisions are made, we must work to keep the layers in mind. Education happens in homes and in schools. It is also debated in government bureaucracies and universities. Some of its policies are set by lawmakers. Ideas on education are written down sometimes as philosophy, sometimes as public policy, sometimes as the psychology of learning, and sometimes as classroom procedure. In some sense, all these levels are education, but in essential ways they are entirely different. Sometimes I see the drama of education as a sort of *Upstairs, Downstairs.* While the philosophers sort out their treatises, the lawmakers are in committees recommending legislation, and the professors are at their conferences, the children are with their teachers in classrooms. An adequate understanding of schooling requires that we differentiate who is upstairs and who is downstairs. We need to remember how infrequently their issues, no less the actual people, ever meet. All levels of work actually go on simultaneously, largely oblivious to, if not actively disinterested in, one another. This fact needs more attention. These different levels are competing realities, and I fear that the reality that is losing, that eludes us, is the actual classroom.

In the 1960s I became a teacher in a New York City public school. Though I taught in a neighborhood quite different from where I grew up, I know I filtered whatever I did through the stardards and expectations I formed in my early years. Even as an inexperienced teacher I determined what happened in my classroom. I made my own lesson plans and I discovered the creativity in that work. If researchers wanted to understand my time in the 1960s, they could look to records and publications of art supervisors at that time. They could also look to see if, in those years, the central office of the New York public schools published directives for its art teachers. They could even look to see if New York City's School Committee ever left art recommendations in its minutes. From these varied records, a researcher might glean certain tensions and priorities that may have filtered to some degree down to me actually making my own decisions teaching in that art room with the door closed. But the fact is, I still had considerable independence.

When Arthur Efland[6] describes art education in those years when I was teaching children, he describes very different ideas from those I had on my mind. What he preserves of the 1960s is intellectual controversy. His is a record of the history of ideas. Efland characterizes the different trends of professors of art education in those years, 1965 to 1975. One trend was for the analysis of the art curriculum according to the field or "discipline." Its advocates were influenced by Jerome Bruner's 1960 book *The Process of Education.* The opposition saw the school itself as a problem. Curriculum, any curriculum, was symptomatic of the rigidity of schools. Curriculum itself was anti-art. Their solution was to bring community artists into schools. Artists were to be themselves—to be artists. Though Efland's description does account for some talk that did take place in the years I was in the classroom, as a new teacher I knew little of what the men and women from universities were arguing about.

My hands and head were full, planning for the day in the art room with the continual flow of twenty-five children changing every forty-five minutes. I was a painter. I had been trained in art history and painting and due to a series of flukes there I was in a classroom. My teaching was influenced by my own history in art and how I had been taught and treated as a child. I was influenced too by teacher preparation courses I had taken. The greatest impact upon me, however, due to a political circumstance, came from the new federal poverty programs. An avalanche of magnificent art materials become available to me in the art room in the Johnson era. Color-Aid paper! Little did I then understand that I launched my teaching career amidst extraordinary material support for education.

Decades from now it is unlikely that many will know the opulence of the antipoverty programs' art rooms of the late sixties, our overnight access to improved facilities, our dazzling art materials order list. It is equally unlikely that people will have an inkling of what happened in our classrooms. The theorists who argued together, wrote books, recommended policy, who leave their records of education, were not in our East Harlem school. They were elsewhere. Yet if we are not careful, their records will overshadow and come to stand for experience. If that threat is real now, it is even more likely to happen when teachers no longer are alive to describe their own experience for themselves. Theories come to stand for the experiences of the multitudes of women and men who actually did the teaching.

To understand who really decides what happens in clasrooms we have to keep that reality in mind. We have to remember *Upstairs, Downstairs,* the various levels of policymakers and classroom teachers all working simultaneously, and we have to remember the teachers in the classroom. Most of the sensitivity, generosity, and good judgment that teachers exercise are known only in the memories of the children who benefited.

Writing about education, including what you are reading at the moment, is largely a narrative by admired, published professors, all of whom traced their paths to us in the written records they have left. What we have from the past are educational ideas, parts of a centuries-old philosophical conversation that will and should go on into the future. But ideas in print are not necessarily events. Ideas are our ideals. Ideas are what the writers *hoped* teachers would put into practice. These treatises, along with government documents, conference proceedings, and political speeches, all differ from teaching and should not be made to stand, or mistaken for, what happens in classrooms.

The traditions I have organized here map the complexity of studio teaching. I isolated each of them to suggest that even within the pressures of changing climates, significant choices are there for each teacher to make. Here again the role of the artist may be an example. Perhaps the single greatest gift the artist has to offer us is the reminder of the responsibility and the pleasure of individual creation. Though as artists we are attentive to styles, to what we have learned in school, to what we are shown in museums and what we see published in art magazines, the power in our work comes from our seizing the opportunity to embody what we love in that work. In the same way, educators need to create lessons in classrooms. The lessons need to feel truly "ours." They need to come from us and from our own practice of art making.[7] Because we cannot help but bring ourselves into our teaching, we might as well make the most of it.

Because teaching always will remain a personalized, individual work carried on by many people with different backgrounds and biases in private spaces across our vast country, I close with the hope that art teachers, many of whom are also artists, will find support for their own growth in doing their own artwork. From what they learn privately in their own studio and from knowing the schools' traditions of art teaching described here, I hope they may continually distill new ideas for teaching, for meeting the everchanging needs of students as they grow older and as our society changes.

NOTES

1. Marilyn Zurmuehlen, *Studio Art: Praxis, Symbol, Presence* (Reston, Va.: National Art Education Association, 1990), 32.

2. Ibid., 64.

3. Edmund Feldman, *The Artist* (Englewood Cliffs, N.J.: Prentice-Hall, Inc., 1982).

4. Howard S. Becker, *Art Worlds* (Berkeley: University of California Press, 1982).

5. Diana Korzenik, "The Artist as Model Learner," in *The Educational Legacy of Romanticism,* ed. John Willinsky (Calgary, Alberta: Wilfred Laurier University Press, 1990).

6. Arthur Efland, *A History of Art Education* (New York: Teachers College Press, 1990).

7. Janice Wall, *The Effect of Teachers' Art-Making on Their Art Teaching on the High School Level* (Boston: unpublished thesis, Massachusetts College of Art, 1991).

Index

Adams, Henry, 96
Adams, John, 161
Addams, Jane, 180-82
Agassiz, Louis, 195
Alba Madonna (Raphael), 25, 26
Albers, Joseph, 156
Alberti, Leon Battista, 45
Alcott, Bronson, 134-35, 137, 163
Alexander, Marguerite, 93
Americanization, 116, 185-86
"America's Making Exposition," 116,
    185-86, 189
Apollinaire, Guillaume, 72, 85
Applied Arts Book, The (anonymous),
    150
Apprenticeship, 123, 141, 150, 156
Arendt, Hannah, 15
Aristotle, 41, 86
Arithmetic, 122, 126
Armory Show (International Exhibition of
    Modern Art, 1913), 115-16, 168
Arnheim, Rudolf, 126
Art and artist, 5, 15, 16, 95, 96, 100, 111
Art and Ethnics (Grigsby), 189
Art and Industry (Read), 157
Art for Young Folks (anonymous), 165
Art Institute of Chicago, 181
Artist, The (Feldman), 196
Artists-in-the-Schools Programs, 95-96,
    108
Art making, 76, 109; and language, 3-5,
    7-16, 59; artists' descriptions, 3-4, 5; E
    (existential) Factor, 18, 31-33, 45; eclec-
    ticism, 41-44; graphic development, 111,
    148; style, 38-39; themes, 62-64, 70
Art of Seeing, The (Woodbury and
    Perkins), 168

Art on the Edge (Rosenberg), 10
Arts and Crafts Movement, 153-55, 157
Arts Education and Back to Basics
    (Dobbs, ed.), 173
Art Students' League, 170
Arts without Mystery, The (Donoghue),
    10
Art Worlds (Becker), 196
Ashton, Dore, 171
Auerbach, Frank, 87
Augie March (Bellow), 12

Baby at Play (Eakins), 134-35
Bailey, Henry Turner, 150-51
Balthus, Jean, 10
Barzun, Jacques, 77, 78, 118
Bauhaus, 155-57
Bearden, Romare, 79
Beauchamp, Robert, 69
Becker, Howard, 196
Beethoven, Ludwig von, 77
Bellini, Jacopo, 8
Benedict, Enella, 181
Bennett, Charles Alpheus, 150,
    156
Berenson, Bernard, 8, 79
Bernard, Emile, 66
Beuys, Joseph, 82, 84
Bihzad, 74
Black Mountain College, 93, 156
Blow, Susan, 135
Boisbaudran, LeCoq de, 122
Bonheur, Rosa, 43
Boorstin, Daniel, 13
Boris, Eileen, 154
Bosch, Hieronymous, 70, 74
Boston Latin School, 143

Boston Society of Arts and Crafts, 153-54
Boucher, François, 44
Braque, Georges, 27, 36, 83
Breuer, Marcel, 156
Brockman, John, 85
Bruner, Jerome, 199
Buber, Martin, 193
Buddha, 9
Buffon, Georges, 39
Burchfield, Charles, 44
Burden, Chris, 82
Bushmiller, Ernie, 43
Butler, Samuel, 83
Butler Art Gallery, 180-81

Cahill, Holger, 187
Caravaggio, Michelangelo, 46
Cassat, Mary, 5
Catullus, 64
Center Academy (New York), 170
Cézanne, Paul, 9, 12, 19, 36, 47, 66, 101
"Chamber's Education Course" (*Elements of Drawing and Perspective*), 163
Chaplin, Charlie, 42
Chapman, John Gadsby, 122
Chicago Public School Art Society, 183-84
Chou, Shen, 70
Christ in the House of Levi (Veronese), 69
Christo, 27
Chuang Tzu, 80-81
Cicero, 45
Civil War, 136, 152
Cizek, Franz, 170
Clark, Edith, 166
Clark, John, 163-64
Clark, John S., 166
Clarke, Isaac Edwards, 146
Classroom, 91, 96, 101; demonstration, 97-98; teachers' choices, 112-14
Clert, Iris, 82
Coe, Sue, 54
Cole, Sir Henry, 146
Color, 45, 46, 60, 101; black and white, 46-48; drawing, 45, 47; form, 45
Common School Drawing Master, The (Schmid), 144
Composition (Dow), 167
Constable, John, 43, 74
Cook, Mary, 165

Cooper Union Art School, 115, 117
Cosimo, Piero di, 87
Craftsman, The (magazine), 154
Creation and creativity, 14, 16, 72, 73-79, 81, 83, 85-87, 96, 102; individual nature, 16, 72; insanity, 77; mediation, 67-68
Creative and Mental Growth (Lowenfeld), 169-70
Cubism and cubists, 10, 36, 81, 82
Cultural diversity, 112, 173-87

Dada and dadaists, 80, 83
Dana, John Cotton, 187
Danae (Titian), 69
Daniels, Frederick H., 150
Dante, 29
Daumier, Honoré, 68, 70
David, Jacques Louis, 30
"Day of the Dead" (Mexico), 194-95
Degas, Edgar, 28, 46
de Kooning, Willem, 11-12, 44, 82
Delacroix, Eugene, 27, 45, 47, 103
Democratic pluralism, 144, 177-82, 185, 188-89
Democritus, 47
Demon of Progress in the Arts, The (Lewis), 10
Denison House (Boston), 184
De Vries, Peter, 12
Dewey, John, 136-37, 151, 185
Diebenkorn, Richard, 44
Disasters of War, The (Goya), 54
Disney, Walt, 44
Dix, Otto, 54
Dobbs, Stephen M., 173
Donlevy, Alice, 165
Don Quixote (Cervantes), 57
Doulton Ware, 124
Dow, Arthur Wesley, 112, 166-68
Drawing for Young Children (anonymous), 164
Dubuffet, Jean, 81
Duchamp, Marcel, 36, 80, 81
Dürer, Albrecht, 69, 70

Eakins, Thomas, 134-35
Eaton, Allen, 185, 187
Education through Art (Read), 188
Efland, Arthur, 128, 199

Ehrenzweig, Anton, 100
Einstein, Albert, 8
Ellul, Jacques, 13
Émile (Rousseau), 132
Entombment (Titian), 3
Ernst, Max, 3
Etant Données (Duchamp), 80
Euclid, 14
Ewing, C. Kermit, 94
Expulsion of the Money Changers, The (El Greco), 43

Fantin-Latour, Ignace, 46
Faulkner, William, 102-3
Feininger, Lyonel, 156
Feldman, Edmund Burke, 196
Fenellosa, Ernest, 167
Field Museum (Chicago), 183
Fitzgerald, F. Scott, 61
Flack, Audrey, 3
Flaying of Marsyas, The (Titian), 69
Fortune Teller, The (de la Tour), 25
Foundations of Modern Art (Ozenfant), 12
Fragonard, Jean-Honoré, 30
Freud, Sigmund, 76
Friedman, Maurice, 86
Froebel, Frederick, 133-34, 136
Fruitlands Museums (Boston), 135
Fryatt, F. E., 165

Gablik, Suzi, 79
Galton, Francis, 77
Garrison, J. J., 46
Gary (Ind.) Public Schools, 155
Gauguin, Paul, 70
Genauer, Emily, 39
Geography, 122, 129, 131, 137-38, 161
Geology, 115, 117, 139
Getty Center for Education in the Arts, 107-8
Giacometti, Alberto, 53
Giotto, 74, 168
Goethe, Johann Wolfgang, 77
Gogh, Vincent van, 3, 12, 77, 171
Golding, John, 36
Gombrich, E. H., 100
Gorky, Arshile, 91
Goya, Francisco de, 46, 74
Graeter, Francis, 134-35, 163

Grammar of Ornament, The (Jones), 178
Graphics: A Manual of Drawing and Writing (anonymous), 161
Green Truck (Brown), 63
Greenwich House (New York), 184
Grigsby, J. Eugene, Jr., 189
Grooms, Red, 79
Gropius, Walter, 155-56
Guernica (Picasso), 54
Guston, Philip, 43

Hall, G. Stanley, 148
Hand, 86, 87, 95, 129, 141, 152-54; copying, 111, 164; manual training, 87-88, 126-27, 147-49; penmanship, 122
Handicraft (magazine), 154
Harnett, William M., 138
Harvard University School of Architecture, 156
Hegel, Georg Wilhelm Friedrich, 85
Herrick, Henry Walker, 165
Hickock, Wild Bill, 69
Hicks, Mary Dana, 166
Hildreth, Gertrude, 140
Hiroshige, 77
Hitler, Adolph, 157
Hoffman, Hans, 30
Hollander, Anne, 46-47
Holmes, Oliver Wendell, 29
Homer, Winslow, 9, 166
Hughes, Robert, 41
Hull-House (Chicago), 180-84
Hunchback of Notre Dame, The (Hugo), 12
Hunt, William Morris, 166
Hunt of the Unicorn (French or Flemish tapestry), 25, 26
Huxley, Aldous, 9, 13

Illinois Institute of Technology, 156
Immigrant Gifts to American Life (Eaton), 185
Immigration, 117, 185-86
Impressionism and Impressionists, 35, 46
Indiana, Robert, 9
Industry and factories, 144, 146-48, 150, 152-53, 155-57, 165
Ingres, Jean-Auguste-Dominique, 34, 45
Innis, Harold, 13
Irwin, Robert, 3

Isenheim Altarpiece, The (Grünewald), 87
Itten, Johannes, 156

Jarry, Alfred, 81
Johns, Jasper, 138, 197
Johnson, Samuel, 24
Jones, Owen, 178-79
Journal of Eugene Delacroix, The, 12
Joyce, James, 85
Judgment of Paris, The (Raphael), 42

Kafka, Franz, 59
Kandinsky, Wassily, 156
Kaprow, Allen, 80
Kiefer, Anselm, 30
Kindergarten, 133-36
Klee, Paul, 47, 156
Kline, Franz, 35
Klumpke, Anna, 166
Knight, Death, and Devil (Dürer), 68, 69, 70
Koestler, Arthur, 10
Korzenik, Harold, 115-17, 138-39
Korzenik, Lillian, 115-17
Kostabi, Mark, 75
Krasner, Lee, 138
Kubie, Lawrence, 77

"Laborphobia," 144, 150
"Ladies Art Association" (New York), 165
LaFarge, John, 166
Lambeth Faience, 124
Last Supper (Titian), 69
Léger, Fernand, 3
Leland, Charles G., 147-50
Leonardo da Vinci, 9, 12, 52, 70, 100, 166, 168
Levi, Albert W., 118
Lewis, Wyndham, 9
Lichtenstein, Roy, 30
Lincoln, Abraham, 69, 70
Little Women (Alcott), 135
Lombroso, Cesare, 77
Lowenfeld, Viktor, 112, 169
Luncheon on the Grass (Manet), 42

"Macondo" drawing (Brown), 59
Maids of Honor (Picasso), 20, 22
Malevich, Kasimir, 25, 80
Malraux, André, 79

Manet, Edouard, 43, 46
Mangold, Robert, 30
Mann, Horace, 135, 144, 146
Mann, Mary Peabody, 135
Manual Training Magazine, The, 150
Marks, Gerhardt, 156
Martin, Agnes, 30
Márquez, Gabriel García, 57
Marzio, Peter, 171
Massachusetts Institute of Technology, 149
Massachusetts Normal Art School, 121, 124, 146, 148
Matisse, Henri, 11, 25, 34, 45, 47-48, 50, 67
Meaning in Art (Read), 157
Melancolia (Dürer), 70
Melville, Herman, 7, 75, 85
Merleau-Ponty, Maurice, 100
Metaphysics (Aristotle), 78
Meyer, Hans, 156
Michelangelo, 25, 41, 42, 70
Mill by the Water (Mondrian), 20, 21
Minifie, William, 145-46
Minor Arts, The (Leland), 147
Miro, Joan, 43
Mitchell, Lucy S., 137
Moholy-Nagy, Lazlo, 156
Mondrian, Piet, 30, 35, 53
Monet, Claude, 30, 35
Montaigne, 4, 60
Morris, Robert, 54
Morris, William, 147, 152-53
Moscow Technical School, 149
Moving Pictures (Hollander), 46
Mozart, Wolfgang Amadeus, 39, 67
Mumford, Lewis, 75
Munro, Thomas, 188
Museums, 111, 114, 135, 180-81, 183
Mystery, 8, 9, 55, 59, 72, 75, 85

Nash, Paul, 44
National Academy of Design, 165
National Education Association, 120, 126, 141
Neel, Alice, 30
Nevelson, Louise, 53
Neville Brothers, 58
New York City Public Schools, 116-17, 198

Nietzsche, Frederick, 84, 101
Ninth Symphony (Schubert), 58
Notebook (Braque), 12

Of Art and the Mind (Wollheim), 120
O'Keeffe, Georgia, 9, 16
Oldenburg, Claes, 9
On the Content of Children's Minds
(Hall), 148
"On Vanity" (Montaigne), 4
Orwell, George, 13
Ovid, 57

Paglia, Camille, 13
Paint, 18-20, 23, 27, 28, 48, 56
Painted Word, The (Wolfe), 10
Parker, Francis W., 134, 136-37
Parker, Virginia, 93
Patinir, Joachim, 74
Peabody, Elizabeth, 133, 135-36, 144-45
Peale, Rembrandt, 161
Pearlstein, Philip, 30
Pedagogical Sketchbook (Klee), 12
Pedestal Table (Braque), 36
Pensées (Braque), 83
Perception and vision, 15, 38, 44, 48-49,
56, 100-101; form and meaning, 15;
memory drawing, 122; metaphorical,
28
Perkins, Elizabeth, 168
Perkins, Lucy F., 166
Perry, Walter S., 166
Pestalozzi, Heinrich, 133, 147
Peto, John F., 138
Philadelphia Centennial Exposition, 120,
124, 134, 147, 149
Philadelphia Public Schools, 147-49
Philadelphia Social Science Association,
148
Picabia, Francis, 80
Picasso, Pablo, 3, 12, 14, 36, 39, 43, 45,
53, 56, 65, 68, 81-82, 91, 102
Piero della Francesca, 29
Pissaro, Camille, 19
Plato, 41, 45, 64, 77, 80
"Playing school," 120
Pollock, Jackson, 34
Postman, Neil, 13
Postmodernism, 73
Poussin, Nicolas, 44

Prang, Louis, 165-67
*Prang Elementary Course in Art Instruc-
tion, The*, 166
*Prang's Complete Course for Form Study
and Drawing*, 166
Process of Education, The (Bruner), 199
Psychologists, 111
Purdue University, 120

Raphael, 41, 166
Rauschenberg, Robert, 82
Read, Herbert, 157, 188
Reading, 122, 131
Real Presences (Steiner), 10
Record of a School (Peabody), 135
Reinhardt, Ad, 31, 34, 47-48, 64
Rembrandt, 20, 46, 69, 74, 97, 166
Remington, Frederick, 92
Representation, 25, 86, 100
Reproductions, 92, 93, 98-99
Reynolds, Sir Joshua, 12, 42, 54
Richmond Hull House (New York), 184
Rimbaud, 81
Riis, Jacob, 185
Robb, David, 46
Robertson, Seonaid, 160, 163
Roderick Hudson (James), 84
Rosegarden and Labyrinth (Robertson),
160
Rosenberg, Harold, 91, 95
Rosenquist, James, 53
Rothenberg, Susan, 30
Rothko, Mark, 170-71
Rousseau, Jean Jacques, 80, 107, 131-34
Rubens, Peter Paul, 44, 77, 82
Ruskin, John, 152-54
Russell, John, 10
Ryder, Albert P., 19, 54

St. Gaudens, Augustus, 186
Samaras, Lucas, 44
Sandusky (Ohio) Public Schools, 120
Sargent, John S., 166
Schmid, Peter, 144-45
School and Society, The (Dewey), 151
School Arts Book, The (magazine), 150,
154, 184-85
"School art style," 128
"Schoolgirl art," 143
Schurz, Mrs. Carl, 135

Schwitters, Kurt, 99
Science, 8, 131, 137-38, 194
Scully, Sean, 44
Segal, Erich, 9
Self-reliant qualities, 134, 164, 170
Seneca, 4
Sequeiros, David, 54
Seurat, Georges, 35
Shahn, Ben, 44
Shakespeare, William, 11
Shelley, Percy Bysshe, 77
Sherman, Hoyt, 94
Sisto, Elena, 43
Sloyd method, 107, 149-50, 152
Smith, Ralph A., 118
Smith, Walter, 112, 146-47, 165, 178
Smithson, Robert, 78-79, 80, 82
Snyder, Joan, 43
Some Curious Schools (anonymous), 165
Some Reasons Why Drawing Should Be Taught in Our Common Schools (Thompson), 120
South End House (Boston), 184
South Kensington Art School (London), 146-48, 153
Soutine, Chaim, 30
Spelling, 122, 138
Spiral Jetty (Smithson), 79
Stankiewicz, Mary Ann, 180
Starr, Ellen G., 180-82, 184
Stella, Frank, 44
Stevens, Wallace, 52
Stickley, Gustav, 154
Studio, 50, 55, 95; effects, 54; light, 53; relation to paintings, 51-53
Studio of the Painter, The (Courbet), 66
Sultan, Donald, 43

Temple School (Boston), 134-35
Textbook for Mechanical Drawing and an Essay on the Theory of Color (Minifie), 145-46
Thiebaud, Wayne, 44
Thompson, Langdon S., 120-28, 131, 163, 173

Thurber, James, 12
Titian, 29, 41, 74
Topham, Pamela, 25
Toynbee Hall (London), 180
Tradition, 74, 85, 86
Travels (Brown), 59
Treason of Images, The (Magritte), 82
Twain, Mark, 12

Untitled Landscape (Brown), 65

Valéry, Paul, 52
Van Der Rohe, Mies, 156
Van Dyck, Anthony, 43, 46, 82
van Eyck, Jan, 35
Vasari, Giorgio, 18
Vedder, Elihu, 166
Vermeer, Jan, 13, 14, 46
Velázquez, Diego, 20, 43, 46
Visual Thinking (Arnheim), 126

Walter Besant's People's Palace, 180
Washing the Feet of Christ (Tintoretto), 69
Washington Crossing the Delaware (Leutze), 93
Weber, Max, 170
Wide Awake (magazine), 164-65
Wife of Tobias with the Goat, The (Rembrandt), 20, 22
Wilde, Oscar, 80
Wirt, William, 155
Wittgenstein, Ludwig, 15
Wollheim, Richard, 120
Women as artists, 124, 143, 165, 180-81
Women of Algiers (Delacroix), 20, 21
Woodbury, Charles, 166, 169
Wordsworth, William, 8, 107
Works Progress Administration, 187
Wright, Frank Lloyd, 134
Wyeth, N. C., 92

Yeats, William Butler, 40
Young Geographers (Mitchell), 137

Zurmuehlen, Marilyn, 193, 195
Zwilich, Ellen Taaffe, 28